Robert Singh's *In Defense of the United States Cons*
and welcome antidote to the frequent charges that ~~the Constitution~~
is outmoded and undemocratic. There are serious problems in our
politics – citizen apathy and ignorance, partisan polarization, and institutional gridlock among them. But as Singh calmly and reasonably
points out, these are problems of our politics and not our Constitution.
This book will lower your blood-pressure and lift your spirits – just the
prescription for our times.

**Cal Jillson**, *Southern Methodist University*

Given the current troubled state of the American polity, calls to amend
the Constitution are once again in vogue. This book is an important
and timely response to these proposals. Robert Singh offers an articulate, balanced, and well-informed discussion of the strengths and weaknesses of the Constitution, one that suggests that the governing problems
that afflict the United States are not necessarily a product of constitutional flaws. Although he agrees that there are certain amendments that
would be real improvements, he concludes that the document's daunting
amending procedure makes change unlikely, and more importantly, that
there are greater dangers than advantages to undertaking a wholesale
process of constitutional revision.

**Michael L. Mezey**, *DePaul University*

Critics argue that American politics are broken and that the Constitution is to blame. Robert S. Singh deflects this blame in this clearly
written, lucid, and timely defense of the Framers' handiwork: Taking
seriously points of view from all sides and origins and arguing in good
faith at every point, Singh dismantles each critique – and the "situational
constitutionalism" orientation articulated by many parties – by pointing
out the flaws in the argument. Singh places blame for what ails American politics where it clearly belongs: on America's polarized politics
and rudderless ship of state. This book will make students in American
politics and constitutional studies courses think critically, and is also a
novel contribution to the literature.

**Jeffrey S. Peake**, *Clemson University*

*In Defense of the United States Constitution* offers a reasonable diagnosis and an achievable prescription for what ails American politics today. Responding to calls for major structural amendments or even a
new constitutional convention, author Robert Singh wisely advises that
"dispensing with the existing settlement is a gamble unlikely to pay off."
The reform we need is partisan, not constitutional: Partisans can reframe
issues so as to re-establish the possibility of ideological compromise.

Without such a rapprochement, constitutional reform is impossible; with it, existing constitutional provisions are satisfactory.

**Randall Calvert,** *Washington University in St. Louis*

Robert Singh has written a timely, carefully researched, and well-reasoned book. Sure to stimulate discussion, his work is in the must-read category for anyone interested in the future of constitutional government in the United States.

**Donald Grier Stephenson, Jr.,** *Franklin & Marshall College;*
*Co-author of* American Constitutional Law:
Introductory Essays and Selected Cases

Rob Singh's accomplished book will command attention and respect. It is a work of wisdom. Culturally and historically sensitive, his defense of the constitution is the intelligent and rigorous account that we need to set twenty-first-century turmoil and discontents in appropriate historical, political, and legal contexts. Here is a scholarly defense of the constitution with which scholars and non-scholars alike should engage.

**Nigel Bowles,** *University of Oxford*

In a time of gridlock and polarizing politics, Robert Singh reminds us why the US Constitution still matters and is worth defending. He lays out why the Constitution is not – and never has been – perfect, but also how it has always aspired to that goal and is closer now than it once was. He argues for some amendments to the document but also counsels against wholesale changes that would involve more costs than benefits. To put it succinctly, Singh shows us why "we the people" are better off with our Constitution than we would be without it or with a fundamentally different one.

**Eric T. Kasper,** *University of Wisconsin-Eau Claire;*
*Director, Center for Constitutional Studies*

Blaming the US Constitution for our present discontents is like blaming a home's foundation for the poor interior decorating choices of its inhabitants: It is a national resource which should be altered only with great care. Singh evenhandedly and comprehensively demonstrates that the problem lies in the realm of politics – his contribution to this important debate will give reasons for dismay to, and should be taken seriously by, both the left and right.

**Andrew E. Busch,** *Claremont McKenna College*

# In Defense of the United States Constitution

Constitutional reform is a topic of perennial academic debate, perhaps now more than ever, amid sharp polarization in the electorate and government. At once a cogent, new contribution to the scholarly literature and appropriate for American politics and government students, this book mounts a provocative, nonideological defense of the US Constitution, directly engaging proposals for reform and providing a rare systematic argument for continuity: our politics may be broken but our system is not. Writing from an international perspective with an array of fascinating data, Singh draws on theory, law, and history to defend the republican order under political stress and intellectual challenge.

**Robert S. Singh** is Professor of Politics at Birkbeck, University of London. His research focuses on contemporary US politics and the politics of US foreign policy.

20170013S3

# In Defense of the United States Constitution

## Robert S. Singh

BIRKBECK, UNIVERSITY OF LONDON

Routledge
Taylor & Francis Group

NEW YORK AND LONDON

Published 2019
by Routledge
711 Third Avenue, New York, NY 10017

and by Routledge
2 Park Square, Milton Park, Abingdon, Oxon, OX14 4RN

*Routledge is an imprint of the Taylor & Francis Group, an
informa business*

*Library of Congress Cataloging-in-Publication Data*
Names: Singh, Robert, author.
Title: In defense of the United States Constitution /
Robert S. Singh, Birkbeck, University of London.
Description: New York, NY: Routledge, 2019. |
Includes bibliographical references and index.
Identifiers: LCCN 2018019601 | ISBN 9780815360735 (hbk) |
ISBN 9780815360742 (pbk) | ISBN 9781351117708 (ebk)
Subjects: LCSH: Constitutional history—United States.
Classification: LCC KF4541 .S54 2019 |
DDC 342.7302/9—dc23
LC record available at https://lccn.loc.gov/2018019601

ISBN: 978-0-815-36073-5 (hbk)
ISBN: 978-0-815-36074-2 (pbk)
ISBN: 978-1-351-11770-8 (ebk)

Typeset in Sabon
by codeMantra

In memory of Martin Clark (1938–2017)

# Contents

# Illustrations

# Preface

On January 20, 2017, Donald J. Trump pledged to "faithfully execute the Office of President" and "preserve, protect, and defend the Constitution of the United States." But in the inaugural address on American "carnage" that followed, the Constitution went unmentioned.

That absence confirmed many critics' fears of a coming constitutional twilight: "an existential moment" posing "a genuine threat to the well-being of our country and the sustainability of our democracy" (Mann 2016) and proof that the "...Constitution is gravely, perhaps terminally, ill. Trumpism is the symptom, not the cause, of the malaise" (Epps 2016). Echoing Plato's *Republic*, Andrew Sullivan (2016) even lamented America having "jumped off a constitutional cliff":

> A country designed to resist tyranny has now embraced it. A constitution designed to prevent democracy taking over everything has now succumbed to it. A country once defined by self-government has openly, clearly, enthusiastically delivered its fate into the hands of one man to do as he sees fit. After 240 years, an idea that once inspired the world has finally repealed itself. We the people did it.

But rather than envisaging imminent constitutional collapse, others responded with more sanguine assessments, suggesting there was much less to Trump than met his ubiquitous "I":

> The reaction in some circles to Trump's election has been a little hysterical. It would be one thing if this result represented the extinction of American democracy. But this is ridiculous. Whatever the many concerns about Trump—and I fully understand them—we live and will continue to live in an exceptionally rambunctious and free republic where the courts, the press, the Congress, and the people will all continue to have their say.
>
> (Dueck 2016)

Ultimately, despite damage, the Republic was not read the last rites, nor was the Constitution trampled under goose steps. But America's long season of discontent did not so much disappear as deepen, suggesting that its constitutional problems were more systemic than a solitary individual. Abiding concerns over whether the Federal Government could govern were not dispelled. Gridlock did not end. Issues from immigration to infrastructure remained unresolved. Congressional deals yielding trillion-dollar budgets, soaring deficits, and a metastasizing national debt were hailed as political breakthroughs while threatening insolvency and leaving future generations to pay the bills.

Unsurprisingly, popular disillusion intensified. In 2017, just 51 percent of Americans said they trusted the Federal Government to "do what is right for the US," while only 46 percent were satisfied with the way democracy was working (Gramlich 2017). In 2018, just 50 percent of Americans said their system of government was basically sound. Eighty-one percent thought the Founders would be upset with the functioning of government institutions; just 11 percent imagined they would be happy. Three in four Americans were either dissatisfied (60 percent) or angry (20 percent) at "Washington" (Monmouth 2018). In 1776, pursuing happiness had been enshrined as an "unalienable right" in the Declaration of Independence; by the second and third decades of the twenty-first century, achieving it seemed increasingly difficult. According to the "World Happiness Report," while the US ranked third happiest among OECD member countries in 2007, it had dropped to nineteenth by 2016 (Sustainable Development Solutions Network 2017).

Although every democracy is unhappy in its own way, America's metrics speak to profound national anxieties: is the American Dream at an end? Do current problems suggest America's success occurred more despite than because of a Constitution now showing its age? Does that Constitution merit elegies, not encomiums, having outlived its usefulness? Or are problems in the United States less constitutional in origin than the result of a divided political class and people who recognize shared challenges as patriots but cannot agree on solutions as partisans?

The latter is the case advanced in this respectfully contrarian book, which examines whether the Constitution is adequate to contemporary challenges or if fundamental change is needed. It makes an emphatically outspoken and unfashionable case that America's form of government remains sound. The Constitution is far from flawless, and some modernizing fine-tuning would not go amiss. But it deserves neither rubbishing nor romanticizing. A haven of unity in an otherwise unruly and disunited polity, the Constitution is not the source of today's problems, nor are constitutional "fixes" the solution. Radical change is, where feasible, mostly undesirable, and where desirable, mostly unfeasible. The constitutional order remains a positive one, at this juncture in American history more than ever.

The Constitution has aged well. But although they remain essential to democracy, America's political parties exist in a state of advanced immaturity. Current problems have less to do with the Constitution than with hyper-partisanship, ideological polarization, and the cultural and technological changes afflicting all western democracies regardless of constitutional arrangements. Among multiple aims, the Constitution's "father," James Madison, intended it to curb the "factious spirit" he identified in *Federalist 10* as the bane of popular governments. But ironically, after many decades as integral elements in making the Constitution work, the parties now seem to be trivializing politics and realizing the Framers' fears. Republicans and Democrats no longer recognize shared realities. Amid an epidemic of "truth decay," this factious spirit is out of control, with a distinctly Manichean and tribal edge that treats politics more as a barrier than as a bridge. As David Mayhew (2017: 3) cautioned, "It is a short step to the view: 'My party can't get what it wants, so the system must be broken.'"

An effective liberal democratic constitution should clearly and consistently achieve four essential goals:

i   Provide a stable framework for government by channeling societal conflict into everyday politics;
ii  Allow the expression in law and policy of majority preferences, while safeguarding protections for individual rights and liberties;
iii Ensure the peaceful transfer of power; and
iv  Permit the means of its own revision through amendments and interpretation.

The US Constitution meets these core requirements, and the six objectives of its own Preamble, more fully now than at any time in American history. It is not merely resilient and adaptive, but "antifragile": gaining strength from the tests to which it is periodically subjected (Taleb 2013). Imperfect, to be sure, and deserving respect rather than unthinking veneration, it has nonetheless weathered storms that capsized less sturdy vessels. A few modernizing changes would improve the system but are unlikely to occur (most notably, the end of equal state representation in the US Senate). But overall, the existing design remains fit for purpose. Radicals, romantics and reactionaries advocating overhaul should be strongly resisted.

The United States is again experiencing one of its periodic dark nights of the national soul. But history suggests this too shall pass. Whatever the Constitution's faults, its virtues loom larger. Comprehensive change is a prospect ultimately more costly than compelling, its risks exceeding its rewards. Political dysfunction is less attributable to parchment constraints than to self-inflicted ones and, from enlightened self-interest as much as goodwill, capable of resolution. Whether, when, and how that occurs is another matter well above my modest pay grade. Yet, as

Churchill remarked in 1931, "Sometimes when Fortune scowls most spitefully, she is preparing her most dazzling gifts."

We occasionally stand too close to the frame to see the whole picture. In a noisily narcissistic, insistently nonjudgmental yet hyper-opinionated age, quiet stoicism is unfashionable. What divides Americans is less impressive than what unites them. Some comparative perspective ought to make clear: the United States is not a failed state; the Republic is not collapsing; democracy is not in its death throes. As a poet once wrote, "There is a crack in everything. That's how the light gets in" (Cohen 1993: 373).

The US Constitution is not broken; it doesn't need fixing.

# Acknowledgments

My sincerest thanks go to Ze'ev Sudry for his interest, enthusiasm, and support for this book, and to Jennifer Knerr and all the Routledge team for their dedication, assistance, and professionalism. I should also thank the six anonymous American reviewers who examined some early chapters and made many valuable suggestions. For the permissions to use their maps in Chapter 2, I'm especially grateful to the generosity of Professor Mark Perry of the American Enterprise Institute and Dr. Jenny Schuetz of the Brookings Institution.

On my side of the pond, I'm grateful to the School of Social Sciences, History and Philosophy at Birkbeck for the research grants that made possible two trips to Washington, D.C. I'm also thankful to friends and colleagues who made it possible to make presentations over 2015–2018 on which this work has drawn, at universities and public events in Bath, Bucharest, Canterbury, Cheltenham, Doha, Lancaster, London, and Warsaw.

For formal and informal exchanges on US matters over 2015–2018, my warmest thanks go to Elliot Abrams, Nigel Bowles, Hal Brands, Anthony Butler, Howard Burdett, Eliot Cohen, Tom Donnelly, Colin Dueck, William Galston, Jeff Gedmin, Michael Green, Jacob Grygiel, Matt Hoelscher, Robert Lieber, James Lindsay, Robert Litwak, Michael Mandelbaum, Aaron David Miller, Rory Miller, Donette Murray, Henry Nau, Pietro Nivola, Tim Nuthall, Michael O'Hanlon, Michael O'Neal, Norman Ornstein, Kenneth Pollack, Bruce Riedel, Gary Schmitt, Tui Shaub, and Keith Willis. As always, thanks go to my incomparable father, Shiv, a constant source of wisdom, kindness, support, and inspiration. The book is respectfully dedicated to the memory of Martin Clark, a former colleague and friend, a fine scholar of modern Italy and a political historian with a rare sense of irreverence for the lecture theaters of the absurd.

That we are all at best footnotes in history, and that higher education enlightens you primarily to how much you don't know, are enduring truths – and always sufficient reason to try to learn more and err less. In that spirit, the usual proviso applies: all errors of fact and interpretation herein are mine alone.

—Robert S. Singh

# Introduction
## Why the Constitution Needs Defending Today

> ... The ground of political dispute in the United States is about the nature and extent of the Constitution, a carefully wrought form of words devised by Englishmen in revolt against the Crown and amended by their successor generations. The ideas contained within it can be revered and disputed at the same time.
>
> Christopher Hitchens (1993)

> Critics say that America is a lie because its reality falls so short of its ideals. They are wrong. America is not a lie; it is a disappointment. But it can be a disappointment only because it is also a hope.
>
> Samuel P. Huntington (1981: 262)

This chapter summarizes the book's core arguments. It begins with the supposed demise of the Constitution that some feared contemporary politics has confirmed. Locating such apprehension within a longer history of American constitutional angst, it then deals with three themes revisited at length in the book: *from whom* the Constitution needs defending; *how* it should be defended; and *why* it needs defending.

### "I, the People"? President Trump's "Teachable Moments"

On April 29, 2017, his 100th day in office, Donald Trump boasted that his accomplishments were the best of any president since Franklin D. Roosevelt. But he blamed his governing difficulties – such as they were – on the Constitution: "It's a very rough system ... an archaic system ... It's really a bad thing for the country" (Borger 2017).

That same month, Allan Lichtman (2017) – a rare political historian who correctly predicted the 2016 election outcome – published *The Case for Impeachment*, calling for Trump's removal. A few weeks later, Laurence Tribe (2017), Harvard constitutional law professor, declared about allegations of collusion between Trump and Russian government officials that, "The time has come for Congress to launch an impeachment investigation of President Trump for obstruction of justice." If impeachment proved impossible, others suggested impairment: the Twenty-fifth

Amendment allowed removing a president deemed physically or mentally unfit to serve (Osnos 2017). After Trump's dismissal of FBI Director James Comey, and the appointment of a Special Prosecutor, Robert S. Mueller III, to investigate the Russia issue, experts debated whether the Constitution allowed a president to use the pardon power for himself (Tribe, Painter and Eisen 2017; Turley 2017).

Such constitutional tumult was unusual but understandable. No election in modern US history had produced as surprising an outcome (Ceaser, Busch and Pitney 2017). Trump was the first president never to have held political office or served in government or the military. Moreover, as Henry Kissinger tactfully noted, Trump was "... a personality for whom there is no precedent in modern American history. And his campaign included rhetorical elements challenging patterns heretofore considered traditional" (Hains 2016). In his first two years in office, the sense that Washington was "broken" deepened. Other than a tax reform law at the end of 2017, the White House and Congress proved unable to enact key campaign promises – such as the repeal and replacement of the Affordable Care Act of 2010 ("Obamacare") – despite Republican control. A massive spending bill passed in February 2018 required Republicans to abandon fiscal responsibility for the kind of stimulus that, when President Obama had championed it in 2009, they condemned. Conservative Hugh Hewitt (2017) lamented that, "We are at a crisis point where citizens are giving up on representative government *en masse*." On the left, E. J. Dionne (2017) claimed that, "Our country is now as close to crossing the line from democracy to autocracy as it has been in our lifetimes."

In the light of how polarized politics has become, perhaps no one should have been surprised. As Levinson and Balkin (2009: 709) noted, "The language of 'crisis' has never been absent from discussions of American politics or American constitutionalism." Even during the 2016 campaign, two contrasting events captured the tension between the Constitution's centrality and fragility.

The most noteworthy event, in terms of national and international attention, came at the Democratic Party convention in Philadelphia, Pennsylvania in July 2016. Khizr Khan – father of US Army Captain Humayun Khan, a Muslim American who died shielding fellow soldiers in the Iraq war – criticized the Republican Party nominee directly: "Donald Trump, you are asking Americans to trust you with our future. Let me ask you: Have you even read the US Constitution? I will gladly lend you my copy." He then pulled a copy of the Constitution from his jacket pocket. "In this document, look for the words 'liberty' and 'equal protection of law'" (CNN 2016).

That Trump had read the Constitution was doubtful, given his repeated public misunderstandings. Earlier that month, Trump had promised that he would be the "best constitutional president ever" and defend

"Article Twelve" – a surprising pledge given the Constitution's seven articles (Siegel 2016). In August, he had proposed an immigration policy of "extreme vetting" for individuals showing

> any hostile attitude towards our country or its principles, or who believed sharia law should supplant American law... Those who did not believe in our Constitution or who support bigotry and hatred will not be admitted for immigration into our country.
>
> (DeYoung 2016)

That prompted former Senate Majority Leader Harry Reid (D-NV) to call for Trump to take a naturalization test to demonstrate his own familiarity with American values. Trump later advocated a "stop and frisk" policy to deal with urban rioting, seemingly oblivious to the Fourth Amendment's limits on unreasonable searches and those on the Federal Government ordering local actions in the Tenth.

A second constitutional moment had occurred a few months earlier. In January 2016, Greg Abbott, Republican Governor of Texas, had highlighted how the Constitution had been violated by an over-powerful Federal Government. Under Obama, the executive branch had exceeded its proscribed limits. What was needed was a new convention to propose constitutional amendments, revive the spirit of the "lost" document, and restore the rule of law (Abbott 2016). After the 2016 election, former Florida Governor Jeb Bush (2016) echoed this call:

> Americans, by wide majorities, agree that Washington is broken, so let's send power back to the people and back to the states. Republicans should support convening a constitutional convention to pass term limits, a balanced-budget amendment and restraints on the Commerce Clause, which has given the federal government far more regulatory power than the Founders intended. The federal government has become too unwieldy, too powerful and too distant— precisely the problem that the Constitution was designed to avoid. The breakdown of our constitutional system isn't a theoretical discussion. It's affecting every American in real ways.

These events – one sparking sales of pocket constitutions, the other barely registering outside Texas – offered contrasting windows into the strange career of the US Constitution. They signaled that much was unwell and framed debate over the "threat" to constitutionalism. In Khan's case, Trump was endangering constitutional norms; his ignorance of core guarantees implied unfitness for presidential office. Implicitly, it also raised questions about how such a powerful institution contradicted the Framers' rejection of monarchical power. In Abbott's case, the need for extensive rewriting implied something defective about twenty-first-century America: that it rejected the Framers' vision of limited government. A new beginning was necessary to restore a system honored more in the breach than in the observance.

But if the Constitution was so universally revered, how it came to be so grievously eroded presents us with something of a mystery. The Constitution provides the anchor for the US ship of state. It defines concretely the nature of the American social contract and forms the constant organizing frame for government and politics, structuring political competition. Approaching its 250th anniversary, the Constitution remains the cornerstone of public life and a rare reference point for national unity. Nothing is more substantial. As former President Bill Clinton often remarked, "The Constitution boils down to one thing. Let's have an argument and then let's make a deal" (Nelson 2018: 147). How and why has it come to suffer such political strain and intellectual challenge?

## From Whom Does the Constitution Need Defending? I: Critics

H. L. Mencken, the great American satirist, rejected the biblical advice of Ecclesiastes 9, verse 11, when he asserted, "The race may not always be to the swift nor the battle to the strong: but that's the way to bet." But to critics who favor strong government action to resolve social, economic, and political problems, the Constitution stands as a permanent antidote to that gamble: more albatross than asset. A case of arrested constitutional development, its unattractive and obsolete design denies decisive victories to politicians, absent very broad support, and consistently frustrates the strong – especially the White House – by denying them the full fruits of their electoral triumphs. The Constitution instead demands deliberation, reflection, and compromise.

To others, the Constitution remains attractive but, at best, a noble piece of paper. Its birth was defective, it excluded minorities, and its effective operation more than 200 years later remains far from assured. Constitutional protections are contingent, sometimes weak to the point of being feeble, and tyrannical government is far from impossible:

> Many of the US government's famous checks and balances only check and balance if you want them to. It has always been possible, given the wrong combination of people and circumstances, or the necessities of war and conflict, to get round the intentions of the framers of the constitution. Ask the Japanese-American internees of the Second World War. In the end, the guarantee has been the people themselves.
>
> (Aaronovitch 2017)

The Constitution represents the ultimate Rorschach test. Akin to those psychologists' inkblots, in which individuals discern different realities in the same amoebic shapes, the Constitution offers ambiguity, elasticity, and "silences" (unanswered questions). Ironically, these are as much the source of its longevity as its better-defined elements: the institutions of government (legislature, executive, and judiciary), federalism and the Bill of Rights (the first ten amendments).

Americans are an unusually patriotic people, proud of their Constitution and heritage. Listen to US political debate for any length of time, and the Founders will be enlisted by politicians on the left and right for or against limited government, gun rights, progressive taxation, and more. Applying history to contemporary problems resonates. That is unsurprising. Emblematic of the republic – the "first new nation" – the Constitution (with the Declaration of Independence) provides Americans their political inheritance. But, where admirers see an exceptional governing framework, detractors perceive an eighteenth-century prison from which twenty-first-century Americans are sentenced to life without parole, unable or unwilling to escape. The wide disparities contained in the Constitution are understandable. The Constitution contains multitudes and admits of disorderly contradictions. Disagreement about constitutional order is nonetheless integral to that order.

In intellectual terms, the direction of recent critical travel has emphasized what is wrong with the Constitution more than what is right. Outside academia, suggesting it needs complete overhaul is heretical. Outside the United States, however, the Constitution has long been regarded as a period piece past its "best before" date. What is striking is that over the last decade, US commentary too has become more negative, disenchanted, and pessimistic. Much as the public lost trust in "Washington" after Vietnam, Watergate, the Iraq War, the Great Recession, and multiple scandals involving presidents and Congress, so have many intellectuals lost faith in America's promise. The gloss appears to have come off the "shining city on a hill." The "decline and fall of the republic" appears all too plausible and well-advanced (Ackerman 2013).

Addressing Washington's dysfunction, for example, in his final State of the Union, Obama conceded, "It's one of the few regrets of my presidency that the rancor and suspicion between the parties has gotten worse instead of better" (White House 2016). For Robert Putnam (2015), the American Dream was in "crisis." Epps (2016) claimed that:

> … we have for some time been living in the post-Constitution era. America's fundamental law remains and will remain important as a source of litigation. But the nation seems to have turned away from a search of values in the Constitution, regarding it instead as a set of annoying rules.

Sounding a similar theme, Robert Samuelson (2017) noted that:

> One mark of a successful democracy is the willingness of the losers to accept election results without questioning the system's moral foundations ... There's a growing tendency to want to replay elections by transforming ordinary political disagreements into impeachable offenses. This is a new norm.

A political system that offered Hillary Clinton and Donald Trump for president in 2016 – a political choice of *Alien vs. Predator* as the two most unpopular candidates since records began – was, at minimum, flawed. But expert voices counseled calm:

> Our country is not poised on the abyss of race war, Civil War, or any other kind of domestic war. Nor are we sliding down a slippery slope toward fascism. Normal people — a.k.a. the general public — continue to live their lives as they did before the election. The voters changed little between 2012 and 2016, although the small changes that occurred were critical for the outcome. Many of Trump's voters were not endorsing his draconian proposals so much as sending a message that they were unhappy with the direction of current policy. Finally, many, if not most Americans thought that the parties had given them a historically poor choice. Believing that change was needed, just enough of them in just the right places rolled the dice to send the candidate of the status quo down to defeat.
>
> (Fiorina 2018)

Constitutional pessimism was, nonetheless, triply unsurprising.

First, despite the Constitution's ubiquitous presence, the Framers could never have anticipated the fractious and febrile United States of selfies, Facebook, Google, Instagram, Twitter, Tinder, Grindr, emojis, twerking, Michael Moore, Judge Roy Moore, Stormy Daniels, Fox News, Ann Coulter, Breitbart News, and the Drudge Report. That the Kardashians and *Game of Thrones* command a seemingly permanent presence in popular culture while prescription opioid abuse convulses America would be shocking. So, too, would be the president's power to order extra-constitutional targeted assassinations executed by pilots in Nevada via drones on the other side of the world, or the National Security Agency's ability to eavesdrop on electronic communications from Paris, Texas to Paris, France. It would be no shame on the Founders to suggest that twenty-first-century America no longer shares their vision or values (thankfully, in important respects). Even genius has its limits.

Secondly, the United States is in the throes of overlapping economic, technological, and demographic changes unlike any experienced since the late 1800s. Popular sentiments see the country as in a figurative and literal mess. Materially, this can literally be seen in crumbling roads, bridges, ports, and airports. Socially, malaise finds expression in rising poverty, unemployment, poor educational results, static social mobility, and severe racial tension. Spiritually, there exists little uniting the heterogeneous people. Other than being fellow citizens, Black Lives Matter devotees and Trump supporters seemingly share little in common. Politically, public cynicism and partisan polarization are mutually parasitical. Americans identifying with one party now dislike, distrust, and fear the other. Visceral divisions manifest themselves on issues from immigration to firearms and climate change. Played out through a fragmented cacophony of rival TV networks, talk radio and social media, Americans' daily lives are lived in a cultural chasm not just between, but also within, "blue" and "red" states. Some Americans may lean left and swipe right, and vice versa, but most appear to actively desire a "conscious uncoupling" not only from Washington's "power elite" but the other half of the country.

Thirdly, no matter who holds power, politics no longer "works" in providing remedies. In 119 separate CBS polls from January 2006 to January 2018, only twice were less than 50 percent of Americans in agreement the country was headed on the wrong track. In 105 instances of asking about their satisfaction with "the way things are going in this country today" between January 2004 and July 2017, not since January 2004 did less than a majority express dissatisfaction (Polling Report). Elections promise new beginnings ("Yes, We Can"; "Make America Great Again"), change and bipartisanship, only to fail to deliver. Regular disappointment with exaggerated promises fuels greater frustration. Cynicism, distrust of public institutions (except the military), and support for "outsiders" result. Politics becomes coarser and corrosive, frustrating consensus building. In 2016, dissatisfied with politics as usual, the populist campaigns of Trump and, in the Democratic Party, Bernie Sanders (I-VT), revealed fault lines as much between "establishment" and "anti-establishment" forces as progressives and conservatives.

Low trust, declining social capital, and divisions too entrenched to overcome lead some even to doubt their own American DNA. In 2011, for example, according to one analysis of "democratic disconnect," 24 percent of millennials (in their late teens or early twenties) considered democracy to be a "bad" or "very bad" way of running the country; 26 percent thought it "unimportant" for people to "choose their leaders in free elections"; and those thinking it would be a "good" or "very good" thing for the "army to rule" grew from one in sixteen in 1995 to one in six by 2014 (Foa and Munck 2016). In 2016, only 130.8 million of 231 million eligible voters showed up; 43.5 percent of the electorate chose not to bother. Fueled by sensationalist "click-bait" media outlets whose business models perpetuate a sense of constant outrage, some on the left and right even discerned conspiratorial plots to destroy America by stealth.

In this light, it is not surprising that the 2000s and 2010s saw the expression of profound constitutional angst. Many critiques attributed American ills – from anemic economic growth to gun violence and substandard education – to a Constitution unfit for its purpose (Levinson and Levinson 2017). At the heart of such arguments was a paradox: many progressives regard the Constitution as having inhibited the growth of a state capable of remedying social and economic woes, but many conservatives view the Constitution as having been relentlessly abrogated to bring an intrusive redistributionist state into being. Can the same constitution be so radically different, "breaking bad" according to political tastes?

On the left, the Constitution is a "relic" (Howell and Moe 2016). Its authors never intended for it to become a "forever constitution" but one in sync with changing times: a "Living Constitution." The limited government that once safeguarded against majority tyranny now inhibits expression of the popular will. On the right, unlimited government – vast, intrusive, unaccountable – is the target. Successive administrations have gone beyond the Constitution's limits since the 1930s. What is required is a return to the "original understanding," as written by its authors.

And if traditional conservatives felt that the left had erected a false regime of progressive values, some outspoken pro-Trump backers feared its replacement by Sharia law. Although Trump represented the antithesis of the intellectual, his populism won support from thinkers – associated with the *Journal of American Greatness* and *American Affairs* – for whom the United States had become "post-constitutional." The republic had degenerated into a collapse of its own making. Only a reassertion of popular sovereignty via a well-intentioned American Caesar could overthrow the decadent elite destroying the nation's fabric and restore the people's natural right to rule (Publius Decius Mus 2016). Redemptive constitutionalism represented the latest expression of disillusionment, not with the Constitution – which remained sacrosanct – but with failure to live up to its promise.

Among academics, festering beneath every political dispute is a more fundamental divide over the Constitution. Consensus about a "broken" system is broad and can be found in *Why Washington Won't Work* (Hetherington and Rudolph 2015), *America's Failing Experiment* (Goidel 2015) and *American Gridlock* (Thurber and Yoshinaka 2016). "Government of the people, by the people, for the people" appears to have morphed into government of two tribes, by lawmakers-turned-lobbyists, for a plutocratic ruling class. Where no consensus exists is on a way out. Perhaps, then, the acceptance of substantial risk in seeking a fundamental constitutional rewrite rather than ritualistic praise of the Constitution should be welcomed? Americans may look at the "World Happiness Report" (Sustainable Development Solutions

Network 2017), note Norway, Denmark, Iceland, and Switzerland at the top, and decide to opt for a more European design in pursuit of "living well"?

That seems unlikely, for three reasons.

First, the 2016 presidential and congressional elections confirmed not the rise of insurgent politics but the "triumph of polarized partisanship" (Jacobson, 2017). For all the populist noise, "politics-as-usual" prevailed, reflecting rather than repudiating the real driver of political dysfunction. Much as Americans express dissatisfaction with Congress but consistently reelect their lawmakers, so partisans on both sides coalesced behind their deeply unpopular nominees. For all the sizzle about new approaches, there was precious little steak.

Secondly, political division and intense partisanship are nothing new. It is even questionable how far the bitter politics of the 2010s approached those of the 1960s and 1970s, amid civil rights struggles, Vietnam War protests, and "stagflation" that crippled the US economy, never mind the intensity of the 1850s and 1860s. The common refrain that today's troubles are unique distorts present discontents as somehow unprecedented and destined to be permanent – "politics will never be the same again" – absent some new constitutional settlement. But the violence that Irish immigrants faced in the 1840s, the Chinese in the 1880s, and eastern and southern Europeans faced at the turn of the twentieth century were of an order and magnitude of conflict unseen today. Historical context denies the unique character of contemporary American dysfunction.

Nor do the problems that exist necessarily imply a vintage Constitution gone rotten. Such "situational constitutionalism" finds regular expression in strident partisan critiques that pose as reflections about constitutionality but are more concerned with policy outcomes: the Constitution works fine when the correct policies prevail. This encompasses many: presidents who claim the Constitution is "shredded" by their opponents but upheld with studious care when they undertake the same actions; constitutional lawyers who fetishize legalism to marginalize law's inherently political aspects; and political scientists who inflate the centrality of power to minimize the influence of laws, norms and conventions to governance. But the Constitution's relevance is, if anything, even greater today in the face of transformational changes. Although critical commentary makes reform politically seductive, it offers no magic bullet and serves only as a detour, not a destination, for real change. Politics can deliver, but it requires dedicated leadership, outside pressure and public support.

Third, as Sehat (2015) argued (albeit more in sorrow than anger), many Americans still think the Founders have answers. US history has seen secessionists and unionists, conservatives and liberals, seek out the Founders to defend their policies. Recently, right and left have used them on issues such as taxes, voting rights, and war and peace. Although this may be unhealthy – Sehat argues against oversimplification of the Founders' divergent views and their misapplication to current problems – it nonetheless binds debates to constitutional rationales.

In short, the Constitution merits defending from critics. If flaws exist – and no design is flawless – that alone is insufficient to compel substantial change without carefully weighing the costs and benefits. Reform manifestos typically offer more than they deliver. The Constitution's mojo is still working, but it won't work fully while the parties remain in a state of polarized antipathy.

In 2012, Mann and Ornstein published *It's Even Worse Than It Looks: How the American Constitutional System Collided With The New Politics of Extremism*. Their argument was that, like an irresistible force encountering an immovable object, polarization had crashed into constitutional rocks. But it seems perverse to seek transformation of the tectonic plates of the system rather than dial down the extremist politics. Arguing for constitutional overhaul is better directed at political persuasion. Politics everywhere in the democratic world is about coalitions and compromise but needs dynamism among parties, interest groups and social movements that accept pragmatism over purity. Democracy is a conversation, requiring dialogue, whereas US political discourse appears like two monologues with minimal exchange: Every issue is parsed through a partisan filter, as if America exists in a permanent split-screen state. In an age of unreason – anti-intellectualism, "post-truth politics," and righteous certainty – the basic purpose of government based on popular consent is called into question. Balancing competing interests is regarded as a denial of politics, not its fullest expression.

One can therefore scrutinize the Constitution in vain for the secret to restoring "functional" government. The solution lies in the "unwritten constitution" (Amar 2012) and, especially, the parties. The biggest obstacles: reflexive partisanship and distrust at dangerous depths. As Vermuele (2013) argued, the Constitution can be conceived of as a means of managing the risks in political life – from corruption and military coups to discriminatory government actions – but pervasive mistrust of official power is not necessarily optimal. Rauch (2016) put it provocatively well:

> Neurotic hatred of the political class is the country's last universally acceptable public form of bigotry. Because that problem is mental, not mechanical, it really is hard to remedy... Populism, individualism, and a skeptical attitude toward politics are all healthy up to a point, but America has passed that point ... Our most pressing political problem today is that the country abandoned the establishment, not the other way around.

## From Whom Does the Constitution Need Defending?
## II: The Public

If the country has abandoned the establishment, has it also abandoned the Constitution? That seems preposterous. To public acclaim, politicians routinely invoke the document to rationalize their preferred positions or castigate opponents. In 2016, constitutionalized discussions were widespread: Did the president have authority to deport 11 million illegal immigrants and ban adherents of a religious faith from entering the United States? Did Hillary Clinton want to "repeal" the Second Amendment? Did the Federal Government have the right to compel states to introduce transgender bathrooms in public spaces? No other nation approximates America in incessantly discussing political issues through the prism of its constitutional framework.

The Constitution's continuing relevance is the tribute that virtue pays vice: a nation that otherwise appears pitted against itself. Elected officials pledge faithfully to defend it. The Founders are invoked to justify positions in a fashion wholly unknown elsewhere. No British politician defends tax cuts or increased spending on the National Health Service by invoking Thomas Hobbes or John Stuart Mill; no German justifies industrial policy by reference to Hegel or Nietzsche; even the Chinese have mostly given up on quoting Marx, Mao and Confucius. American politicians can face no more damaging an accusation than that they are disrespecting the Constitution.

Invoking the Constitution encompasses everything from the profound to the mundane. For example, the First Amendment assures the liberty to enjoy literature, art and political communications of every type, from the most refined to the crudest. But every celebratory beer at a sports game also owes a debt of gratitude to the Twenty-first Amendment (1933), which repealed the Prohibition the Eighteenth Amendment (1919) established. No wonder that the ever-stylish Saul Goodman, "Attorney at Law" in *Breaking Bad* and *Better Call Saul*, decorated the interior of his Albuquerque, New Mexico office with wallpaper of the Constitution's text.

But, in contrast to critics clamoring for change, the relative silence of the public is deafening. There is minimal debate among the public about the Constitution's continuing viability or the need for revision. Whether this is the result of sincere contentment or a lack of association between the discontent felt towards "Washington" and the Constitution is unclear. But the constitutional health of any order is inextricably tied to the people whose decisions and non-decisions give life and meaning to its promises, permissions and protections. No constitution is self-executing. The question of whether the Constitution is actively supported or just tolerated through myopia, ignorance or indifference is important.

American sentiments in this regard are rather mixed. Leading up to its 200th anniversary in 1987, Gallup found barely half of Americans (53 percent) agreeing the Constitution was "basically sound and meets the needs of our country"; 44 percent thought it required "some basic changes or amendments" (Saad 2017). At the same time, most Americans endorsed the division of governmental responsibilities across the executive, judicial, and legislative branches. Seventy-three percent of adults said the separation of powers was good because "it keeps any one branch from becoming too powerful." Just 19 percent said checks and balances were a "bad idea" because they "get in the way of efficient government" (Saad 2017).

Most Americans have had faith in the Constitution's longevity, though a sizeable minority has been more skeptical. In 1995, for example, Gallup asked about the likelihood that within twenty years, the Constitution would no longer be used as the basis for governing the United States. One-third thought it likely, while two-thirds said unlikely (Saad 2017). In a 2011 poll, three-quarters of Americans said the Constitution was "an enduring document that remains relevant today," while one-quarter said it needed modernization (Associated Press/GfK Roper). Most Americans are seemingly content with their "Hotel California" constitution: content to "check out but never leave."

What was also clear, though, was that Trump's unfamiliarity with the Constitution was not unusual. Although famously concise in its brevity (slightly more than 7,500 words, compared to the roughly 77,000 words of the first Harry Potter book), relatively few Americans know a great deal about the document that is the cornerstone of their way of life. For instance, in 2011, *Newsweek* convened 1,000 Americans to take a standard citizenship test; only 62 percent passed (Romano 2011). Forty-four percent could not define the Bill of Rights. Thirty-three percent did not know when the Declaration of Independence was adopted (July 4, 1776). Only 37 percent knew there are nine Supreme Court Justices. In a poll conducted for its 200th anniversary, nearly half the respondents believed the Constitution contains Karl Marx's phrase "From each according to his ability, to each according to his need" (Calandra 2010). The Annenberg Public Policy Center (2014) found that: only one-third of Americans (36 percent) could name all three government branches; one-third (35 percent) could not identify one branch; and one in five (21 percent) incorrectly believed that a 5–4 Supreme Court decision goes to Congress for reconsideration. Another Annenberg survey (2015) found that one in ten (12 percent) thought the Bill of Rights guarantees the right to own a pet. A poll of college graduates commissioned by the American Council of Trustees and Alumni in January 2016 found that 10 percent believed Judge Judy sat on the Supreme Court (American Council of Trustees and Alumni 2016).

Nor are elites more reliable. In his 2009 State of the Union, Obama declared that, "...we find unity in our incredible diversity, drawing on the promise enshrined in our Constitution: the notion that we're all created equal." But those words are from the Declaration of Independence. When *Seinfeld* and *Veep* star Julia Louis-Dreyfus was photographed naked with the Constitution written on her back for the April 24, 2014 cover of *Rolling Stone*, one prominent name – John Hancock – had never signed it, being a signatory to the Declaration. In 2009, then House Minority Leader John Boehner (R-OH), at a Capitol Hill rally, held a copy of the Constitution, pledging to "stand here with our Founding Fathers, who wrote in the Preamble that: 'We hold these truths to be self-evident...'" – the opening lines of the Declaration (Kady II 2009). Boehner was then lampooned by MSNBC's Rachel Maddow, who denied that a "Preamble" existed – before apologizing and asking viewers to join her in singing the Schoolhouse Rock version (Sheppard 2009). Even a pocket Constitution purchased in London in 2017 misleadingly included "We hold these truths..." from the Declaration on its first page, before adding "Signed, September 17, 1787" on its second (Penguin Classics 2017).

Perhaps we should not read too much into all this. But if constitutional literacy is limited, basing the case for change on public opinion – or the composition of a new convention on a random public ballot, as some suggest – may be less compelling. Constitutional arguments for change or continuity can only succeed with real-world acceptance from an engaged public.

## How Does the Constitution Need Defending?

Is there a bright future on the horizon if only sufficient Americans demanded constitutional renewal? Most works on the Constitution identify some provisions, usually concerning structure or rights, as inappropriate or outdated. But the case for continuity relies on its meeting the four criteria elaborated in the Preface, its own goals in the Preamble, and on four broad themes:

i   *Functionality and Risk Aversion*. The Constitution is in rude health and has aged well. Many criticisms are less convincing than proponents claim, nor do proponents' solutions reliably address the problems they seek to rectify. Some remedies would exacerbate dysfunction. Anyone peddling "Constitutional Solutions" needs to be treated with enlightened skepticism. In the risk-reward balance, there is a strong case for caution.

ii  *Partisan Polarization*. Constitutional engineering is an art, not a science. The Constitution is an imperfect but effective governing arrangement for American conditions. Having been amended to address the most damaging aspects of its original design, it is a *better* fit now. The core problem underpinning political dysfunction is the unyielding polarization in the priorities and preferences of political elites and the mass public. According to the Bureau of Indian Affairs, there exist 566 federally recognized tribes in the US. But in terms of "political tribes" there are only two that count (Chua 2018). Ironically, it is precisely these kinds of strongly held differences that the Constitution was designed to contain. But as long as the two parties are so strongly opposed and evenly matched, the Constitution cannot fashion effective policy outcomes and polarization hampers effective governance at home and abroad (Schultz 2018).

iii  *Comparative Metrics.* All states have tried to construct viable constitutions. On most metrics, not least political stability and the peaceful transfer of power, the United States continues to provide an unmatched level of success. You don't miss your water until the well runs dry: before deriding American faith, it behooves non-Americans to cast critical appraisals on their constitutions. Most offer pale facsimiles. In our obsession with what is new, age and antiquity do not necessarily imply outdatedness. The US Constitution is a fine example of the benefits of combining unusually learned and applied vision – what Lincoln described as "the mystic chords of memory." The Constitution's words repay careful reading. America remains a democratic republic because the people's voice counts (if not, measures from the minimum wage to civil rights would never have succeeded). But it is also a liberal republic because freedom of the press, judicial independence and the rule of law are not held hostage to popular vote. Invocation of the Constitution acts as a necessary if insufficient bulwark against the trivialization of political discourse and a reminder of the higher law that legislation and executive actions must meet.

iv   *Cost-Benefit Analysis.* "If it ain't broke, don't fix it." In *New York Trust Co. v Eisner* (1921), Justice Oliver Wendell Holmes claimed "a page of history is worth a volume of logic." But one paradox about the Constitution is that despite its achievements, the intellectual initiative is dominated by critics. Rather than viewing the document either as so sacrosanct as to be beyond criticism or as causing America's problems, the Constitution remains an effective basis for successful government. It is no relic. The distrust in which major institutions are held is a sharp contrast to the Constitution. The imperative facing Americans is less rolling the dice to transform it than reviving its relevance and "efficient secret": compromise. Mostly, where constitutional changes are feasible, they seem undesirable; and where desirable, infeasible. Many reform proposals exist, but when all is said and done, like the Wizard of Oz, there may not be all that much behind the curtain.

## Why Defend the Constitution Today?

Constitutional analysis is not exactly everyone's cup of tea. Writing about arcane subjects from secluded retreats (#ivorytowers), rarefied academic musing rarely reaches popular attention. Many scholarly criticisms remain fringe ideas. Even disgruntled (or less than "gruntled") academics advocating change generally concede its infeasibility. That does not mean that criticism is the triumph of hope over experience or the definition of insanity (mad professors doing the same thing over and over and expecting a different result). But in an era where the path to fame and fortune is through books proclaiming "failure" in their titles, it might appear quixotic to make a case for success. So, why write this unfashionably upbeat renegade tome?

For four reasons.

First, while some might claim the Constitution is not at risk, arguments for change have been growing over recent years. Admittedly, amendment proposals introduced into Congress each session are typically more about scoring political points than serious efforts to change the document. Academic monographs on constitutional change also typically encounter a tsunami of public indifference and languish unread and unloved. Some might therefore say – according to political tastes – that outside the DC cocktail party circuit, Harvard common rooms or Mar-a-Lago, the Constitution is in no danger.

But across the left and right, important forces are mobilizing behind reform. The National Popular Vote Compact has been seeking to alter the ways presidents are elected, for example. The push by conservative groups such as the Balanced Budget Amendment Task Force (BBATF) and Convention of States (COS) has given serious impetus to a new constitutional convention. By the spring of 2018, the BBATF had gained twenty-eight of the thirty-four states needed for a convention, while a COS resolution had passed in one or both chambers of twenty-one state legislatures. Progressive concern about issues such as campaign finance and elections add to the possibility that a Constitution long taken for granted as an immovable feature of the landscape could be encountering the irresistible force of public exasperation with politics-as-usual.

Strident political arguments may metastasize into constitutional ones. The more that gridlock continues, the more that concerned citizens will look for structural rather than political or policy solutions. On the right, the focus is on constitutional means to conservative outcomes: reinvigorating federalism, a balanced budget amendment. On the left, calls for greater equality and social justice are increasingly dissatisfied with indirect presidential elections, the separation of powers and judicial review. Perceptions of crisis heighten anxieties and fan the flames for systemic change. Although most Americans strongly defend the Constitution, the Overton Window – the range of acceptable ideas in public debate – may yet encompass radical reform. "Low risk, high impact" though it may be, the notion that a new constitutional moment is impossible is no longer tenable. So, the case for the Constitution is preventive: getting the defense in early.

Second, few of us searching for adrenaline-fueled, life-enhancing activities consume learned treatises on the Constitution as guilty pleasures. Many works are important but inaccessible. Excessive jargon is the enemy of clear thinking. This is unfortunate, not only because the topic is fascinating but also because it deserves a wide readership. Few documents are better worthy of careful study and persistent reflection. Readers will not find all this book's arguments, as lawyers say, dispositive, and may find some provocative. But in an era that is not exactly overflowing with reasoned rather than censorious debate, thinking seriously about the Constitution should not be limited to September 17 each year (Constitution Day). If, as contended here, dysfunction is more about politics and culture than institutional design, then "change the Constitution" proposals are, in some ways, intellectually lazy responses to the sources of, and inadequate solutions to, America's real problems.

Third, popular culture (not least, American popular culture) abets an unreflective, vulgar constitutionalism that treats the US foundation as a kind of peculiar, boutique effort of limited or freakish appeal. Cartoonish notions that the United States is locked in a time warp and politics is systemically corrupt require debunking. Outstanding shows such as *House of Cards* and *Veep* nonetheless portray "public service" as a contradiction and Washington as a swamp that merits "draining." They reinforce a certain historical amnesia and a simplistic caricature of dubiously venal politicians and the Constitution as the fount of original American sin: "Americans can't get gun control because of the Second Amendment," "Americans are racist, they wrote slavery into their Constitution," "The First Amendment allows you to say anything you like in America." Even in an age of American politics that is all-too-difficult to satirize, we should perhaps aim higher.

Fourth and finally, when asked to name a concise, up-to-date defense of the Constitution, I've been snookered. Many excellent works offer highly negative assessments. But while critics have thrown down the gauntlet, it has not been picked up. There exist few coherent defenses of the Constitution as it is: neither lost nor in exile nor precluding social progress; imperfect, complex, yet impressively suited for the United States compared to all alternatives. That does not mean that America's is the best of all possible constitutional worlds, nor does it require defending every element in the existing design. Like those who support a sports team, one can defend the team but still want some transfers in and out to breathe new life into its prospects for success. Lest it be thought too traditionalist, the pages that follow do not exhibit a zero tolerance for constitutional reform – quite the contrary. Although they are politically unlikely to occur in my lifetime, some areas would clearly benefit from modernizing revision: most importantly, an end to equal state representation in the Senate, but also a line-item veto, changed presidential eligibility conditions, judicial term limits and mandatory retirement, a proportional method of allocating state electoral votes, and a more relaxed set of constitutional amendment requirements. But even so, the Constitution still works well and – for the reverence in which it is held – remains rather undervalued.

Full disclosure: As an Englishman with no skin in the game, my perspective on US politics is more that of a war correspondent than a participant. But my constitutional enthusiasm remains uncurbed nonetheless. Although many now treat the Constitution as so ordinary as to no longer be original, that is testament to its remarkable success. It is worth offering at least two, if not three, cheers for the Constitution, and providing some intellectual ballast to a positive case for constitutional continuity and against major change.

## The Structure of the Book

To make my case for the defense, after reviewing various contemporary critiques in the next chapter, I then adopt the same sequence as the Constitution itself. In Chapter 2, I consider the "beginning." The Preamble's importance stems from its integrative power as "the part of the constitution that best reflects the constitutional understandings of the framers" (Orgad 2010: 715). The pledge to create a "more perfect" union was not utopian but one that has been substantially fulfilled. It helped to meet two of the four conditions of an effective constitution: providing a stable framework for government by channeling conflict into everyday politics and ensuring the peaceful transfer of power.

Chapter 3 then assesses the governing institutions. A serious governance crisis exists. But while the flaws that critics identify are serious, their remedies are mostly unpersuasive. Change merits careful evaluation but these promise less a road to better days than a dead end. Moreover, the governing arrangements meet the third criterion of effective constitutionalism: allowing the expression in law of majority will while safeguarding rights and liberties.

In Chapter 4, I turn to the amendment process and judicial review. These provide key mechanisms by which the constitutional order is updated and revised. Though often pitted against one another, amendments represent a beginning, not an end – they require interpretation, an inherently political as well as legal process. By permitting the means of its own revision and reinterpretation, the fourth condition of an effective constitution is met.

Finally, in the conclusion, I offer some reflections on four aspects of contemporary debate: the Constitution's "cult" status; "constitutional crisis"; the problems of a new convention; and the possibility of political renewal without constitutional rewrites. That discussion reaffirms that the Constitution is not calcified but bespoke for American conditions. There is no Holy Grail of constitutional overhaul that can solve political problems about which Americans disagree. To paraphrase Churchill's famous comment about democracy, for America, "the US Constitution is the worst form of government except all those other forms that have been tried from time to time."

America's institutional system is strong, even if the state of the union is not. Across the sweep of US history, the Constitution has been repeatedly on intellectual trial since its inception. The case for the prosecution has been made, with varying levels of success, by multiple advocates across the political spectrum. A robust case for the defense is made in the pages that follow.

# 1 Constitutional Critiques

## The Reemergence of Jeffersonian Constitutional Angst

> Some men look at constitutions with sanctimonious reverence, and deem them like the arc of the covenant, too sacred to be touched. They ascribe to the men of the preceding age a wisdom more than human, and suppose what they did to be beyond amendment ... (But) laws and institutions must go hand in hand with the progress of the human mind.
>
> Thomas Jefferson, letter to Samuel Kercheval,
> July 12, 1816 (Leicester 1904)

> When America has doubts, these seldom extend to the ideals of its Constitution, which are on the contrary invoked as inviolable precepts to condemn those who govern badly. The American dream is thus reborn from the worst errors and survives all reports of its death.
>
> Pascal Bruckner (2010: 91–92)

## Introduction

Nothing is more calculated to antagonize the nationalist sensibilities of folk outside the United States – "to make America grate again"– than to point out how, on multiple indices, the United States remains number one. But America's is the oldest codified constitution in existence. It was, when composed, a revolutionary document advancing an entirely new form of government. More than two centuries after its ratification, this remarkably short Constitution remains unique, confirming that "less is more" (the Constitution contains approximately 7,500 words, the Ten Commandments some 200, the Declaration of Independence 1,300, and the Magna Carta 4,000). In the twenty-first century, tenacious adherence to a text written by fifty-five eighteenth-century gentlemen for an entirely different society and time might seem perverse. But the Constitution has endured through adapting to immense changes while retaining its structure and animating values essentially intact.

Constitutions, to give them their formal definition, are "codes of norms which aspire to regulate the allocation of powers, functions, and duties among the various agencies and officers of government, and to define the relationships between these and the public" (Finer, Bogdanor and Rudden 1995: 1). Most are, at best, incomplete guides to practice. Some are ominously aspirational (for example, North Korea's Constitution states that its aim is reunification of the Korean Peninsula under the Kim family's control). Many are ineffective (ignored, suspended, or violated) or promise illusory goals. America's is different. Admired and emulated, the Constitution has nowhere been bettered as a revolutionary design for republican government: providing a stable framework for government, reconciling the need for collective action by the state with the consent and representation of the governed and respect for civil liberties and rights, ensuring the peaceful transfer of power, and allowing its own revision.

Most states now possess codified constitutions. Each provides the crossroads where a nation's values and institutions meet. But in no other does the foundation exert such extensive influence, both on the way government acts and in the nation's daily life. In its brevity, structure, and institutions, no constitution comes close to approximating America's fusion of concision and complexity – including the constitutions of the individual states devised before and after the federal one.

As important, the Constitution has a meaning to its citizens – a lived authenticity – that no other can match. There exists no more compelling a political object for patriotism – what Orwell (1994) called the "devotion to a particular place and a particular way of life" – that transcends all other divisions. In an era where the new and youthful exercise inflated influence, infatuation with an aged parchment provides a conspicuous contrast. The repository of national values, the Constitution provides the steadiest of tectonic plates for a polity that has otherwise been reliably fractious.

One of the happier by-products of the unhappy state of politics is the revival of works examining the Constitution. Historically, these have surfaced amid periods of major stress on the political system (although the strains of the 1950s and 1960s produced relatively little constitutional criticism; the exception that proved the rule). The last fertile period was the 1970s, when the United States appeared to succumb to the "crisis of governability" that shook many Organization for Economic Cooperation and Development (OECD) member countries. The question of whether America was impossible to govern preoccupied many, including the White House. With the Reagan Era (1981–1989), those concerns dissipated, but a few lingering analyses lamented the Federal Government's inability to run a balanced budget and the negative consequences of divided party control of the White House and Capitol Hill (Sundquist 1992).

Not until recently, however, has there been such an outpouring of critical constitutionalism. Reflecting the sense of a system creaking under multiple pressures, many scholars track the ills to the Constitution. Unlike prior eras, these problems are not isolated. The targets of anxiety are not only the presidency and Congress, but courts, the electoral and party systems, and federalism. Unlike earlier iterations, however, division exists over the nature of the problems and available solutions. Is the United States in democratic deficit or surplus? Is the system insufficiently responsive to popular demands or much too attentive?

In this chapter, I argue that constitutional critiques can be divided broadly into Madisonian and Jeffersonian approaches to change, and Jeffersonian and Hamiltonian approaches to the size of government. After elaborating three types of critique, the chapter examines the twenty-first century revival of constitutional debate. Finally, I identify the most influential criticisms before revisiting their key suggestions for reform in later chapters.

## Madison v Jefferson (v Hamilton)

The Constitution can be revered and disputed without contradiction. It offers a source of hope and disappointment. An important part of that enduring dualistic tradition concerns the relative merit of constitutional continuity versus change. King (2012: 154) wrote that, "More than two centuries after its ratification, the hold that the American Constitution still has on the American imagination is almost impossible to exaggerate... the founding fathers, if only they knew, would be astonished as well as delighted." But while their astonishment would surely be universal, the delight would probably be more selective. The Founders disagreed over much, including the merits of an enduring constitutional settlement. This finds ample expression in the divergent perspectives of two key Founders.

For James Madison, the "father" of the Constitution, no constitution was "too big to fail." Although a calcified constitution was to be undesirable and best avoided, "veneration" of the Constitution was necessary for it to survive. For the American experiment in self-government to be sustainable and provide a stable foundation for the republic, the Constitution needed to be more than merely a passing interlude between successive rewrites. The draft assembled in 1787 through a succession of painful compromises – including concessions to the South over slavery and Anti-Federalists over the Bill of Rights – was not guaranteed to survive.

Madison was far from satisfied with the Constitution that emerged and held it to be flawed rather than sublime. But he was nonetheless convinced that its prospects depended on commanding respect, rather than inviting revision. For revisionists, the "rationality" of reform may be obvious, but for Madisonians, constitutions are not national lifestyle choices to be adjusted season by season according to passing fashion. That Madisonian thread, emphasizing the benefits of continuity, still informs many critiques that are cautious about change and risk averse towards experimentation. To be effective, constitutions must be conservative forces, providing for and prioritizing stability.

But Thomas Jefferson – reflecting his role in America's revolutionary break from colonial rule – believed that criticism of the constitutional order was desirable and healthy. New generations would and should author their own versions as they deemed necessary. In human affairs, constitutional failure – partial, if not total – was predestined to occur. Regular renewal was not to be feared. In a famous letter on political obligation, Jefferson wrote to Madison that "by the law of nature, one generation is to another as one independent nation is to another ... The earth belongs to the living and not the dead" (Lepore 2010: 29). The authority of America's founding documents was contingent, since "each generation" should "choose for itself the form of government it believes most promotive of its own happiness" (Lepore 2010: 309). Little solace should be taken by Americans that the United States is the last codified Constitution standing if it no longer remains fit for its purpose.

The Jeffersonian embrace of change lends itself easily to critics and arguments for reform. (President Kennedy once commenced a White House dinner for Nobel Prize winners on April 29, 1962 with the words, "I think this is the most extraordinary collection of talent, of human knowledge, that has ever been gathered together at the White House, with the possible exception of when Thomas Jefferson dined alone" [Kennedy 1962].) Those seeking to identify an "original" constitutional meaning are hamstrung by the conflicting views of its authors and the compromises they struck. Those viewing it as "holy writ" for "Americanism" face the problem that Jefferson – author of the Declaration of Independence and an admirer, though not signatory, of the Constitution – never viewed the design as permanently set in stone. Zakaria (2011) provided one example of Jeffersonian ambivalence:

> I believe that the Constitution was one of the wonders of the world – in the 18$^{th}$ century. But today we face the reality of a system that has become creaky... And if one mentions any of this, why, one is being unpatriotic, because we have the perfect system of government, handed down to us by demigods who walked the earth in the late 18$^{th}$ century and who serve as models for us today and forever ... America's founders would have been profoundly annoyed by this kind of unreflective ancestor worship.

Given such sentiments about symbolism versus substance, one might imagine that Americans would have taken up the call to abandon ancestor worship – not just because their ancestors were flawed, but also because they would have hated it (though that, too, would logically have been a form of abiding by their wishes). To please the Framers, a revision of constitutional order and the tree of liberty would seem in order (if not necessarily accompanied by the blood of patriots and tyrants). Or, as former Republican governor of New Mexico and 2016 Libertarian Party candidate for president Gary Johnson put it, "The fact that the founders anticipated our two-party morass and warned against it ought to be enough incentive to look beyond it" (Johnson 2016).

But Americans have never shown too many constitutional inhibitions. Although many Americans construct their own personal shrines to the Constitution – displaying copies in their offices, homes, or, like the late Senator Robert Byrd (D-WV), carrying pocket versions – there exists no shortage of critics claiming that the god they worship is a false idol. Assembling all their collected works would constitute quite the spectacle. The seas may run dry before critical works on the Constitution cease being published.

A rough estimate would suggest that – between the two Virginians – Madison has proven victorious in the overall war, while losing some battles. Passion for the Constitution has mostly been matched by reservation about reform, and failure to achieve it. Since 1791, only seventeen amendments have been enacted, the last in 1992. The ratio of proposed amendments introduced in Congress to those ratified is over 1000:1. But Jeffersonians periodically wage spirited new campaigns when, as now, politics no longer seems to "work."

That is especially ironic since there exists a second important debate about constitutional development relevant to politics today: the size of the Federal Government. But in this debate, between Jeffersonians and Hamiltonians, it is the Jeffersonian view that typically is least congenial to those seeking far-reaching change.

On this, Jefferson was more the status quo figure, an advocate of the view that, "That government governs best that governs least." Government closest to the people – states and local units – rather than a remote but robust national government was preferable. Jefferson's rival, Alexander Hamilton, instead saw a strong national government and an "energetic" chief executive as essential if the new nation was to prosper. A strong proponent of government's implied powers (those going beyond the enumerated ones listed in the Constitution), Hamilton wrote in *Federalist 31* that:

> A government ought to contain in itself every power requisite to the full accomplishment of the objects committed to its care, and to the complete execution of the trust for which it is responsible, free from every other control but a regard to the public good and to the sense of the people.

The Hamiltonian approach anticipated the future trajectory of political thought that has, mostly, championed expansion of the state. Hamilton believed the Federal Government could be a positive instrument for addressing common problems that no individual or locality could re-solve alone, such as maintaining a strong defense or creating a national currency. As Abraham Lincoln later put it, "Government is people coming together collectively to do that which they could not do as well, or at all, individually" (Hallard 1996: 9).

In a sense, then, constitutional genealogists – tracing the genetic imperfections of US democracy to constitutional causes – ultimately fall on one side of the twin historic divides between Jefferson and his contemporaries. We are arguably witnesses to a surprisingly symmetrical struggle today. On one hand, there is the reemergence of Jeffersonian constitutional angst in pursuit of Hamiltonian ends: progressives who want reform to allow a stronger government to intervene more decisively in social, economic, and political life. Against this, there is a counterpoint in conservatives, who favor Madisonian reverence for the "original" Constitution as an anti-Hamiltonian method of rejecting federal intervention, seeking a more "lean and mean" Jeffersonian government.

Although, therefore, talk of revising the Constitution is often seen as heresy, criticism has a long history. John Vile (1991) even identified eight distinct post-Civil War periods of critical constitutionalism from Reconstruction to the late twentieth century, in which forty proposals to rewrite the Constitution were advanced. Contrary to Zakaria's *faux* indignity, no one has been ostracized by adverse appraisals. Moreover, to those seeking to scribble a polemic against the prevailing political system, the Constitution is a gift that keeps on giving. Since little in public life cannot ultimately be traced to its design, critical commentaries appear with metronomic frequency.

Their content, however, is less predictable. It varies from utopian schemes of comprehensive overhaul to proposals for incremental adjustments. Coolly forensic criticism is more attached to aspects of the Constitution than the entire design. More idealized critiques tend to imply that the parts are rather less than the whole. What these appraisals share is an emphasis on the document's deficient origins, oddities, and decay. Taken together, it is outdated and inappropriate. Or, as Garrett Epps (2016) asserted, "Constitutional rot has spread from a feckless Congress to a desperate executive, and is now enfeebling the judiciary."

One way to identify critiques employs their ideological leanings. On the left, the Constitution is typically viewed as noble but errant. Its promise as a "Living Constitution" remains unfulfilled and only when substantial reform occurs will it be worthy of popular veneration. On the right, the problem is more about mistaken interpretation. For Burkean conservatives, an instinctive "bring backery" – yearning for the past – is in their DNA. What they cherish most about constitutional order is typically vanishing, changing, or threatened. On this reading, the Constitution was invariably "best before... (insert date of presidency, congressional session or Supreme Court ruling here)."

One of the ironies about the conflict between these constitutionalists – one a set of avowed futurists, the other nostalgic – is that neither side can ever be content with the status quo. The right looks back at a constitution whose meaning has been erased and replaced with new writing, mere traces of the original remaining; the left looks askance at the existing version and forward to a comprehensive rewrite to offer a better egalitarian dispensation for the masses.

However, some on the right were unpersuaded that America's political system could be remedied. Populist nationalists more than conservatives, they wanted the prevailing disorder overthrown by a candidate voicing the popular will. This was dramatically elaborated in the essay "The Flight 93 Election." The author, "Decius," drew an analogy between the state of America and Flight 93 on 9/11, where, faced with the knowledge of certain death, the passengers bravely took a chance to regain control of the aircraft, only to tragically crash in Shanksville, Pennsylvania. He claimed that America faced a comparable choice between political reaction and national suicide.

According to this analysis, a partial list of reasons why "the republic is dying" included: illegitimacy, oppressive government, high taxes, crumbling infrastructure, declining morality, political correctness, crumbling families, and failed schools that turned out "disruptive punks." Establishment conservatives who called for civic renewal and incremental change were blind to the gravity of America's predicament. The existential challenge was so profound and the issues so fundamental that America had to turn to an insurgent. "Decius" drew on the work of theorist Leo Strauss to distinguish "tyranny" from "Caesarism." A tyrant takes absolute power by overthrowing a constitutional republic. A Caesar also takes absolute power, but only when a republic has already collapsed. Decius argued that Donald Trump probably wasn't a Caesar, because "he will serve no more than his Constitutionally permissible two terms." But even if he was, it might serve America right. By overthrowing an unaccountable elite, Trump would reassert "the people's sovereignty" and "their natural right to rule themselves." "Have we not degenerated to the point that we are ready for Caesar?" Decius wrote:

> Caesarism is not tyranny. It is rather a sub-species of absolute monarchy, in which the monarch is not an unjust usurper but the savior of a country with a decayed republican order that can no longer function.
>
> (Publius Decius Mus 2016)

Some might dismiss this as hyperbole, vulgar constitutionalism, or worse. But the author using the pseudonym Decius, Michael Anton, went on to serve as Deputy Assistant to the President for Strategic Communications in the National Security Council from 2017–2018.

How far his prescriptions were realized remained unclear. Nonetheless, regardless of the merits, the severity of the crisis he detailed suggested a constitutional order under pressure.

## Three Types of Constitutional Critique

An alternative to classifying critiques by ideology is to identify the scope of change they advocate. In this more neutral taxonomy of scale, the ecosystem of constitutional studies comprises three general forms. Each makes a case that the Constitution is problematic.

Those finding fault with aspects of American life are drawn to constitutional criticism like moths to a flame. For the severest critics – "external jeremiads," "radicals" and "reactionaries" – the Constitution is in perpetual crisis. This stern genre of *constitution noir* – pessimistic, fatalistic, and downbeat, like its *film noir* counterpart – exists regardless of whether most Americans are aware of or share the sensibility. To more incrementally minded observers, imperfections exist, but these are not necessarily serious enough to rise to crisis level.

### (i)  External Jeremiads: Constitutional Critiques from Abroad

As far back as colonial days, the "promised land" of a "new Atlantis" was something that preoccupied non-Americans as much as Americans. Strange tales were told of America, with "dogs that didn't bark" and other exotica to be discovered. Latterly, travelers such as Charles Dickens and P. G. Wodehouse offered their own assessments: some positive, others less so. Invariably pitched in terms of the "how do we explain these peculiar Americans and their exotic practices?" formula, writers from De Tocqueville to Levy (2006) offered complex appraisals. Some are empathetic, but many are unimpressed by a people so credulous as to believe in the American Creed. Most seek to account for the unrequited love of Americans for their Constitution, a love often depicted as more blind than romantic.

Foreign assessments reveal as much about the nations and nationalities of the writers as they do the United States. Even today, critics outside the United States cannot resist cheap shots at the constitutional order that contain more than a hint of visceral anti-American sentiment (Singh 2005). Where Bill Clinton once articulated the essence of the American Creed in his first inaugural address in 1993 – "There is nothing wrong with America that cannot be cured by what is right with America" – what unites these critiques is a palpable sense that there is nothing wrong with America apart from its being populated by Americans.

Comparative assessments differ in damning the document with the faintest of praise. A few offer backhanded compliments that "the American system works, or has worked, *in spite of* its constitution – hardly *thanks to* its constitution" (Sartori 1994: 89 [italics in the original]). Some minimize the extent to which the Constitution has resulted in different outcomes to the wider industrialized world (Baldwin 2009; Wilson 1998). Others, however, lament Americans believing in their own propaganda about exceptionalism. For example, in a review of James D. Zirin's *Supremely Partisan*, English historian Dominic Sandbrook (2016) wrote:

> The basic problem, it seems to me, is not the supposed partisanship of the judges. After all, you can hardly expect extremely clever, highly experienced, supremely well-educated people not to have strong political opinions. The deeper problem lies in imagining that you can run a vast 21$^{st}$-century continental empire according to the principles of a document drafted by 55 men in wigs and breeches in the summer of 1787. But that thought, I suspect, has never occurred to Zirin at all.

Many comparative works rehearse familiar themes: the Constitution is old, the Founders neither solved existing problems nor anticipated new ones, the language protected slavery, and the Constitution was difficult to alter to accommodate change. A central objection is anti-statism: a "moral vacuum" at the Constitution's core (Putley 1997). The Constitution is the preeminent example of "path dependency": once established, the constitutional order has assumed an inexorable logic that only external shocks disturb.

What tends to unify external critics is less the design but more a disapproval of the policy outcomes inferred to be the result of that design: legal private ownership of firearms and less generous social welfare provision than European states, for example. For British critics, the preference for "strong" government is the "Westminster model," in which one party with most seats in the House of Commons (the lower house of the national parliament) typically can rule with minimal trouble from opposing parties. Such a model, fusing executive and legislative power, provides more rapid and decisive state action, offering responsible governments that can be held accountable for their program at the next election. On this accounting, a parliamentary system could change US politics for the better (Manuel and Cammisa 1999).

What is problematic about such criticisms is fourfold. First, the comparative achievements of the Westminster model are not obviously better. Second, the costs in a more diverse nation are higher. The US model may make it difficult for society to gain, but it also prevents society from losing, through government action. Third, issues of representation and accountability plague a system that no longer works in the classical sense, if it ever did. For example, coalition government between the Conservatives and Liberal Democrats occurred from 2010 to 2015. Fourth, legitimacy questions undermine governments elected on minority votes. The

Conservatives under Margaret Thatcher and John Major (1979–1997) and Labor under Tony Blair and Gordon Brown (1997–2010) each held power for more than a decade with most parliamentary seats when most voters – at every election from 1979–2010 – voted *against* those parties.

The holier-than-thou aspect of some external critiques has declined in recent decades, partly due to the rise of the US as a global power, its economic influence, and advances in civil rights. The decline has also reflected a humility about their own constitutions' defects. For example, their density leaves constitutional discussions as a rarefied matter for lawyers rather than the people. (Few EU citizens can name relevant provisions of the Treaty of Rome and other turgid texts.) Popular loyalty to constitutions is much less present elsewhere. But even so, there remains a sense among external critics that while other states have emulated the United States in devising their own Bill of Rights, they have wisely avoided importing the separation of powers, checks and balances, and "vetocracy" (Fukuyama 2014; King 2012).

### (ii) Radical and Reactionary Critiques

Radical and reactionary critiques echo external ones, but with nationalistic rather than cosmopolitan features. Sometimes, however, they go further in their quest for transformation and stigmatizing the Constitution. Some authors even seem to be guilty of, in that southern phrase, "losing their religion" (getting angry). But none are unserious.

Historically, radical works tend to fault the Constitution less for aging disgracefully than for original sin: being flawed by design. They endorse the poignant critique advanced by the first African American Supreme Court Justice, Thurgood Marshall, on the Constitution's bicentenary:

> I do not believe that the meaning of the Constitution was forever "fixed" at the Philadelphia Convention. Nor do I find the wisdom, foresight and sense of justice exhibited by the Framers particularly profound. To the contrary, the government they devised was defective from the start, requiring several amendments, a civil war and momentous social transformation to attain the system of constitutional government, and its respect for individual freedoms and human rights, we hold as fundamental today.
>
> (Marshall 1987)

Typically, this denunciation attributes American ills to the Founders and their errant intent, codified in a static constitutional order that inhibits change as it perpetuates private property and white privilege. Where defenders see a set of ideas that have proved incomparably successful – property rights; separation of powers; limits on the power of the state; protection of the rights of conscience, assembly, speech, and self-protection; guarantees for local government over central planning; and a free market economy – radicals perceive Americans imprisoned by an order that is so "natural" as to be immune to rational challenge or change.

Sehat (2015), for example, laments the "Jefferson rule," whereby politicians and the public employ an outdated context – invariably citing Jefferson to rationalize their preferences – to make sense of contemporary concerns. Such ancestor worship and oversimplification distort historical truth and obscure today's issues. From Jefferson until now, Americans have looked to the eighteenth century to solve their problems, even though the Founders themselves were a querulous and divided group who rarely agreed. Caught up in the cult of Constitution-worship, Americans fail to locate the source of their maladies even as it is right before their noses. As Max Lerner (1937: 1294) put it:

> To understand the fetishism of the Constitution, one would require the detachment of an anthropologist. Every tribe needs its totem and its fetish, and the Constitution is ours. Every tribe clings to something which it believes to possess supernatural powers, as an instrument for controlling unknown forces in a hostile universe.

Constitutional anthropologists are less in vogue on campus these postmodern days than the American-style Jacques Derridas who are busy deconstructing the hidden truths of oppressive power behind the document's idealistic facade. Historians and political scientists have long recognized that legal institutions facilitate the formation of modern states by monopolizing and legitimizing violence, protecting economic transactions and property rights, and justifying taxation and military conscription. In a distinguished tradition of writers from historian Charles Beard's *Economic Interpretation of the Constitution* (2011) to Lazare's *The Frozen Republic* (1996), the "cult" of the deified Constitution is a common theme for righteous censure. As Lazare noted, constitutional change was at the center of the original Progressive agenda. Populists called for a system of national referendums, while Socialists pushed amendments for a graduated income tax, women's suffrage, and abolition of the presidential veto. In calling for a nonviolent, pro-democratic coup by the House of Representatives to rid America of the Founders' anti-democratic elements, Lazare (1996: 293) argued that:

> Not just the Constitution would be toppled, but so would checks and balances, separation of powers, and the deeply inculcated habit of deferring to the authority of a group of eighteenth-century Country gentlemen ... The traditional American distrust of political power, rooted in the ideology of the eighteenth-century Country opposition, would undoubtedly disappear as well.

On this reading, the rotten Constitution was motivated not by republican ideas but by parochial economic interests, and the resulting design "paralyzes" democracy, leaving the republic "frozen." The Constitution's otherwise admirable parsimony becomes an austere conservatism, its promise more suited for avaricious "Masters of the Universe" at Goldman Sachs, Halliburton and ExxonMobil than the citizenry. One recent expression of this approach (Smith, Esparza, and Blau 2017) claims that "'United Statesians' lag behind almost all other nations: constitutional guarantees of 'negative rights' neglect the 'positive' human rights that are now enshrined in other constitutions worldwide" (no matter that most of these rights are studiously ignored by the states promising them).

Like zealots pursuing a secular moral inquisition, these efforts at censuring the Constitution and its authors tend to be less a call for selective reform than for counter-constitutionalism. Although subtle and sincere in their radicalism, they are nonetheless proclaiming the urgent need for, and the feasibility of, constitutional transformation. Rather than mild adjustments, they pursue far-reaching change that seeks to salvage something of promise from the wreckage of constitutional disorder. Mindful of the warning of the German economist Werner Sombart that "all socialist utopias come to nothing on roast beef and apple pie," they are preternaturally disposed toward times of crisis or, as Huntington (1981) termed it, "Creedal Passion" – when the gap between American ideals and reality can no longer be tolerated (such as the Revolutionary War, the Jacksonian age, the Progressive era, and the 1960s).

Present discontents in the United States give ample cause for concern that the Constitution's traditional strengths are being eroded from within. Traditionally, the United States has been the exemplar of the distinction between what Easton (1965) termed "regime legitimacy" and "government legitimacy." People may feel that the government is not ruling well, and current arrangements are not working for them, but this only reinforces their appreciation for the broader system that allows them to protest, organize, and vote the government out of office. The distinction between *the* government and *government* (the constitutional edifice) matters and is clear, not blurred.

But there is strong evidence now that – even prior to the Trump presidency – systemic strains exist, and consolidated democracies are experiencing increasing signs of serious wear and tear. For example, as Foa and Mounk's (2016) analysis of World Values Survey data indicated, on four key measures – citizen support for the system; belief in key institutions, such as civil rights; willingness to advance political goals within the existing system; and openness to authoritarian alternatives, like military rule – democracies may be in the early stages of deconsolidation. That might cheer some radicals on the left, but, more recently, some reactionaries on the right have also felt the call of duty, typically arguing that the Constitution has been robbed of its original meaning. To "constitutional conservatives," the real Constitution has been rent asunder by illegitimate government encroachment, progressive usurpation, and the feckless exercise of "raw judicial power."

The Constitution of civics textbooks and under glass in the National Archives in Washington is no longer the one practiced by the elected branches or enforced by the courts. Since constitutional judicial review was proclaimed in *Marbury v Madison* (1803), but especially since the 1930s, the courts have been cutting holes in the original Constitution and its amendments to eliminate the parts that preserve and protect liberty. From the Commerce Clause and the Necessary and Proper Clause, through the Ninth and Tenth Amendments, to the Privileges or Immunities Clause of the Fourteenth Amendment, the courts have rendered each of these increasingly toothless. In the process, the written Constitution has been lost (Barnett 2013, 2016; Lee 2016). Americans are akin to constitutional strangers, their Constitution exiled from Main Street.

The relentless enabling of an intrusive federal regulatory state has also downsized the original content and deprived Americans of their proper polity. (Concern that, especially since 9/11, the national security state tramples civil liberties is one of the rare instances of shared convictions by civil libertarians on the left and right.) Agreement on how to differ – by reference to a shared Constitution – was traditionally a unifying mark of political discourse. But now, the Constitution itself generates division. In a twenty-first century populist expression of "radical conservative nostalgia," "for many Republicans, the modern structures of public power and authority are illegitimate departures from the purity of the Framers' original design" (Peele 2014: 17). Some even claim that Islamist terrorism represents an ideological war "targeting core American constitutional and philosophical principles" (Bolton 2016).

No matter their divergent ideological leanings, radical critiques exhibit something of the reactionary strand in Romanticism that contains a visceral dislike of, and aversion to conceding, progress; Steven Pinker (2018: 39–52) termed such critics "progressophobes." But thus far, neither the radical nor reactionary critiques, nor the external ones, have won substantial popular support, perhaps as they are out of sync with the basically positive predisposition of American culture toward the future. That could occur. But for our purposes, more incremental Jeffersonian criticisms have greatest salience. These seek less to destroy the US house than to mend some important features in serious disrepair.

### (iii) Incremental Critiques: Repairing America's Fences

Most recent critiques see the devil in the detail when it comes to constitutional reform. These authors offer two cheers for the Constitution – one more than external critics, radicals, and reactionaries, but not the full-throated three.

Historically, such critical interpretations were to be expected when genuine crises threatened to tear the United States apart – in the revolutionary era, prior to the Civil War, and during the Great Depression. At such moments, widespread discontent supplants complacency, cynicism, and hypocrisy; authority and expertise are questioned; traditional values of liberty, individualism, equality, and popular control of government dominate public debate; politics is highly polarized amid constant protests; hostility toward concentrated power, wealth, and inequality grows intense; social movements flourish; and new forms of media devoted to advocacy and adversarial journalism arise. With uncanny timing, Huntington (1981) even predicted that, given the historically cyclical nature of responses to the gap between America's promise and reality, a "major sustained creedal passion period" would be due in the second and third decades of the twenty-first century.

Even in less momentous times, concerns that government wasn't working, and the political system was "broken," generated constitutional anxiety. In the 1970s, for example, after the serial frustrations of the Carter presidency, senior legal counsel Lloyd Cutler argued that "... it is not now possible 'to Form a Government.' The separation of powers between the executive and legislative branches, whatever its merits in 1793, has become a structure that almost guarantees stalemate today." By fractioning power and preventing accountability, a "permanent centrism" was guaranteed:

> ...in this century the system has succeeded only on the rare occasions when there is an unusual event that brings us together and creates substantial consensus throughout the country on the need for a whole new program.
>
> (Cutler 1980: 127)

Cutler concluded that, "The structure of our Constitution prevents us from doing significantly better."

That familiar assertion now resembles a premature capitulation and a reflection more on Jimmy Carter than on the Constitution. But constitutional reflections tend to be products of their historical contexts. The notion that what ails America is a "permanent centrism" seems quaint. A temporary, never mind "permanent," centrism would be a welcome departure from decades of polarized antipathy. Nonetheless, that criticism may be an artifact of its era does not mean it lacks purchase. In the contemporary context – when such widespread perceptions that the system is "rigged" for privileged and powerful elites exist – the revival of serious constitutional criticism is unsurprising, but nevertheless striking in the breadth and depth of its targets. Before outlining some of the most important, it is worth looking at what is wrong with politics to see if this new moment of creedal passion has truly arrived on schedule.

## The Return of Dysfunction in American Government

After Bill Clinton left office in 2001 and bequeathed George W. Bush a federal budget in surplus, the United States suffered the 9/11 terrorist attacks, its longest ever war in Afghanistan, the botched occupation of Iraq following the 2003 invasion, the 2008 financial crisis and Great Recession, a national debt over $20 trillion, and Russian interference in the 2016 election. "Textbook" models of politics seem outdated, with the two parties unable to compromise and engaging in brinkmanship that saw the Federal Government shut down because of a failure to agree its funding in 1996, 2013, and 2018. As it has evolved from what Byron Shafer (2016) termed the Era of Divided Government (1969–1992) to the Era of Partisan Volatility (1993–2016, and beyond), US politics appears to have gone "insane" and, without proper remedial treatment, promises only to worsen (Rauch 2016). But, as Shafer detailed (2016: 196–200), analysts – such as James MacGregor Burns and James Sundquist – have periodically switched supposed solutions from party-focused remedies to more institutional fixes.

As Tables 1.1 and 1.2 illustrate, "Washington" is not viewed favorably. More precisely, the public does not perceive officials as working for the general benefit, but rather to line their own coffers. According to Gallup, in the month following Barack Obama's reelection as President in 2012, even 68 percent of Democrats felt that politics in Washington was "causing serious harm." Independents and Republicans agreed by still higher margins.

Moreover, this lack of confidence has long been in gestation. Congress is the most reliably unpopular branch. Even so, the recent decline in its job approval ratings has been marked. From a brief and unrepresentative high in 2001–2002 following 9/11, the decline has been steep, punctuated only by a brief resurgence in 2009–2010 (following the Democrats winning the White House and both houses of Congress).

Disapproval is not confined to Congress. Confidence in the entire Federal Government has substantially declined (Table 1.3). By 2015, only one in four Americans expressed "a great deal" or "quite a lot" of

*Table 1.1* Politics in Washington Is Causing Harm (2012)

| | Causing Serious Harm (Percent) | Effects Not Serious (Percent) | No Opinion (Percent) |
|---|---|---|---|
| Republicans | 87 | 13 | – |
| Independents | 79 | 16 | 5 |
| Democrats | 68 | 28 | 4 |

Source: Gallup (Newport 2013a).

Question: Do you think the way politics works in Washington these days is causing serious harm to the US, or are the effects not that serious?

*Table 1.2* Congressional Job Approval Ratings (2001–2017)

| Year | Approval Rate (Percent) |
| --- | --- |
| 2001 | 84 |
| 2003 | 58 |
| 2006 | 27 |
| 2009 | 39 |
| 2012 | 13 |
| 2014 | 9 |
| 2015 | 20 |
| 2016 | 13 |
| 2017 | 19 |

Source: Gallup (Brands 2017).

Question: Do you approve or disapprove of the way Congress is handling its job?

*Table 1.3* Average of Americans' Confidence Ratings of the Three Branches of Government (1991–2015)

| Year | Confidence Rate (Percent) |
| --- | --- |
| 1991 | 50 |
| 1992 | 36 |
| 1994 | 33 |
| 1995 | 37 |
| 1996 | 35 |
| 1997 | 40 |
| 2000 | 38 |
| 2002 | 46 |
| 2004 | 43 |
| 2005 | 36 |
| 2007 | 31 |
| 2008 | 23 |
| 2009 | 36 |
| 2010 | 28 |
| 2012 | 29 |
| 2013 | 27 |
| 2014 | 22 |
| 2015 | 24 |

Source: Gallup (McCarthy 2015).

Note: Confidence measured by those expressing "a great deal" or "quite a lot" of confidence.

confidence. Neither Bush (who promised to be a "uniter, not a divider"), Obama (who promised to transcend partisan differences), nor Trump (who pledged to "drain the swamp") reversed the tide of disillusion. All three together proved the most divisive presidents in modern history, each more polarizing than their immediate predecessor.

Moreover, declining public trust goes beyond Washington. As Table 1.4 illustrates, Americans have "a great deal" or "quite a lot" of confidence in almost no major institutions (except the military). Even here, public praise conceals some troubling statistics. For example, according to one striking study, 55 percent of respondents didn't know whether they had confidence in the military to perform well during wartime (Schake 2016; Schake and Mattis 2016).

Most Americans remain highly patriotic. In 2013, for example, 85 percent stated that they were proud to be American. But they had a more negative response when asked if the Founders would be pleased by how America had turned out (see Table 1.5). According to Gallup, in 2013, 71 percent of Americans said the Declaration of Independence's signatories would be disappointed; only 27 percent said pleased.

*Table 1.4* Many Institutions Lost Ground (2006–2016)

| Institution | June 2006 (Percent) | June 2016 (Percent) | Difference (Percent) |
|---|---|---|---|
| Military | 73% | 73% | 0 |
| Police | 58% | 56% | –2% |
| Church or organized religion | 52% | 41% | –11% |
| Medical system | 38% | 39% | +1% |
| Presidency | 33% | 36% | +3% |
| US Supreme Court | 40% | 36% | –4% |
| Public schools | 37% | 30% | –7% |
| Banks | 49% | 27% | –22% |
| Organized labor | 24% | 23% | –1% |
| Criminal justice system | 25% | 23% | –2% |
| Television news | 31% | 21% | –10% |
| Big business | 18% | 18% | 0 |
| Congress | 19% | 9% | –10% |

Source: Gallup (Norman 2016).

Note: Confidence measured by those expressing "a great deal" or "quite a lot" of confidence.

*Table 1.5* Founders' Views of the US (1999–2013)

| Year | Pleased (Percent) | Disappointed (Percent) |
|---|---|---|
| 1999 | 44 | 55 |
| 2001 | 54 | 42 |
| 2003 | 50 | 48 |
| 2013 | 27 | 71 |

Source: Gallup (Newport 2013b).

Question: Overall, do you think the signers of the Declaration of Independence would be pleased or disappointed by the way the United States has turned out?

## The New Constitutional Critics

Faced with popular discontent about politics, the Constitution has once again attracted a new set of critics who trace political dysfunction in large part to a constitutional source. Moreover, there is more to the renaissance of constitutional angst than merely old wine rebottled. Six examples from the revival of constitutional critique in the twenty-first century are especially illustrative.

First, in 2006 (and again in 2017), constitutional law scholar Sanford Levinson advanced a scathing critique that argued the Constitution stymies "modern ideas":

> The US Constitution is radically defective in a number of important ways … To the extent that we continue thoughtlessly to venerate, and therefore not to subject to truly critical examination, our Constitution, we are in the position of the battered wife who continues to profess the "essential goodness" of her abusive husband.
>
> (2006: 11, 20)

Levinson singled out five features:

i    the state rather than population-based composition of the US Senate (meaning that 25 percent of the Senate is now elected by just twelve of the fifty states, which together contain a mere 5 percent of the total population);

ii   the indirect rather than popular method of electing presidents through the Electoral College;

iii  the rampant growth of presidential power and the undemocratic nature of the presidential veto;

iv   the Supreme Court's problematic exercise of constitutional judicial review and the life tenure of the Justices; and

v    Article V (that requires three-quarters of the states to ratify a constitutional amendment and thereby allows a minority of just thirteen states to block amendments – the failure of the Equal Rights Amendment in the 1970s being the most recent and significant).

Levinson (2012) later doubled down against America's "imbecilic" Constitution, highlighting:

> … the Senate and its assignment of equal voting power to California and Wyoming; Vermont and Texas; New York and North Dakota. Consider that, although a majority of Americans since World War II have registered opposition to the Electoral College, we will participate this year in yet another election that

"battleground states" will dominate while the three largest states will be largely ignored.

To remedy these defects, Levinson called for a national convention:

> New York, in fact, had had five constitutions over its history, and, of course, there have been a number of amendments, many of them coming through previous conventions. I believe that the United States Constitution would be a far better Constitution if, in fact, the national electorate had the same opportunity. And I think it is a serious blemish on our democracy that we venerate the Constitution, we celebrate it, but often very thoughtlessly. And we prefer to attack each other and to attack the deficiencies of certain alleged leaders or political parties rather than to confront the possibility that it's the 1787 Constitution itself – in its surprisingly un-amended form – that is afflicting our politics in the year 2016.
>
> (Dubner 2016)

Second, political scientist Larry Sabato (2007) published the state-of-the-art *A More Perfect Constitution?*, in which he proposed comprehensive changes to revitalize the Constitution and make the US "fairer" (summarized in Figure 1.1). Sabato's remains the most sustained case for reform.

Third, Michael Klarman (2010), a constitutional historian, offered a "Constitution Day" critique focused on four problems:

i   the Framers' constitution represented values that Americans today should abhor and reject;
ii  parts of the Constitution are inappropriate today – most notably the composition of the Senate and the native-born eligibility requirement for the presidency;
iii the Constitution is mostly irrelevant to the current political operation of the nation, especially in the extensive and unaccountable role played by the administrative state;
iv  the rights celebrated as enshrined and protected today are mostly the result of the evolution of attitudes among the public, not the aggressive intervention of courts based on close textual study of the Constitution's language and meaning.

Fourth, John Paul Stevens (2014) published *Six Amendments: How and Why We Should Change the Constitution*. The retired Supreme Court Justice singled out his former institution for criticism, asserting it had "had such a profound and unfortunate impact on our basic law that resort to the process of amendment is warranted" (Stevens 2014: 11).

1. More representative Senate – ten largest population states get 4 senators, next fifteen three senators each.
2. Appoint all former presidents & VPs as 'national senators.'
3. Mandate non-partisan redistricting for House elections.
4. House terms to 3 years, all Senate terms to coincide with each presidential election.
5. Expand House to 1000 members, but staffing and budget levels remain the same.
6. (Generous) term limits to assure rotation in office.
7. Balanced Budget Amendment (with safeguards and escape clauses).
8. Continuity of Government procedure (appointment of replacement lawmakers etc.).
9. Establish a new 6-year presidential term, including a fifth-year extension referendum that could result in an additional two years in the office.
10. Limit some presidential war-making powers and expand congressional oversight to renew assent to on-going wars at regular intervals.
11. Give the president a line-item veto to remove specific items from appropriations bills.
12. Replace the unfair constitutional prohibition against non-natural-born presidents with a requirement that candidates need only have been a US citizen for 20 years.
13. Eliminate life tenure for Supreme Court Justices for a single, non-renewable term of 15 years for all federal judges.
14. Grant Congress the power to set a mandatory retirement age for federal judges.
15. Expand the Supreme Court from nine to twelve members.
16. Give federal judges more financial independence with guaranteed cost of living increases.
17. A new, separate constitutional amendment for politics.
18. A regional lottery for presidential primary nominations.
19. Grant more states additional electors (in proportion to population or enhanced Senate representation).
20. Reform campaign finance by allowing Congress to pass reasonable limits on campaign spending by the wealthy and mandate partial public funding for general election House and Senate campaigns.
21. Adopt automatic registration for all qualified US citizens.
22. Require all able-bodied young Americans to devote two years to serving their nation as a universal civic duty, a Bill of Responsibilities.
23. Convene a new Constitutional Convention, using the state-based mechanism for so doing.

*Figure 1.1* Larry Sabato's 23 Proposals for Constitutional Change.
Source: Adapted from Sabato (2007).

Among other pressing problems, amendments were needed to address campaign finance, redistricting, the death penalty, and gun control.

Fifth, an analysis offered by presidential scholars William Howell and Terry Moe (2016) argued the Constitution – rather than partisan polarization, campaign spending or other influences – is responsible for political institutions' failure to tackle modern challenges. The parochial Congress at the center of the Federal Government is ill-equipped to address the problems of a complex, postindustrial nation. The solution is to update the Constitution through reforms that push Congress and its pathologies to the periphery of the policy process, and bring presidents – who, they claim, have a concern for their legacy that impels them to seek coherent policy solutions – to the center of decision-making. The remedy to dysfunction is a more powerful presidency, with greater control of the legislative process through "fast-track" powers, analogous to those available already on trade negotiations.

Sixth, and finally, was public intellectual Francis Fukuyama. In examining political order through history, he contended that:

> The US political system has decayed over time because its traditional system of checks and balances has deepened and become increasingly rigid. In an environment of sharp political polarization, this decentralized system is less and less able to represent majority interests and gives excessive representation to the views of interest groups and activist organizations that collectively do not add up to a sovereign American people.
>
> (Fukuyama 2014: 25–26)

This list of distinguished critics is extensive but by no means exhaustive. In the Jeffersonian tradition, Levinson, Sabato, Klarman, Stevens, Howell, Moe, and Fukuyama together offer serious indictments of existing constitutional arrangements. How persuasive are they?

## Appraising the Constitutional Critics

An important distinction exists between these writers' arguments and the radical critiques that argue for replacing the Constitution. Although Levinson *et al.* are proposing major changes, they largely retain the classical, established framework: "reformist" rather than "revolutionary."

Is that sufficient? To radicals like Lazare, the Constitution is simply an analogue framework for a digital age. Incremental critics merely offer tactical adjustments – a "US Constitution Lite" – in the face of a need for a strategic change of direction. But while wholesale transformation may appeal to utopians, they represent the intellectual equivalent of overkill and are not the mainstay of constitutional debate. Not only is there no "off the shelf" constitution that radicals offer as a feasible substitute, but the prospects for systemic overhaul are politically limited.

Moreover, much of the radical critique is not so much about the constitutional design, as such, but government. The Constitution is an impediment to ideological goals: socialism, for the left, a night-watchman state for the libertarian right. The appropriate government role remains a subject of deep division today as much as in 1787. While it is tempting for some to take a "smash the system" approach to change, this is politically unsatisfying. As one commentary on two very different US Senators, Bernie Sanders and Ted Cruz, observed:

When given a choice, about a third of Americans say government should take active steps in every area it can to improve the lives of its citizens, presumably a position that Sanders thinks reflects most Americans' opinions. And about a third say government should do only the things necessary to provide basic government functions, Cruz's core philosophical position. The rest are somewhere in the middle ... Americans remain torn about what the federal government should or should not be doing. The public eschews simple, sweeping and unrealistic proposals for the way government should work, and recognizes that hard work and slogging compromise are necessary.

(Newport 2016)

For the most part, it seems more sensible to examine the pragmatic changes suggested by reformists. Taken together, these make a powerful case for change. Their critique is comprehensive and coherent, the changes they prescribe are rational, and the implication – that few would grieve the passing of certain elements of the existing framework – is suggestive. It may be tempting to succumb to the appeal of comparative constitutional engineering. Whether going the whole nine yards or being more selective, the promise that altering institutional arrangements will yield a more functional politics with better public policies and improved results is inviting.

But the prescriptions should mostly, though not completely, be resisted. The case for change is based on a misdiagnosis of the problems ailing the United States and offers a palliative, not a real remedy. To understand why requires reconsidering what the Constitution promised and achieved as well as the menu of options for reform. Critics can seem dissatisfied, grumpy figures but often resemble thwarted romantics. In seeking to perfect the foundational framework, they sometimes make the perfect the enemy of the good.

A measured assessment must begin with the observation that constitutions are nowhere self-executing entities. What a constitution means, whether it "works," how accurate a road map of state power or rights it offers – all these depend not on the words alone but whether and how the constitution is executed. A constitution can be no more and no less than those who staff the governing institutions and accept and abide by its prescriptions and prohibitions. It is in this sense that, whether conservatives approve, the Constitution is a "living" presence in public life. And in many respects, it is also in this sense that the Constitution acquits itself well. For those frustrated with the existing rules, the question arises of whether changing them is worth the risk.

The problem with the "Constitution-as-train-wreck" interpretation is that it begs the question: if the constitutional order has been so manifestly unfit for purpose, why did the train not derail long ago? Why, instead, does it continue to roll steadily, if punctuated by occasional delays? It is under the same framework that the United States has transformed from an agrarian collection of thirteen states to the world's leading power. It is under the same edifice that change has empowered citizens of all races, genders, sexual identities, and religions. It is under the same arrangements that the United States survived a brutal Civil War, prevailed against Nazi, fascist, and militarist tyrannies through World War II, and defeated Soviet communism during the Cold War. Moreover, the recent polarization is less a departure from the historic norm than a return to the levels of polarization that prevailed from the 1870s to the 1920s. If there exists an aberrant era in US history, it was the mid-twentieth century of less ideologically distinct, more internally factionalized and incoherent parties.

A better way to comprehend the Constitution is as the permanent organizational frame for American politics (albeit one that has itself altered by amendment and interpretation). The Constitution establishes the basic rules of the political game and thereby – through the separation of powers and federalism in particular – structures the incentives and opportunities for the players. But it does not (any longer) predetermine those players, identify their strategies and tactics, or shape their concerns and their popular appeal. As Shafer (2016) compellingly argued, the "moving pieces" in US politics are threefold: the *party balance* (the comparative standing of the two main parties in American society); *ideological polarization* (the programmatic distance between parties and their electoral coalitions); and *substantive conflict* (the policy content that is at stake in a given historical epoch). Where many political commentators go wrong is to mistake the sources of dysfunction at the organizational frame rather than the interplay between the active partisans, their supporters, and the key issues of the day that have – mostly – little direct relationship to the Constitution as such.

Seen in this way, it is not surprising that critics invariably mislocate the source of their ire at the rules of the game, rather than the more contingent elements of how it is played and by whom. That is, those frustrated by policy outcomes often identify structural weaknesses to correct, only then to despair about this occurring. Often the lament is that the Constitution is a conservative force, even if that conservatism preserves revolutionary ideals and allows for what, in more sober moments, critics concede is transformational political, economic, and social change. The socialist Karl Liebknecht once observed, "Despotically ruled people are never conservative, because they are never content," but omitted to state the converse: contented people tend to be relatively conservative in the absence of despotic rule.

Health checks of the US diagnose multiple ills of varying severity. Whether from the left, right, or center, there exists plenty to dislike about the status quo. The political system – slow, deliberative, veto-ridden – offers a target-rich environment. And Zakaria is surely right that no stigma should be attached to thinking through a new design. If the rules of the game no longer appear fair and balanced, no one need eat humble pie for agreeing that something needs to change. But prescribing appropriate remedies is harder and open to a few second opinions as to just how chronic the condition truly is.

The difficulty here is that few prescriptions appear disinterested. The breadth and depth of partisan antagonism and ideological distance between the parties is such that each party's core perceives the other as all too capable of despotic rule. Democrats and Republicans, reflecting their activist bases, seem tenaciously committed to making Congress a mausoleum to compromise. Liberals and conservatives no longer recognize the other side's values, much less view them as legitimate. Partisans view a president of the other party less as a political opponent than as an enemy. Lawmakers of the other party are not fellow Americans of good faith with different views, but creatures from another culture, pursuing regressive designs and animated by malign motivations.

The extent to which internecine warfare characterizes party politics can be exaggerated, especially when compared to those nations and regions of the world where genuine tribal conflicts daily threaten life and limb. But "negative partisanship," where each party's identifiers actively dislike the other party, and fear what the other party will do to them and the nation, has grown alarmingly (Abramowitz 2012, 2018). Key voters in Michigan, Ohio, Pennsylvania, and Wisconsin who had previously voted for Obama endorsed Trump in 2016. But most partisans have few friends across the divide. And members of each party view the other as more ideologically extreme than their own, which they consider moderate. In contrast to Obama's Democratic Party convention speech in 2004, denying there existed a "blue" and "red" America, there do appear two nations to millions of Americans. The Democratic–Republican duopoly is like a dysfunctional couple in a loveless marriage, moving slowly yet inexorably apart but trapped by the constraints of an arrangement too costly to abandon.

## Conclusion

The Constitution remains, for better and worse, the holy writ of America's civic religion. As Anthony King (2012: 206) observed, "The fact that American society is so deeply divided, psychologically and ideologically as well as demographically, helps to explain the continuing coexistence within the American political system of ancient constitutional practices and doctrines alongside their more modern radical-democratic opposites." The delicate balance may not offer total satisfaction all the time, but serious attempts to alter the balance could themselves prove damaging and even dangerous.

But what that also means is that, at times, the Constitution can seem like a political piñata for the ills of current politics. Recent years have seen a resurgence of Jeffersonian angst with proponents of change inhabiting the moral high ground. As one critic calling for a constitutional "makeover" pithily summarized the case against the Constitution, it may be magnificent, with features that make it a work of genius, "But let's be frank: It's an 18th-century work of genius. We've reached a point where our outmoded political architecture is betraying the ideals it was designed to protect" (Caryl 2016). Combine gridlock, history, and the Founders' flaws, and the Constitution's defenders are easily depicted as elitist, complacent, and out-of-touch, weaponizing a sterile document to freeze-dry America and thwart progressive change. In pledging to "make America great again," Donald Trump was hardly alone in harking back to a "golden age."

In a polarized era, though, golden ages typically exhibit distinctly red or blue hues. As Levin (2016) persuasively argued, *both* left and right exhibit forms of nostalgia about finding a way back to a time when there existed plentiful jobs providing good incomes with which to support families that stayed together in a culture of freedom and respect. Not only does this neglect the flaws of a conformist, illiberal era – one consigned to history's ash heap under the same Constitution – but it falsely promises a "back to the future" stability that technological transformations, cheap labor, specialization, and globalization mostly preclude.

Correlation is not causation. But since the Constitution is a constant, it is tempting to conclude that social, economic, and political problems that have constitutional dimensions – that are contingent and coincidental – are somehow constitutional in origin. There is a danger in these debates: that in being careful not to lionize the Constitution, we lose sight of the distinction between constitutionalism – whose central aim is good government – and everyday politics. Constitutional quality control requires the possible downsides to supposed remedies to be examined. Closer scrutiny suggests the Constitution is neither "radically defective" nor "imbecilic." What follows is a careful rebuttal of the critiques, beginning with the Preamble.

## Summary

- While Madison believed that constitutions required veneration to endure, Jefferson held that regular revision was desirable.
- Three broad critiques exist: external jeremiads, radical and reactionary critiques, and incremental reform proposals. It is the latter

that offer the most politically feasible – if not necessarily desirable – types of constitutional change.

- Although US government has often been criticized as dysfunctional across American history, the political, economic, and social problems of the early twenty-first century have generated new and urgent debates over the need for constitutional reform.
- The Constitution sets the rules of the political game in the United States, but it does not, and cannot, predetermine the outcomes.

# 2 The Preamble, Then and Now

## A More Perfect Union

The Framers of our Constitution triumphantly declared to whom the government of the United States belonged: it was "WE THE PEOPLE." These three beautiful words are among the most important ideas in our nation's history: the idea that government's power is vested in the nation's citizens – the people to whom we owe our ultimate and sacred allegiance.

President Donald J. Trump (Schwartz 2017)

I think we can say that the Constitution reflected an enormous blind spot in this culture that carries on until this day, and that the Framers had that same blind spot. I don't think the two views are contradictory, to say that it was a remarkable political document that paved the way for where we are now, and to say that it also reflected the fundamental flaw of this country that continues to this day.

President Barack Obama (Patten 2008)

## Introduction

To assess how well the Constitution works, it is first necessary to understand its purpose. With the Preamble's six objectives as a structuring device, supplemented by some empirical comparisons and metrics, this chapter makes the case for its overall success. Serious socioeconomic and political problems remain. But attributing these to constitutional rather than political choices is problematic. The evidence is mixed but the mixture of evidence points to the Constitution meeting its goal, not of a "perfect," but a *more* perfect union.

The United States is a diverse nation of approximately 324 million people covering a landmass of 3.5 million square miles (9.2 million km$^2$). The nation boasts the world's third most populous country, the largest economy, a per capita income of $57,638 and median household income of $59,039 (Davidson 2017), energy abundance, the world's largest prison population, and in-migration that partially counters the effects of its aging population, with a median age of thirty-eight. According to Gallup, 80 percent of Americans were satisfied with their overall quality of life in 2018 (Norman 2018). But majorities said the Federal

Government did not provide enough help for older (65 percent), poor (62 percent), middle class (61 percent), or younger people (51 percent), while nearly two-thirds of Americans (64 percent) said it provided too much help for the wealthy (Pew 2018a).

The Constitution comprised its share of the good, the bad, and the ugly. It was more a product of political struggle than disinterested political philosophizing (Klarman 2016; Robertson 2013). Creditors and debtors, urban dwellers and backcountry farmers, northerners and southerners fought for their competing interests with the weapons of ordinary politics: disparaging adversaries' motives, character assassination, and threats of violence (as the French saying has it, "the more things change, the more they stay the same"). Although celebrated as a "brilliant solution" (Berkin 2003) to the problems facing the fledgling nation after the Revolutionary War, the Framers wrote a Constitution whose features were designed not to maximize democracy but to insulate the national government from full popular influence.

Subsequent history expanded democracy, but opposition to power, and suspicion of government as its most dangerous embodiment, has remained the thematic core of American political thought (Huntington 1981: 39). The size and structure of government, and the Constitution's practical meaning, nonetheless changed more after the 1930s than at any time previously. The New Deal and World War II transformed the Federal Government into a much more centralized entity administering a far different state than the Founders envisaged. Federal authorities assumed responsibility for regulating a national banking system and financial institutions, securing citizens' legal equality and economic welfare, waging war and projecting global power, sustaining a permanent national security state, and regulating a transnational market economy. Most of these changes went undocumented in formal revisions to the constitutional text. But while they drastically altered a once limited government, the Preamble's goals remain intact as a yardstick by which to judge the operative Constitution:

> We the People of the United States, in Order to form a more perfect Union, establish Justice, insure domestic Tranquility, provide for the common defense, promote the general Welfare, and secure the blessings of Liberty to ourselves and our Posterity, do ordain and establish this Constitution for the United States of America.

## The Past as Prologue

"To see what is in front of one's nose," Orwell wrote, "needs a constant struggle" (1946). In that spirit, the strongest argument in the Constitution's defense is deceptively simple: it works. More precisely, it works as intended, and better than feasible alternatives, for US conditions. At its most elemental, that is the task for which constitutions are designed: to meet not universal conditions, but those specific to a people and place. History records many nations adopting constitutions, but hundreds failing to fulfill their basic purpose. As a nineteenth-century Russian remarked of one of his nation's less impressive efforts, "Every country has its own constitution; ours is absolutism moderated by assassination" (Herbert 2010: 19).

Few doubt that the writing of the Constitution was a seminal moment in US, and world, history. As the American Revolution's final chapter, the first secular, quasi-democratic republic was its legacy (no constitution excluding its own citizens can be considered properly democratic). The shape of nations has been rewritten by this epic struggle for self-government. The decision to adopt a concise yet complex constitution, in the first-person plural – to transcribe into law the preexisting, precontractual ties of "we the people" – distinguished the United States as a departure from, and challenge to, all existing forms of government. US naturalization law still requires citizenship applicants to be "attached to the principles of the Constitution."

That attachment owes much to the Constitution and Declaration of Independence together establishing something unique: a nation-state self-consciously created by politics. America remains a nation apart in its comingling of nation building and constitution drafting, defined by ideals – civic nationalism – that indelibly encoded values into the people's DNA. Although millions embrace the "elective nationality" of the American Creed, in choosing to *become* Americans they assume a bond founded irrevocably on certain principles, not ethnicity:

> The United States is surely the Manhattan skyline, the Kansas plains, the redwood forests, the Mississippi river. But it is, far more importantly, the Declaration of Independence, the Constitution, and the Gettysburg Address. You could cut down the forest or dry up the river and the country would be infinitely the poorer for it, but it would still be the United States of America. If Americans jettison the Bill of Rights and the ideas enshrined in it, they become a different country altogether.
>
> (Cohen 2017)

Although scholars have challenged that idealistic conception – emphasizing instead multiple identities, nativism, racism, religiosity, repression, and American political cultures rather than culture (Ellis 1993) – civic nationalism exerts a tenacious hold on popular imaginations. Pervasive oppression and exclusion denied millions America's promise, yet the attraction of those ideals and the challenge of realizing them still act as a global magnet. At a time when many are seeking to exit the nations of their birth, millions are trying to get into the United States. American identities are many, and overlapping, but their fabric is interwoven by a unifying thread: *e pluribus unum* (out of many, one).

But, to paraphrase Martin Luther King Jr., what is the enduring content of the Constitution's character?

To many, a work of incomparable genius marries effective governing arrangements to specially protected rights. The Constitution bakes key ideas into American political culture: republicanism, democracy, rule of law, political and economic freedom, individualism, and anti-statism. It remains the optimal environment in which freely associating individuals, under a self-governing republic, can pursue what revolutionaries fought for in the war against colonial oppression: "life, liberty, and the pursuit of happiness." The Constitution offers the nation's USP: a Unique Selling Point of what political philosopher Isaiah Berlin termed "negative liberty" – freedom from oppression rather than entitlement to concrete material ends.

To critics, that is an epic fairy tale. Dulling the minds of an entire people, the Constitution narrows the range of possibilities they entertain for a better existence. So central is the Constitution to the meaning of citizenship that, instead of providing a clear window into reality, it blinds the masses into collective denial. Mindless ancestor worship of a parchment promise long past its prime is the result. The Constitution's dirty life and times warrants a health warning. It causes Americans to judge the rationality of new laws and policies by reference to dead white European men rather than results. To many (not least those supposedly included all along in the new nation's promise, but who required special amendments to make that happen), Americans are conned by their Constitution.

On one thing, though, admirers and detractors agree: "constitutionalism" is the medium of American values. No problem lacks a constitutional dimension. From the right of "exotic" dancers to ply their trade nude to that of grandparents to visit their grandchildren or that of airplane operators to refuse to allow "emotional support animals" on flights, issues the Framers never conjured receive solemn constitutional adjudication. "Only in America" is more than a popular comment of amused bewilderment at "things American." What the drafters created was a carefully calibrated Constitution for an exceptional nation-state.

Whether one regards that as unique, better, or just different is debatable. But the newly independent nation was determined, if not destined, to be unlike others. In terms of comparative generalizations, the United States would typically provide the qualifier "except" rather than "especially" in America. As the Declaration put it, "a decent respect to the opinion of mankind requires that they should declare the causes which impel them to the separation." In other words, a prudent respect for the rest of the world required revolutionary Americans to explain why they were doing things differently. Although some still think it means respecting others by emulating what they do, this is mistaken. The statement was a clarion call to doing things the American way, unilaterally, even if that offended foreign sensibilities.

The Constitution, then, inherited many aspects of English common law traditions but was tailored for a distinct body politic embarking on a novel journey of self-government. It fitted imperfectly when designed. But as the shape of the United States has evolved, it fits better now through alterations and refinements. With new generations of more diverse backgrounds, the Constitution's special and singular role in uniting a heterogeneous people behind ageless ideals is regularly affirmed anew.

## Who Are "We the People"?

The Constitution's story is not so much well-trodden ground as trampled. May 25, 1787 saw fifty-five delegates gather in a cramped room in Philadelphia, Pennsylvania with armed guards outside to create a wholly new nation at a time of immense crisis for the newly independent country. Forty-one of them had served in Congress, and ten were still lawmakers at the time of the Constitutional Convention.

Religious men, they wrote a secular Constitution that made no mention of God to welcome those wishing to practice their religion freely, those escaping religious persecution, and the faithless. The Constitution created a "wall of separation" between Church and State. That said, although the Constitution never explicitly references one nation under the divine, the terms are mentioned at least once in each of the fifty State Constitutions (Sandstrom 2017). (The Pledge of Allegiance, adopted by Congress in 1942, added the phrase "under God" in 1954.)

Propertied men (many of whom counted as property their fellow human beings), they established a republic with qualified democratic accountability. Unlike regimes elsewhere, the national government would contain elements of monarchy (the indirectly elected presidency), oligarchy (the US Senate, appointed by state legislatures, until the Seventeenth Amendment of 1913), and democracy (the US House of Representatives, popularly elected directly by white males, until the enfranchisement of women, with the Nineteenth Amendment of 1920, and of African Americans, with the passage of the Voting Rights Act of 1965).

The failing Articles of Confederation, the first attempt at organizing the thirteen colonies, brought the delegates to Philadelphia. The central government had too few and inappropriate powers. The Framers bestowed on this decentralized "states-union" more powers and relevant authorities and created multiple countervailing power centers. The new Constitution's core was to empower the Federal Government and restrain excess by compelling competing forces to bargain and compromise – "ambition must be made to counter ambition," in Madison's words.

Anticipating the excesses of the mob during the 1789 French Revolution, with memories of King George III still strong, the Framers worried about the dual challenges of majority and minority tyranny. Their solution was a system wherein authority and power were dispersed, with buffers and gatekeepers between the people and government: "as much an anti-state as a state" (Deudney 1995: 207). By European standards, central government remained small and weak. The Constitution was a deal of seismic proportions: an exercise in national postcolonial conflict management that entrenched its own historical experience in the institutional framework it created. Its terms were ones of "calculated ambiguity."

But it was not "democratic." As King (2012: 62) observed:

America's 1787 Constitution was, by the standards of the contemporary civilized world, many decades ahead of its time. But, simultaneously, it was far from creating arrangements in which the people at large were to be either the sole or the dominant political power. The people were given a place, to be sure, but they were also to be kept in that place, as securely as could be arranged. The founding fathers' profound ambivalence about the American people – and indeed, about people in general – manifested itself in everything they did.

First, the Constitution vested sovereignty in "We the People," the most elegantly concise expression of the republican principle that governments are instituted to secure the people's natural rights. Many Americans today take those simple yet profound seven words – We the People of the United States – for granted. At the time, they were among the most extraordinary ever written. But, though representing the first modern codified assertion that might does not equal right, the American people themselves never drafted nor voted to accept their constitution. The text that emerged stated that it was to become a constitution for those who ratified it when nine states did so (Article VII). Since it couldn't be known, during drafting, which states would ratify, the solution was a "stroke of political genius" (Finer, Bogdanor, and Rudden 1995: 10): "We the People." But as Posner (2003: 154) argues, that was more an assertion of adoption by democratic choice than a claim of establishing a democracy.

Second, as those origins attest, the Constitution was a controversial document in its own time, never mind in ours. That some of the Founders thought it necessary to "sell" the new arrangement via *The Federalist Papers* was indicative. The Constitution was an elitist draft that simultaneously empowered but checked the people. It is less the authors than the content that matters. "Democracy," like "privacy," went unmentioned. What was created was more qualified and "is better described as elite democracy than as either deliberative or populist democracy" (Posner 2003: 154). The Founding Fathers designed the Constitution precisely to create a buffer between the leaders and the citizenry. The Founders wanted to ensure that empowered states would create a powerful counterweight to the central government – one of the many checks and balances built into the system.

The Framers were suspicious of direct democracy. Madison argued in *Federalist 10* that direct democracies had "in general been as short in their lives as they have been violent in their deaths." Instead, in *Federalist 39*, he defined a republic as "a government which derives all its powers directly or indirectly from the great body of the people and is administered by persons holding their offices during pleasure, for a limited period, or during good behavior." The people do not voice their opinions directly but, rather, convey them through representatives. As he wrote in *Federalist 10*, a republic would, unlike a direct democracy:

> [R]efine and enlarge the public views, by passing them through the medium of a chosen body of citizens, whose wisdom may best discern the true interest of their country and whose patriotism and love of justice will be least likely to sacrifice it to temporary or partial considerations.

Third, as Ware argued (2011: 168), "American democracy tends to emphasize government by the people at the expense of government for the people; and the question of who actually constitutes the people is one that is always contested." In one sense, this was a matter of who would be admitted to citizenship, a question that plagued American identity from slavery through racial apartheid to the exclusion of non-Europeans from 1924–1965 and even now. (The Trump administration's attempts to ban individuals from certain majority-Muslim nations, upheld in *Trump v Hawaii* (2018), offered another example.) It was only after 1965 that the United States fully democratized in terms of citizenship, ballot access, and voting rights.

In another respect, the question implicated two competing notions of "We the People." Those who viewed this collectively believed popular sovereignty resided in the group, which favored a "democratic" constitution facilitating majority rule. But those who saw popular sovereignty as residing in individuals contended that a "republican" constitution was needed, to secure their preexisting inalienable rights against majority abuse. The Bill of Rights provided a shield for individuals and a sword against intrusive government. Dispute over the nature of government "of the people, by the people, for the people" has been constant because rival notions of popular sovereignty yield competing schools of constitutional interpretation (explored further in Chapter 4).

Fourth, the constitutional toolkit was incomplete. The Constitution made no mention of features that ultimately ensured its functioning, such as political parties and judicial review: a parallel but "unwritten" constitution (Amar 2012). Part of the paradoxical reason the Constitution compels reverence is, nonetheless, its incomplete status as a permanent work-in-progress. For generations, the challenge has been to realize its aspirations. This living history affords a human dimension that other constitutions lack. The Constitution was the first, but not last, act in a perpetual national melodrama.

More than any prior or subsequent effort at distilling the essence of ordered liberty, the Framers established bold goals for the new dispensation. If all presidential elections rest in part on Ronald Reagan's question in the 1980 presidential debate – "are you better off than you were four years ago?" – the Preamble offers metrics to evaluate matters of more panoramic scope: is the US improving or regressing? Can we regard the Constitution as allowing the conditions for a better America or is that only possible by defining down the terms of success? As the elegant expression of its rationale, the Preamble therefore repays close reading. (Some even praise it as a "legend" [Orgad 2010] and an "anomalous," "upbeat, affirmative, and inclusive" contrast to the "snarly and negativistic" Bill of Rights [Blau 2017: 14]). Its fifty-two words represent the Constitution's sweet spot and state its purpose concisely:

i    to form a more perfect Union
ii   establish Justice
iii  insure domestic Tranquility
iv   provide for the common defense
v    promote the general Welfare
vi   secure the blessings of Liberty to ourselves and our Posterity

### A More Perfect Union

Establishing a "more perfect" union did not offer the hostage to fortune of an end-state or utopia. But it implied something within reach: national self-improvement. Is the state of the union – as presidents invariably insist in their annual addresses to Congress – still "strong"?

On balance, yes. Although once divided by a devastating civil war that cost over 600,000 lives, since the 1860s, national consolidation has advanced steadily. By any standard, a rational citizen would prefer today's America to any prior era. The United States has fought terrorist organizations since 2001, suffered a major recession, and experienced multiple social and economic dislocations. But it is not at war with another great power; only 1 percent of its population is serving, voluntarily, in the armed forces; GDP and per capita prosperity is greater than ever; and technological, cultural, and social advancement make America the destination of choice for most emigrants worldwide.

These achievements have been recorded through a political culture of substantial continuity. Americans are often regarded by outsiders as insular, self-referential, and failing to "see us as others see us," in Robert Burns' words. Whether that is so, one way to bring out how distinct the United States remains is to compare it with others. Figure 2.1 summarizes some differences with America's leading challenger, China.

Geography and ideology have been mutually reinforcing. Good fortune has abetted American self-perception of the United States as an exceptional nation: protected by two vast oceans, distant from warring neighbors, abundantly resourced and continent-sized. The emphasis on liberty has reinforced a skeptical view of government, an embrace of risk and innovation, and a focus on the here and now. A traditionally inclusive approach to immigrants has helped innovation and growth. There have been downsides to these features, but their persistence has marked the United States as distinct and refutes more negative verdicts, in three respects.

First, while critics have rightly castigated the 1787 settlement as flawed, those very criticisms imply the vast improvement thereafter. Remedial action to advance gender, racial, and sexual equality has occurred under the same order. Inclusion has neither required overthrowing the Constitution nor importing "un-American" ideas. The union has been self-correcting on its own terms.

While the optics of politics looks ugly, comparisons with earlier eras point towards the better present. Although important exceptions exist, on almost every dimension – life expectancy, income, employment, prosperity, living conditions, civil and political rights, and more – the United States is immeasurably better than previously. Technological change, mechanization, and globalization together pose immense challenges to old ways. But nostalgia for a "golden age" is misplaced. In terms of material indices and quality of life, conditions remain advanced.

|  | America | China |
|---|---|---|
| Self-perception | "Number one" | "Center of universe" |
| Core value | Freedom | Order |
| View of government | Necessary evil | Necessary good |
| Form of government | Democratic republic | Responsive authoritarianism |
| Exemplar | Missionary | Inimitable |
| Foreigners | Inclusive | Exclusive |
| Time horizon | Now | Eternity |
| Change | Invention | Restoration and evolution |
| Foreign policy | International order | Harmonious hierarchy |

*Figure 2.1* America and China: Clash of Cultures.
Source: Adapted from Allison (2017: 141).

Second, it is worth emphasizing the sheer scale of the United States, which is often forgotten when comparisons are made between "democracies," "industrialized" or federal states. When we compare the United States with other states, we are frequently comparing apples and oranges. In this sense, at least, the United States is different. The entire United Kingdom (UK) is smaller in geographic area than Oregon, can fit three times into Texas, and seven times into Alaska. It takes only slightly longer to fly non-stop from Boston to London than it does to fly from Boston to Los Angeles. London is closer to Kim Jong-Un's stock of missiles in North Korea than L.A.

As Figure 2.2 illustrates, the huge size of the US economy is sometimes forgotten. With a $18.6 trillion economy in 2016, California produced $2.60 trillion of output, compared to the UK's $2.63 trillion. But California's labor force was 19 million, the UK's 33 million: the US worker was much more productive. Florida produced a GDP of $926 billion, the same as Indonesia ($932 billion), but the Sunshine State's labor force of 9.8 million was 8 percent the size of Indonesia's 127 million. Saudi Arabia, with its immense oil wealth, had a $639 million GDP, less than Illinois ($791).

Third, the same convulsive phenomena disrupting the public worldwide – globalization, rising economic inequality, illegal immigration, dysfunctional welfare states, mounting public debt – afflict

*Figure 2.2* US States Renamed for Countries with Similar GDPs (2016).

Notes:

- The comparison uses nominal GDP data from the BEA on US states and IMF data on countries.
- AEI analysis of data from the Bureau of Economic Analysis and International Monetary Fund.

Source: Mark Perry, www.aei.org/publication/putting-americas-ridiculously-large-18-6t-economy-into-perspective-by-comparing-us-state-gdps-to-entire-countries-2/. With permission.

Americans. But other states are not faring substantially better in countering these forces. Mayhew (2017) offered a compelling comparison. He assessed US performance across thirteen "impulses," or transnational phenomena, that nations worldwide experienced, from the eighteenth century to today:

   i  launch of a new nation
  ii  continental expansion
 iii  mid-nineteenth century consolidation
  iv  building an industrial economy
   v  taming corporations and the rich
  vi  rise to world power
 vii  responding to the Great Depression
viii  building a welfare state
  ix  post-World War II prosperity
   x  civil rights revolution
  xi  neo-liberalizing the economy
 xii  addressing climate change
xiii  containing debt and deficit

Mayhew concluded that, with the one exception of climate change, the United States has been a "high-performing outlier." If the Constitution is "radically defective," as Levinson claimed, it is not in terms of cross-country outcomes.

Metrics can be problematic, of course. The world America inhabits has become increasingly complex, multidimensional, and interdependent. In the prevailing global order (or disorder), the nature of power is more complex and diffuse. "Soft power," or the power of attraction, complements "hard power" (military resources and economic heft), so that power *with* others can prove more effective than power *over* others. But how does one measure soft power?

Research by a strategic consultancy, Portland, and the University of Southern California's Center on Public Diplomacy, assessed the "Soft Power Thirty" on six dimensions: digital, culture, enterprise, engagement, education, and government. As Table 2.1 shows, the United States was in the top three annually from 2015 to 2017. Although it slipped to third in 2017, America ranked first for digital, culture, and education; eighth for enterprise (behind Singapore, Switzerland, South Korea, Ireland, Japan, Denmark, and Sweden); fourth for engagement (behind France, the United Kingdom, and Germany); and twelfth for government (behind Norway, Switzerland, Sweden, Finland, Netherlands, Denmark, Germany, New Zealand, Canada, Ireland, and the United Kingdom). America remained unrivalled in higher education, cultural production, and technological innovation but, in reputational terms, "Brand America" suffered from the Trump presidency's embrace of "America First."

*Table 2.1* The Soft Power 30 (2015–2017)

| Overall Ranking | 2015 | 2016 | 2017 |
|---|---|---|---|
| 1 | UK | USA | France |
| 2 | Germany | UK | UK |
| 3 | USA | Germany | USA |
| 4 | France | Canada | Germany |
| 5 | Canada | France | Canada |
| 6 | Australia | Australia | Japan |
| 7 | Switzerland | Japan | Switzerland |
| 8 | Japan | Switzerland | Australia |
| 9 | Sweden | Sweden | Sweden |
| 10 | Netherlands | Netherlands | Netherlands |
| 11 | Denmark | Italy | Denmark |
| 12 | Italy | Spain | Norway |
| 13 | Austria | Denmark | Italy |
| 14 | Spain | Finland | Austria |
| 15 | Finland | Norway | Spain |
| 16 | New Zealand | New Zealand | Belgium |
| 17 | Belgium | Austria | Finland |
| 18 | Norway | Belgium | New Zealand |
| 19 | Ireland | Singapore | Ireland |
| 20 | South Korea | Ireland | Singapore |
| 21 | Singapore | Portugal | South Korea |
| 22 | Portugal | South Korea | Portugal |
| 23 | Brazil | Poland | Greece |
| 24 | Poland | Brazil | Poland |
| 25 | Greece | Greece | China |
| 26 | Israel | Hungary | Russian Federation |
| 27 | Czech Republic | Russian Federation | Czech Republic |
| 28 | Turkey | China | Hungary |
| 29 | Mexico | Czech Republic | Brazil |
| 30 | China | Argentina | Turkey |

Source: Data from the Soft Power 30, http://softpower30.com/?country_years=2017.

Historical and comparative records partially explain American pride in the Constitution. Most constitutions fail to last a single century. By contrast, the United States is anticipating its 250th anniversary as a nation in 2026 partly because its Constitution has enabled the transition from a predominantly rural and agricultural set of colonies on the Eastern seaboard into a continent-sized country with a prosperous and diverse population. But a "more perfect" union also depended on achieving the Preamble's other five goals.

## Establish Justice

"Justice" is a slippery concept. For some, it is procedural: "equal treatment" or "equality before the law." For others, "treatment as an equal" implies a more substantive concept of what individuals merit, sometimes requiring preferential treatment. Establishing justice is difficult to appraise in a neutral manner. Moreover, whereas in the United States, justice usually connotes legal procedure, elsewhere it typically refers to the distribution of power and issues of socioeconomic equality. But if we take the minimalist conception that individuals should receive equal treatment, has America "established" justice?

Critics regard that notion with contempt. It has only been in recent decades that African Americans, women, and sexual minorities have approached equality before the law. For much of American history, millions were wronged by a Bill of Rights whose promise and protections were a hollow hope. Although legal aspects of inequality have mostly ended, the toxicity of race relations – the legacy of slavery, state-enforced segregation and bigotry – remains. So, too, do sexism, misogyny, and homophobia, all antithetical to core egalitarian American values.

To understate, these are not exclusive to the United States. Despite intense ethnic, racial, and labor violence across its history, the American "melting pot" has also seen blending occur and belief in its promise remains, if anything, as important as the reality. Americans "find ethno-nationalism discomfiting both intellectually and morally" at home and abroad (Muller 2008). And, although a multiethnic, multiracial nation-state, in some important respects, America is less multi- than monocultural. Although subcultures differ between and within each community, white, black, Latino, and Asian Americans remain Americans:

> The United States has never been entirely sure what to do about race. Alone among the countries in the world, it has attempted to construct not just a state of different tribes, but a nation of them — white and black, Christian and Muslim, and many others, too. Its sense of nationalism has evolved unevenly, slowly incorporating an ever-growing chunk of the people within its borders, and it has made steady progress.
>
> (Vance 2016)

Nonetheless, that progress is eternally tainted by America's "birth defect." The tragic contradiction at America's core – the marriage of slavery and freedom – was 1787's Faustian bargain. The freedom some Americans achieved in the Revolution rested on the enslavement of others. Before then, slavery helped dampen class conflict within the white population (Morgan 2013). Subsequently, interstate compromises legitimated slavery even as they provided the framework for its abolition: the Thirteenth, Fourteenth, and Fifteenth Amendments. That racialized legacy runs as a scar through American history and identity. For millions, the Constitution was merely a piece of paper. Racial apartheid represented an affront to human dignity whose emotional resonance remains undeniable. Black Americans have a naturally complex relationship with a country in which one of seven human beings was once owned as property and America's founding promise passed them by.

The racialized character of politics has a powerful impact. As whites approach the era when they become a minority in the United States, estimated to be around 2045, it was significant that Donald Trump won a majority in every white demographic other than Jewish Americans in 2016: men, women, whites with college degrees and without, and every age cohort. "Racial anxiety" was the single best predictor of a Trump vote (Abramowitz 2018). Whether America remains divided *by* or *because* of race, disparities in life chances, educational attainment, employment, and income are stark. The deeply race-conscious origins of a supposedly race-blind Constitution represent a cancer yet to be properly excised.

But the notion that "justice" is absent requires four qualifications.

First, the United States cannot be evaluated in ahistorical terms. Tragic as its genesis was, no other nation promulgated as progressive a design for the times. None prohibited slavery. None allowed women the franchise. None empowered the working class or guaranteed universal access to the ballot. Without compromise over the "peculiar institution," there may well have been no United States. It is unreasonable to judge by today's standards rather than the context of the times. This does not exempt the Framers from moral censure nor argues against social change but places their politics in context.

Second, past tragedies inform but do not define the Constitution. Even without their origins in full popular sovereignty, governments can become legitimate. As Michelle Obama declared to the Democratic Party's national convention in 2016:

> That is the story of this country …The story of generations of people who felt the lash of bondage, the shame of servitude, the sting of segregation, who kept on striving, and hoping, and doing what needed to be done. So that today, I wake up every morning in a house that was built by slaves. And I watch my daughters – two beautiful intelligent black young women – play with the dog on the White House lawn … Don't let anyone ever tell you that this country is not great. That somehow we need to make it great again. Because this right now is the greatest country on Earth.
>
> (Samuels 2016)

Third, there can be no doubt that African Americans have made substantial, but insufficient, progress. The Obama presidency hardly represented a "post-racial" America's arrival. But it was a remarkable achievement to which few other majority-white states compare. Only

Ireland, which elected a head of government of Indian ancestry in 2017, even registers among European nations. The extent of black and minority Europeans' inclusion as full citizens of their nations is, if anything, more distant.

Fourth, in the face of numerous challenges, African Americans still seek not to replace but to realize the Constitution's unfulfilled aspirations. The genius of the civil rights campaign to delegitimize Jim Crow was to ground it in the principles of the Declaration and Constitution – to challenge apartheid by reference to the "inalienable" rights enshrined there. The Founders' extraordinary achievement was to elevate a set of ideals that inserted a self-destruct mechanism in the edifice of slavery. The system they designed eventually transcended their own failures of morality and courage.

The Movement for Black Lives (2016) issued *A Vision For Black Lives* in August 2016. The manifesto focused on harms perpetuated against black Americans in order to demand universal health care, divestment from fossil fuels, and jobs programs. But the Constitution was barely mentioned. Beyond overturning *Citizens United* (2010), the document demanded that judges "Develop and promote robust interpretive frameworks that go beyond fighting corruption as compelling values that our Constitution protects" and that Americans "Fight back in the courts to establish an enduring interpretation of the Constitution that empowers the people." Jaffe (2016) heralded a "political revolution":

> These activists seek long-term radical changes — radical in the sense of "to get to the root of something," because to make the kind of changes that these activists demand will require deep changes at the heart of political structures, while most elected officials seem content to tinker on the surface, disconnected from the pain most Americans are feeling.

Yet the Constitution remained conspicuously untouched. American radicals remain more American than radical. Even in seeking transformative changes at a time of immense social tension, activists echo earlier eras in attempting to alter America through the same framework that once abetted their forebears' oppression. America's progress on race, ethnicity, and other social divisions has been far from linear, smooth, or swift. But, as Amy Chua (2018: 204) rightly notes, "There is a world of difference between saying that America has failed to live up to its ideals, with egregious injustice persisting today, and saying that the principles supposedly uniting us are just smoke screens to disguise oppression." Although the unity necessary for common dedication to the American experiment in self-government is under stress, the overall trajectory has been unequivocally positive and toward justice.

## Insure Domestic Tranquility

Few observers would think of "tranquil" as a good adjective to describe the noisy and raucous United States. American politics is as far from serene as can be imagined. But on closer examination, if what we mean by "domestic tranquility" is taken in context, five aspects stand out.

First, "domestic tranquility" is not another term for "conformity." The Framers anticipated a fractious republic. Without division, there is no politics. Unity can be a positive force but "group-think" of the "best and brightest" led to the Vietnam War. If there was a "golden age" when the United States was tranquil, when was this: the revolutionary era? The Civil War? The Progressive Era? It is tough to identify an epoch where politics was a delicate spectator sport of little consequence and minimal passion.

Second, tranquility did not mean the absence of rival conceptions of the good life. The Framers recognized what is now termed multiculturalism. To paraphrase Robert Nozick, "Steven Pinker, Taylor Swift, Ted Cruz, Beyoncé, you and your parents. Is there really one kind of life which is best for each of these people?" The Framers anticipated a negative answer and crafted a constitutional order to facilitate the "pursuit of happiness" as distinct individuals saw best.

Third, while the optics of American politics suggests an untranquil polity, this can be misleading. Certainly, much empirical evidence confirms what Piereson (2015) termed a "shattered consensus." The narrowness of presidential elections since 1988, in which almost no candidates manage to secure more than 55 percent of the vote and landslides are a distant memory; the era of competitive congressional elections and frequent changes in partisan control (a stark contrast to the uninterrupted Democratic Party dominance of the House of Representatives from 1954–1994); and, in terms of undivided versus divided government, every possible outcome at the federal level occurring from 1992–2016. A closely divided America is not necessarily a deeply divided America (Fiorina 2017). But while the public distrusts government, politics, and politicians, most Americans still have a lengthy "to-do" list for the Federal Government, from disaster response to education.

Fourth, "tranquility" implied self-defense. The Founders strongly opposed a standing army (a permanent military). The Second and Third Amendments together were designed to ward off threats to the people by, respectively, allowing their right to keep and bear arms and prohibiting the government from housing soldiers in their homes during peacetime. How far private gun ownership has benefited a peaceful nation is a heated debate. But many Americans believe strongly that their constitutional right offers "freedom's insurance policy" against the state (Waldman 2014).

Fifth, unlike elsewhere, no *coup d'état* has occurred. In many nations, turnover in rulers comes more from deaths, retirements, and forcible replacements – revolutions, military overthrows – than the peaceful transfer of power. Foreign rulers have frequently identified the United States president with the American state. But although many presidents have pushed executive authority to the fullest, and some acted unethically and even illegally, none has pursued a putsch. For all the conspiracy theories, Manchurian candidates, and "deep state" speculation, the republic has proceeded with metronomic regularity, not regime change. Uninterrupted elections since 1788 have occurred every two years, even in the wartime conditions of 1864 and 1944. And in scenes unimaginable elsewhere, presidents have resigned from office under congressional pressure (Nixon), been impeached by partisan opponents (Clinton), and been sued in office by members of the armed services (Trump).

A wealthy state with the world's most stable constitution, Americans have never experienced political traditions besides liberal democracy. It is a testament to the health of republican democracy that multiple voices are heard, even if this sometimes reaches a cacophony. Politics is highly contentious. Polarization may even deter Americans from public service and compound cynicism about the political class. America's ideological "sorting" into two camps – progressives in the Democratic coalition, conservatives in the GOP – has advanced a discordant public life. The partisan divide reflects an America where people experience different social realities. As Figure 2.3 illustrates, even American television shows a marked regional bias. And, according to Pew, during the 2016 presidential campaign, just one quarter of voters who supported Trump had a lot or some close friends who were Clinton supporters. Even fewer Clinton backers (18 percent) had friends who supported Trump (Pew 2016).

But is this truly new? The eighteenth and nineteenth centuries were no genteel idyll. The years before and after the Civil War saw the most intense struggles. Ardent supporters of Lincoln were unlikely to share many Confederate buddies. It is difficult, when viewed in historical context, to see the contemporary landscape as fundamentally different and, mercifully, it lacks the social unrest and assassinations of the 1960s. A fractious democracy can also coexist with an underlying political consensus on the rules of the game (see Israel). Moreover, consensus can sometimes congeal. The Framers understood that conflict points made the achievement of genuine consensus difficult but more enduring once attained. By 1787 standards, "tranquility" – the avoidance of strife that threatened the nation's existence or broke the social fabric – was an ambitious goal. But in comparative terms, as Mayhew (2017: 5–6) argued, the United States "...has been *extraordinarily* stable. It is not even close. The American system is often seen, along with the British, as the gold standard for long-running constitutional stability."

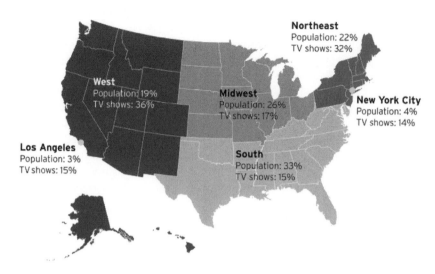

*Figure 2.3*   The South and Midwest Are Flyover Country on TV.

Notes:
- TV show settings by Census region, 1950–2010. Values are averages across decades.
- Brookings analysis of data from the U.S. Census Bureau, Writers Guild of America, The Independent (UK), and www.classictv.com.

Source: Jenny Schuetz, "Does TV bear some responsibility for hard feelings between urban America and small-town America?" The Avenue, Metropolitan Policy Program at the Brookings Institution, February 12, 2018. Map 1. With permission.

## Provide for the Common Defense

The Constitution was born through, by, and for war. Not only were the Articles of Confederation inadequate but "We the People" gained definition against the British, French, Spanish, native Americans, and Barbary pirates who threatened what Hamilton, in *Federalist 1*, termed "an empire in many respects the most interesting in the world."

Providing for national defense is the most important duty of government. As ever, though, the United States chose to do things differently, if one construes the "common defense" more broadly. In that regard, there is some crossover with domestic tranquility. The quality that Max Weber considered essential to a functioning state was a monopoly on legitimate violence. But alongside the state and its law enforcement instruments – the army, police, FBI – ordinary citizens could assume the responsibility for their own protection. As noted, the Framers opposed a permanent set of military forces, and the "right to keep and bear arms" is controversial. But that tradition now sits in parallel with the more familiar statist mechanisms of defending the nation and a vast, professional military.

With the most powerful military in the world, and the most impressive number of formal and informal allies every assembled, the common defense has been well provided for. Since the republic was founded, America has been directly attacked on only three occasions: the War of 1812, Pearl Harbor in 1941, and September 11, 2001. Few nations have proven so safe. Enlightened self-interest helped to maintain US primacy by shaping a global order conducive to American interests and values. As one scholar argued:

> If the US did not have constitutionalism, legality, democracy, re-ligiosity, enormous wealth, a certain history, a special position in the world, and so forth, nationalistic slogans would fall flat. Because there is *some* truth to our hyperbolic, aspirational, self-congratulatory civic rhetoric, we would find total realism deflating and in a sense misleading.
>
> (Posner 2003: 54)

The United States has long sought, with difficulty, to harmonize its power with its principles. It was not just British sovereignty under George III that revolutionaries questioned but his government's legitimacy. Americans have only responded with near unanimity to using force when both national security and American values have been threatened (World War II and 9/11 being the key examples). And there has long been an idealistic, even utopian, streak that has believed that rejecting power politics can inspire other nations to follow suit. During the 1920s, for instance, Republican administrations negotiated a series of naval arms-reduction treaties culminating in the Kellogg-Briand Pact of 1928, which outlawed war "as an instrument of national policy." When the biggest war in history began a decade later, the United States and the world paid a high price for their lack of pre-paredness. Suspicion of standing armies nonetheless meant that the United States lacked permanent military forces. These disbanded after each conflict, including initially after World War II, until the Cold War forced their revival.

Since then, the United States has become a national security state of immense power, operating mostly without strong judicial or legislative oversight, and upon thin legal underpinnings on matters from extrajudicial assassinations to domestic and foreign surveillance. As Wright (2016) noted:

> the inescapable fact is that American national security policy is a hierarchical enterprise. There are some checks and balances, but they are fewer than in the domestic space. No one can make the commander in chief do something he does not want to do. They can't make him threaten force or use it to uphold an alliance. They cannot make him sign a trade agreement or a treaty. And they cannot make him support democracy and human rights around the world.

The development of intercontinental ballistic missiles (ICBMs) in the Cold War shattered America's vulnerability to existential attack. Even the 9/11 attacks, by comparison, were less significant. America today, therefore, faces serious threats: nuclear proliferation, terrorism, climate change, and cyberattacks. Combating these threats poses every administration and Congress with difficult trade-offs between liberty and security, budgetary resources, and diplomacy and coercion. But the remarkable record of a secure homeland is often overlooked. Terrorism is, statistically, less of a threat than car accidents. The US nuclear arsenal, combined with the most advanced military and the most extensive network of allies, ensure that deterrence has worked. The United States leads a loose alliance system of some sixty states that together account for roughly 70 percent of world military spending and a similar fraction of total world GDP. Except in the Middle East, almost all these allies are fellow democracies. While the United States spends more on defense than the next eight largest-spending nations combined, hawks and doves differ over how well this has worked and at what cost. But Washington has global responsibilities that no other nation does. Moreover, the share of national wealth spent on defense – approximately 3.6 percent of GDP in 2016 – is modest, and much less than during the Cold War. Whether this is sufficient is another matter.

American statecraft has had to contend with anti-internationalist sentiment from outset. Jefferson may have envisaged an "empire of liberty" but others saw simply imperialism. Many Americans concur that theirs is a nation built on expansion – not just territorial and geopolitical but of liberty and prosperity. Some celebrate this, others denounce it. For some, America is too good for the world to warrant "foreign entanglements." For others, the world is too good for America, which needs to resolve its own problems before addressing others'. For neo-isolationists on the left and right, American "empire," with 800 bases worldwide and troops from Japan to Germany more than seventy years after World War II ended, repudiates republican values. But to others, defending the "world America made" after 1945 was worth the price in blood and treasure. Harry Truman, the thirty-third President, understood that US power was more effective when exercised in cooperation with other nations, and pioneered the creation of multilateral organizations that endured for decades. The Marshall Plan was very much in American interests. But its passage required facing down the America Firsters of Truman's day. Its opponents could not understand why Washington would spend so much money to rebuild Western European economies.

A central function of government is to conduct relations with the almost 200 other nations in the world. But the number of nations and regions where majorities disapproved of US leadership more than tripled from fifteen in 2016 to a record fifty-three in 2017 (Loschky 2018). Americans have long differed over the right balance of speaking softly, carrying a big stick, and packing the biggest gun. A rules-based international order compromised US sovereignty and freedom of action but expressed an enlightened national self-interest to sustain an open global system congenial to democratic capitalism. This has had its flaws but has proven better than conceivable alternatives. In 2016, defense spending was 3 percent of GDP and 15 percent of the federal budget, while welfare programs ("human resources") accounted for 15 percent of GDP and 73 percent of federal spending. Only in 2018 did a substantial increase in the defense budget, to $700 billion, win approval from Congress in the face of rising global threats and revived beliefs that a strong America remains the best guarantor of world peace. To many, the opportunity cost of a more turbulent world at war makes the common defense cheap at the price. But the right balance of means and ends in US grand strategy remains in flux.

## Promote the General Welfare

The "general welfare" and hyper-individualism have coexisted since the republic's earliest days. Among others who agonized over atomization, Tocqueville wrote with concern about frontier America and rugged individualists who "owe nothing to any man." The 2012 presidential election had powerful echoes when Obama cited a claim that "you didn't build that" to highlight the shared obligations, and benefits, of public works that underpinned "self-reliance." For Tocqueville, civic engagement – participating in local government, churches, and more – inoculated democracy from individualism's negative side by inculcating lessons on interdependence. But he would surely recognize the tensions that remain.

The Legatum Institute – a pro-market think tank – annually measures 148 countries on nine metrics. As Table 2.2 shows, the US ranked eighteenth in 2017. Although scoring highly on business environment, education, and social capital, it fell behind on economic quality, governance and personal freedom, health, the natural environment, safety, and security. America's economic quality has regained only half the ground it lost since the 2008 crash. Alongside Canada, the United States led the world in social capital as recently as 2012, but the North American region now ranks ninth. This reflects a decline in civic participation, with fewer Americans donating to charity and volunteering. Equally, US citizens report less freedom to make life choices, growing intolerance of religious expression, and increasing threats to their personal safety. Similarly, according to the United Nations (2016), the United States ranked tenth in its "human development index" in 2016, behind Norway, Australia, Switzerland, Germany, Denmark, Singapore, the Netherlands, Ireland, Iceland, and Canada. And, according to the "World Happiness Report" (Sustainable Development Solutions

Table 2.2 The Legatum Prosperity Index (2017)

| Overall Ranking | Economic Quality | Business EV | Governance | Education | Health | Safety & Security | Personal Freedom | Social Capital | Natural EV |
|---|---|---|---|---|---|---|---|---|---|
| 1 Norway | 8 | 8 | 2 | 4 | 7 | 3 | 8 | 5 | 1 |
| 2 New Zealand | 3 | 2 | 3 | 16 | 17 | 23 | 1 | 2 | 13 |
| 3 Finland | 14 | 10 | 1 | 3 | 14 | 15 | 9 | 12 | 3 |
| 4 Switzerland | 6 | 9 | 5 | 1 | 3 | 8 | 19 | 20 | 16 |
| 5 Sweden | 1 | 13 | 4 | 14 | 6 | 13 | 12 | 19 | 8 |
| 6 Netherlands | 4 | 14 | 6 | 2 | 8 | 9 | 6 | 11 | 46 |
| 7 Denmark | 5 | 11 | 8 | 11 | 21 | 14 | 14 | 4 | 19 |
| 8 Canada | 15 | 4 | 9 | 13 | 24 | 24 | 2 | 6 | 18 |
| 9 Australia | 20 | 7 | 14 | 5 | 10 | 22 | 15 | 1 | 10 |
| 10 UK | 7 | 5 | 10 | 8 | 19 | 17 | 18 | 16 | 9 |
| 11 Germany | 9 | 12 | 12 | 15 | 12 | 16 | 17 | 17 | 12 |
| 12 Ireland | 19 | 16 | 13 | 10 | 27 | 10 | 5 | 8 | 27 |
| 13 Iceland | 16 | 15 | 11 | 28 | 20 | 2 | 4 | 3 | 21 |
| 14 Luxembourg | 11 | 31 | 7 | 30 | 1 | 11 | 3 | 22 | 6 |
| 15 Austria | 12 | 18 | 16 | 12 | 5 | 6 | 22 | 15 | 15 |
| 16 Belgium | 17 | 17 | 15 | 9 | 11 | 33 | 11 | 25 | 26 |
| 17 Singapore | 2 | 6 | 17 | 6 | 2 | 1 | 97 | 26 | 11 |
| 18 USA | 10 | 1 | 20 | 7 | 30 | 60 | 28 | 9 | 34 |
| 19 France | 25 | 19 | 23 | 19 | 18 | 37 | 25 | 43 | 4 |
| 20 Spain | 37 | 33 | 30 | 25 | 16 | 12 | 16 | 29 | 17 |

Source: Data from The Legatum Institute, www.prosperity.com/rankings.

Notes

- *Economic Quality* refers to the openness of the economy, macroeconomic indicators, foundations for growth, economic opportunity, and financial sector efficiency.
- *Business Environment* measures entrepreneurial environment, business infrastructure, barriers to innovation, and labor market flexibility.
- *Governance* measures performance in effective governance, democracy and political participation, and rule of law.
- *Education* ranks countries on access to education, quality of education, and human capital.
- *Health* measures a country's performance in basic physical and mental health, health infrastructure, and preventative care.
- *Safety and Security* is based on national security and personal safety.
- *Personal Freedom* measures national progress towards basic legal rights, individual freedoms, and social tolerance.
- *Social Capital* measures the strength of personal relationships, social network support, social norms, and civic participation.
- *Natural Environment* measures the quality of the natural environment, environmental pressures, and preservation efforts.

Network 2017), the United States in 2016 ranked nineteenth, a decline from third place in 2007.

Is the American Dream alive and well, but in Norway? American political culture from the outset prioritized equality of opportunity over equality of outcome. Even so, America today exhibits some chastening metrics. Social, economic, and political inequalities are vast. Class, while crosscut by race, ethnicity, and religion, has been a constant element in the American story. According to Census Bureau reports, the share of households reliant on food stamps more than doubled from 2000 to 2013, from one in sixteen to one in eight Americans (Chokshi 2015). The "real unemployment" level remained one in ten in 2016. Secure permanent employment is uncommon. "Quality of life" is highly contingent on location and identity (a "zip-code" lottery). Although 63 percent of Americans were satisfied with the opportunity for a person to get ahead by working hard in 2018, only 32 percent were satisfied with the way that income and wealth are distributed in the US (Norman 2018).

That said, indicators differ. As Table 2.3 shows, the US ranked fourth in the global human capital index of the World Economic Forum (home to the annual Davos, Switzerland meeting of global political and economic elites). Moreover, its welfare state – though less generous than OECD peers – predated many others (the United States legislated for the minimum wage some sixty years before the United Kingdom). The regulatory state's expansion has produced multiple entitlement programs (Social Security, Medicaid, Medicare) and federal agencies (the EPA, Veterans Administration) that refute notions of an unregulated "free market." The Federal Register – recording the regulations conditioning individual and corporate activity – sometimes slows but never ceases growing. And, as Table 2.4 shows, the United States is relatively "clean." Although lower than OECD peers in 2016, it scored much better than China and India (both at 40) and Mexico (30).

*Table 2.3* Global Human Capital Index (2017)

| Rank | Country | Score |
| --- | --- | --- |
| 1 | Norway | 77.12 |
| 2 | Finland | 77.07 |
| 3 | Switzerland | 76.84 |
| 4 | USA | 74.84 |
| 5 | Denmark | 74.40 |
| 6 | Germany | 74.30 |
| 7 | New Zealand | 74.14 |
| 8 | Sweden | 73.95 |
| 9 | Slovenia | 73.33 |
| 10 | Austria | 73.29 |

Source: World Economic Forum (2017).

*Table 2.4* Corruption Perceptions Index (2012–2016)

Scores

| 2016 Ranking | 2016 | 2015 | 2014 | 2013 | 2012 |
|---|---|---|---|---|---|
| 1 Denmark | 90 | 91 | 92 | 91 | 90 |
| 2 New Zealand | 90 | 91 | 91 | 91 | 90 |
| 3 Finland | 89 | 90 | 89 | 89 | 90 |
| 4 Sweden | 88 | 89 | 87 | 89 | 88 |
| 5 Switzerland | 86 | 86 | 86 | 85 | 86 |
| 6 Norway | 85 | 88 | 86 | 86 | 85 |
| 7 Singapore | 84 | 85 | 84 | 86 | 87 |
| 8 Netherlands | 83 | 84 | 83 | 83 | 84 |
| 9 Canada | 82 | 83 | 81 | 81 | 84 |
| 10 Germany | 81 | 81 | 79 | 78 | 79 |
| 11 Luxembourg | 81 | 85 | 82 | 80 | 80 |
| 12 UK | 81 | 81 | 78 | 76 | 74 |
| 13 Australia | 79 | 79 | 80 | 81 | 85 |
| 14 Iceland | 78 | 79 | 79 | 78 | 82 |
| 15 Belgium | 77 | 77 | 76 | 75 | 75 |
| 16 Hong Kong | 77 | 75 | 74 | 75 | 77 |
| 17 Austria | 75 | 76 | 72 | 69 | 69 |
| 18 USA | 74 | 76 | 74 | 73 | 73 |
| 19 Ireland | 73 | 75 | 74 | 72 | 69 |
| 20 Japan | 72 | 75 | 76 | 74 | 74 |

Source: Adapted from Transparency International, www.transparency.org/news/feature/corruption_perceptions_index_2016.

Note: The scale of 176 countries runs from 0 (highly corrupt) to 100 (very clean).

Major problems remain. For example, health-care provision remains far from universal and is deeply uneven, reflecting public divisions. Pew found in 2017 that while most Democrats (52 percent) favored single-payer health care, only 33 percent of the public did (Kiley 2017). Another Kaiser Health poll found that 53 percent of the public favored single-payer, but opinions were "modestly strong but malleable": if, for example, respondents heard single-payer coverage increased taxes, a majority then opposed it (Hamel, Wu and Brodie 2017).

Or consider the tax code. Prior to the 2017 reforms, the tax rate on US business was among the highest, but tax revenue was among the lowest. Lobbying efforts helped businesses craft exemptions, rebates and more. A "submerged" or "hidden" state facilitated tax incentives and relief that was not as visible as tax expenditures that benefit Americans. In 2017, for example, Google spent more than any other company ($18 million) to lobby Congress, federal agencies, and the White House on issues such as tax reform, anti-trust, and immigration (Shaban 2018). But, while media focused on corporations and wealthy individuals, the contributions to overall revenue were often lost in the mix. For example, in 2016, the top 1 percent of earners supplied 39 percent of overall income tax revenue, the top 10 percent supplied 70 percent, and the lower 50 percent supplied just 3 percent (Greenberg 2017). Forty-five percent of Americans and 77.5 million of US households (60 percent of the total) paid no federal individual income tax at all in 2015–2016 (about half because they had insufficient taxable income and half because tax breaks erased their liabilities) (Hill 2016).

Moreover, the general level of US prosperity compares favorably with other states. Inequality levels in nations such as Russia, China, and India, are now comparable or more acute. On average, the US median household income, at a little under $60,000, exceeds most other countries, barring Luxembourg, Norway, and Switzerland. The US *poverty* level was higher than the *median income* in several nations, including Chile, the Czech Republic, Estonia, Greece, Hungary, Israel, Mexico, Poland, Portugal, Slovakia, and Turkey. And the US political system acquitted itself comparatively well in coping with the Great Recession after 2008 (Wittes and Nivola 2015). None of this negates the existence of huge inequalities. But these have been the result of political rather than constitutional battles. As Peter Gourevitch puts it:

> It is important not to confuse institutional limits with a dislike of preferences and policy outputs. Policies fail to happen not because the formal institutions prevent them but because they are not able to mobilize sufficient public support.
>
> (2002: 328)

Federalism permits dramatic variations in policy outcomes between states, from taxation rates to environmental standards. The costs of a "compound republic" are not light. The relative coherence of a unitary state is absent, replaced by a patchwork of laws and regulations. The [e]quality of national citizenship varies by state and locality. But important benefits coexist. The states remain "laboratories of democracy," innovating on workfare, crime and criminal justice reform, and drugs regulation. The horizontal and vertical division of government can be beneficial for the diffusion and contagion of ideas. Expression of local priorities and preferences in policy reinforces federalism despite centralizing imperatives: most variance between states relies on the ideological leanings of state populations. The existence of multiple decision-makers complicates and slows policy-making but can also reduce lasting errors, encourage innovation, and promote legitimacy (and stability) of public policies. The United States lacks the central coordination of other states, but national policies nonetheless reflect heavy regulation, democratic participation, and the inclusion of diverse interests.

Nonetheless, according to the Steuerle-Roeper Fiscal Democracy Index, more government revenue is allocated by prior decisions establishing permanent programs than by current democratic processes (Steuerle 2012). The portion of the federal budget automatically spent by choices made years previously is approaching 90 percent. The growing elderly population consumes an ever-greater share of national resources. The entitlement state provides Social Security and Medicare to the elderly, who happen to vote at higher rates than younger groups. The result risks a less dynamic, growth-oriented nation.

One of the best measures of national economic progress is whether wages are rising. But over the past forty years, overall US wages, adjusted for inflation, were essentially flat, registering about 0.2 percent growth (Shambaugh, Nunn, Liu, and Nantz 2017). Purchasing power, a good proxy for living standards, was also flat. The trend in real median household income, a measure that incorporates increases in the number of family members who work, is similarly poor. From 1960 to 1985, the income of the typical American household doubled. From then on, it remained flat while a tiny minority of Americans' income surged. In 1999, for example, the real median household income was $59,000 per household in 1999, following many years of rising female participation in the workforce. But it was also approximately $59,000 in 2017 (Davidson 2017). Many Americans live on the edge of financial danger. The 2016 Federal Reserve Board survey of household well-being found that 46 percent of adult Americans could not meet a $400 emergency expense without borrowing or selling something they owned; one quarter could not pay their monthly bills in full (Federal Reserve Board 2016).

On some influential analyses, economic inequality is not only about fairness or efficiency but the very survival of the Constitution. Ganesh Sitaraman (2017) argued that growing inequality endangers the "middle-class Constitution." Over two centuries, Americans repeatedly defended the republic against plutocratic oligarchy and tyranny. Each time, Americans mobilized to restore the Framers' middle-class precondition for republicanism. Jacksonian Democrats abolished property qualifications for voting and rejected a national bank. Lincoln's Republicans ended slavery and its downward pull on free working people. Populists and progressives subdued the Gilded Age's trusts and robber barons through progressive income tax, business regulation, and curbing the influence of money in politics. New Dealers restrained Depression-era "economic royalists" with economic regulation. A period of relative equality emerged from 1945 through the 1970s, when women and people of color began to share in America's prosperity. Each struggle was framed in constitutional terms and produced constitutional change: Andrew Jackson vetoed the national bank on constitutional grounds; the Thirteenth Amendment outlawed slavery and involuntary servitude; the Sixteenth authorized a progressive income tax; the Twenty-fourth abolished the poll tax. The New Deal yielded transformative Supreme Court rulings upholding business regulations and labor laws. But this tradition of middle-class constitutionalism is now under strain.

How much this represents a constitutional paradigm shift remains to be seen. In material terms, although it is not about to reach complete "energy independence," the United States is formidably well-equipped to face the future thanks to the explosive growth in shale oil production, surpassing Saudi Arabia and second only to Russia. Although competition among firms precludes the United States dominating the energy market in the way that state firms such as Saudi ARAMCO can, its market share makes it a crucial player (Gross 2018). Geopolitically, the new energy abundance powerfully strengthens American global power (O'Sullivan 2017). In terms of the wider culture, equality of opportunity has produced a meritocratic aristocracy with the old elite's aloofness but not its sense of obligation (Murray 2013). Yet the American Dream still has a powerful resonance since, despite rising inequality levels, the (white) working class reliably resents professionals while admiring the rich (Williams 2017). Moreover, adopting too narrowly a material perspective on the sources of the Constitution's resilience can neglect other important factors, not least the rights and liberties it protects.

## Secure the Blessings of Liberty

In no other state are the blessings of liberty so fully secured as in the United States. Although each confronts threats, the freedoms of speech, assembly, the press, and of religion are protected from government intrusion by the First Amendment. Individual freedom, a quintessential constitutional value, encourages a libertarian impulse that transcends left-right differences. The demand for autonomy, choice, and to be "left alone" by the state is one that those seeking to decriminalize pot and reduce taxes both share. Americans want government off their backs, out of their bedrooms, or away from their boardrooms – or all three.

As Bacevich (2017: 62) argued, the pledge to "secure the Blessings of liberty to ourselves and our Posterity" has a dual meaning: "Put the emphasis on 'ourselves,' and this passage suggests a narrow, even selfish orientation. Put the emphasis on 'our Posterity,' however, and it invites a more generous response." For future generations to enjoy the freedoms Americans currently enjoy, measures must be taken to achieve a "liveable planet, reasonable assurances of security, and a national household in decent working order" allowing the individual and collective pursuit of happiness. But the possibility of large-scale environmental collapse, and the divisions and demoralization among Americans inhibiting the identification and pursuit of a common good, represent major threats to liberty.

The Trump ascendancy occasioned much concern over the erosion of long-cherished freedoms. Freedom House highlighted not only a regression in liberty worldwide (Freedom House 2018). According to its "Freedom in the World Report 2018," 45 percent of nations and

39 percent of the global population could be considered "free"; 30 percent of nations and 24 percent of people were "partly free"; and 25 percent of nations and 37 percent of people were "not free." In the United States, too, it claimed:

> The past year brought further, faster erosion of America's own democratic standards than at any other time in memory, damaging its international credibility as a champion of good governance and human rights. The United States has experienced a series of setbacks in the conduct of elections and criminal justice over the past decade— under leadership from both major political parties—but in 2017 its core institutions were attacked by an administration that rejects established norms of ethical conduct across many fields of activity. President Trump himself has mingled the concerns of his business empire with his role as president, appointed family members to his senior staff, filled other high positions with lobbyists and representatives of special interests, and refused to abide by disclosure and transparency practices observed by his predecessors.

While the Trump presidency generated outspoken criticism, however, American institutions and a vibrant hyper-pluralism proved remarkably resilient. Congress refused to cooperate on many Trump administration initiatives, courts blocked or ruled unconstitutional others, and the free press was, if anything, reinvigorated in unprecedented ways. The typical strategies of genuine populists in power – state colonization, mass clientelism and systematic repression – also confronted huge obstacles in the mass media, interest groups, and civil society. The fragmented media environment that assisted Trump's rise also limited his reach. If a more centralized media ownership environment had existed – or had Trump been shrewder in his purchases – a one-sided Berlusconi-style Italian media would have proven far more Orwellian. Fragmented media make factual politics difficult; centralization guarantees disaster.

But perhaps the most striking comparative illustration is China. In 2013, an internal Communist Party memo known as Document No. 9 expressly warned against "Western constitutional democracy." An ongoing crackdown on journalists, faith leaders, students, academics, social activists, and human rights lawyers is increasing, assisted by new technology that helps Chinese authorities control information flows and monitor citizen behavior. Chinese authoritarianism includes plans for a "social credit system,"

> fusing big data and artificial intelligence to reward and punish citizens on the basis of their political, commercial, social, and online activities. Facial recognition software, combined with the ubiquity

of surveillance cameras across China, has even made it possible for the state to physically locate people within minutes.

(Campbell and Ratner 2018)

And in March 2018, the National People's Congress approved President Xi Jinping's proposal to abolish presidential term limits to keep him in power indefinitely. As He Weifang, a law professor at Peking University, noted, "If the constitution of one nation can be amended by the most powerful person according to his or her will, the constitution is not a real constitution" (Rauhala 2018).

In the United States, by contrast, Tocqueville's "associations" remain a cacophonous preserve of liberty. As Chapter 4 details, balancing competing rights and liberties remains a constant challenge, especially amid illiberal threats to free expression from both the left and right. Proponents of "religious liberty" clash with those who prize secular values, opponents of "offensive" language collide with proponents of uninhibited free expression, and more. But on multiple measures, America remains an inclusive and tolerant haven. A plurality of goals and preferences exists within a diverse, morally heterogeneous United States whose demographics are inexorably departing a monochrome era. From NGOs to community groups, multiple forces embracing democratic norms influence agendas, attitudes, and public policy. Numerous devices of popular accountability mean that America has no peer in how fully society influences a porous state and how deeply embedded civil rights and liberties have become in the political culture.

## Compared to What, Where? Just and Unjust Constitutions

Nations tend to approve new constitutions only when they emerge from some calamity, as in Germany and Japan after World War II, or to avoid one, as in South Africa in the 1990s. Although the United States has no monopoly on constitutional wisdom, Americans have never had to tip their hats to a new constitution or take a bow for a new revolution. The Constitution exists not simply as the apex of the national legal structure but the heart of its political culture. Partly as a result, constitutional debate is as much symptom as cure: self-critical but also self-referential. Scholars discuss the Constitution in its own terms and by reference to American experience. That relative insularity is entirely reasonable. But as a metric for assessing merits and flaws, it is incomplete.

The Framers' genius is more fully vindicated by comparative assessment. Although imperfect, America's can appear an Apple Constitution to others' IBM. In many ways, the most useful measure of the Constitution is "compared to where?" Or put another way, "whose problems would you rather have?" As far as the recipe for enduring constitutional success goes, other nations have had the ingredients and borrowed the instructions but mostly failed to bake equally appetizing offerings (Billias 2009; Elkins, Ginsburg and Melton 2009).

In terms of their most recent constitutions, Japan's dates from 1947, Italy's from 1948, Germany's and India's each from 1949, Spain's from 1978, and Poland's from 1997. While it is untrue that French libraries file the nation's constitutions under "periodicals," since 1791, the French have experienced nine orders, including five republics: The First Republic (1792–1804), the First Empire (1804–1814), the Monarchy (1814–1848), the Second Republic (1848–1852), the Second Empire (1852–1870), the Third Republic (1870–1940), Occupation (1940–1945), and the Fourth Republic (1946–1958). The current Fifth Republic appears more durable. China has experienced six constitutions since 1911. Two pre-communist constitutions were enacted in 1912 and 1946. After 1949, the People's Republic devised four more in 1954, 1975, 1978, and 1982. The turnover offers another reason for enduring American difference. While most nations' citizens are not nostalgic about their country's checkered past, the main episodes and actors in American political history still tend to evoke more reverence than revulsion.

Some argue that the United States has undergone comparable change. Acemoglu and Johnson (2017), for example, contended that:

> Most Americans tend to believe that they've lived under the same form of government, more or less, since the country was founded in late 1700s ... In fact, formidable challenges at the end of the 19th century were met by fashioning a transformation so thorough it could effectively be deemed a "Second Republic." This new republic came with significantly different economic and political rules — and, as a result, enabled the American system to survive and even thrive for another century. Today, faced with serious economic and political dysfunction, we are in need of another round of deep institutional renewal: a Third Republic.

But that claim is too strong. The Progressive Era ushered in major reforms that the New Deal strengthened to adapt to economic and technological change. But these were mostly matters of policy rather than alterations to the constitutional fabric. Although, as Ackerman (1993) argues, "constitutional moments" have ushered in new eras, the basic design has remained intact. There has been neither the need nor desire to proclaim a wholly new republic.

In another illustrative case, the EU took inspiration from the United States to pledge "ever closer union." In a sense, it succeeded. European integration advanced and, until the United Kingdom voted to leave on June 23, 2016, appeared unstoppable. But a distinction exists between "more perfect" and "ever closer." The EU became closer but not more perfect. Elites were more invested in "EUtopia" than their peoples. On the crux of the project – whether to centralize control or cede more autonomy to member states – the political class was far ahead of the masses. Integration has proven more difficult than Europe's "Founders" imagined: citizens value their national interests over the supranational EU. No pan-European identity has crystallized. Instead, the reassertion of identities has created a crisis of governance, identity, and purpose. In 2017, in ten EU countries, a median of 50 percent were dissatisfied with the way democracy was working, compared with just 48 percent who were satisfied (Stokes 2018). The choice facing the EU is of dissolving into a dysfunctional confederation of noncooperative member states or becoming much more centralized, bureaucratic, and even more undemocratic. That Europeans mismanaged state building – with advantages of knowledge, historical experience, and technology denied their 1787 American counterparts – only puts US achievements in an even more flattering light.

The earlier examples are drawn from the democratic world. A more systematic comparison would include those states with constitutions promising heaven but delivering hell – such as Russia, with the worst wealth inequality in the world, where 111 people own 19 percent of the nation's wealth and millions lack even the flimsiest rights or basic liberties (Bennetts 2016). Plenty of cases exist where government is not based on the consent of the governed and equality before the law is a cruel myth. For those looking to a "deep state," for example, there is Pakistan, where no Prime Minister since the founding of the Islamic republic in 1947 has completed a full five-year term.

One final observation: the United States has advanced under a remarkably short federal constitution. It compares favorably with non-American ones, but also with those of individual states. As comparison with Florida's Constitution in Figure 2.4 shows, the federal one is concise. This has a dual benefit. Firstly, the US Constitution avoids excessive prescription. Secondly, although it sets minimal standards, it allows individual states to go further on matters from gun rights to environmental protection. The federal design assists stability. Allowing differences in a heterogeneous nation reinforces the liberty at the core of constitutional order.

For all that there is to admire about Norway, the American Dream remains distinctly American, even if critics increasingly emphasize the unreality of its promise to many. There exists no Slovenian or Scottish Dream. Millions still regard the United States as a beacon for freedom and escape from political oppression, religious persecution, and economic exclusion. Moreover, the Dream was not part of the Constitution but a by-product of its success. Anger and cynicism about ideals are less about their inherent falsity than the failure to realize them fully. Although their relevance is undiminished, there remains a divide between Americans who believe that liberty is overvalued, and equality undervalued, and those believing the reverse.

| US Constitution (1789) | Florida Constitution (1968) |
|---|---|
| First constitution of the nation | Sixth constitution in the state's history |
| Seven articles | Twelve articles |
| Bill of Rights added | Begins with a declaration of rights |
| Establishes executive, legislature, judiciary at the national level | Establishes executive, legislature, judiciary at the state level |
| Broad framework of government | Detailed provisions specified (e.g. a state lottery, conservation, transportation) |
| Establishes state government | Establishes local government |
| Does not establish public education | Establishes public education |
| Allows for amendment, does not require regular review | Requires a commission to review the constitution every 20 years |

*Figure 2.4* The US Constitution and the Florida State Constitution.

There is a compelling arc to America's constitutional maturation. In the metanarrative, the Preamble helped to make the Constitution an essentially conservative force for revolutionary values. It has, at least since the Civil War, offered an unmatched stability. Constitutions should not be judged by stability alone. But nor should this attribute be underestimated. Americans are not perfect – no more than any people – and many aspects of the US story are shameful. But the national trajectory has been, and remains, positive. The task of perfecting a great nation is a work in progress but much of that enterprise has less to do with constitutional engineering than social and economic change. Compared to art-house constitutions elsewhere – quirky, with devotees, but no mass audiences – the United States has a Hollywood constitution.

## Conclusion

Although predictions of America's imminent decline accompanied almost every decade of its rise after 1945, every civilization has believed in its invulnerability, until it fell. Each failed because it could not fully grasp its own flaws or the severity of the threats it faced until it was too late. So, even if those who pronounce the American experiment as "failing" (Goidel 2015) are premature, constitutional complacency is misplaced. The content of America's constitutional character nonetheless merits extensive, if qualified, admiration. The Constitution's authors were fallible men who acknowledged their imperfection and limited prescience. But they crafted a document that produced and adapted to the most polyglot nation in history. Despite their flaws, the term "genius" – "an exceptional intellectual or creative power" – remains appropriate.

Freud once observed that few people can "subsist on the scanty satisfaction which they can extort from reality." And despite the Declaration's lauding "the pursuit of happiness," Americans "are laggards among their first-world peers, and their happiness has stagnated in the era sometimes called the American Century" (Pinker 2018: 283). Less than one-third rate themselves "very happy," a proportion that has not improved since 1947, despite the much-increased wealth that accompanied the decades that followed (271).

Yet the Preamble's ambitions were realistic. Its promise has been substantially realized. The United States has become a less imperfect union, with invaluable assets: peace, security, prosperity, republicanism, liberty, and government based on the consent of the governed. Its comparative ranking is mixed: on some indicators exemplary, on others wanting. Although the economy remains strong, the political power of cultural differences and politicized identities increasingly places America's social fabric under strain, a reality that is unlikely to abate as the share of white Americans declines further and the foreign-born population of the United States – currently at 13 percent – rises to match its 1890 historic peak of 14.8 percent. But popular preferences ultimately drive policies, and the market of ideas within and between parties tends to generate solutions to balancing competing imperatives (some of the most interesting ideas about combating inequality advocate expanding, rather than contracting, markets [Posner and Weyl 2018]). Constitutional order has responded to a heterogeneous society, social change, and power shifts abroad. A more perfect union, justice, domestic tranquility, the general welfare, common defense, and blessings of liberty have been substantially achieved.

No simple truths confirm how well the Constitution has fared, nor its fitness for the future. Every investment prospectus proclaims that past performance cannot guarantee future results. The conflict between political liberty and equality is universally intractable. Moreover, economics is the "dismal science" for good reasons. It is reductionist to treat constitutions purely or predominantly in economic terms; the financial pages do not offer a reliable gauge of fundamental soundness. A constitution is not a ten-year economic plan but ultimately an instrument to preserve a preexisting nation. As one critic observed:

> Americans' relative success, and the ease with which success has come, have involved not only favorable physical and geographic circumstances but also a domestic society that has suffered fewer of the sorts of disruptions and destructive divisions that have beset many other countries. This is easy to forget amid political gridlock in Washington and a related partisan and ideological competition

that has become more intense and uncompromising in recent years. That competition is overlaid on a more fundamental long-standing consensus about politics and society that is centered on the tenets of liberal democracy.

(Pillar 2016–2017: 710)

In terms of adaptation, the same foundation facilitated a transformative advance of equal rights, institutionalization of civil liberties, creation of a welfare state, and an international role unimaginable in 1787. That this helped to sustain a stable framework for government that channels conflict into everyday politics rather than violence and allows the peaceful transfer of power is remarkable. For critics, continuity bespeaks a conservative design that thwarts change. But only ineffective constitutions are *not* conservative. There are few people, whatever their politics, who are not conservative about the things they truly treasure.

By agreeing how to disagree, in reference to the Constitution, the United States has been spared the existential crises of other polities. The Constitution remains the optimal fit for American conditions even as its governing institutions, to which we turn next, have become objects for unrelenting criticism.

## Summary

- The Constitution was the product of intense political conflicts, compromises, and agreements to differ from the outset.
- Although its famous declaration of "We the People" was revolutionary, the Constitution did not establish a popular democracy but a republic.
- The Preamble sets out six goals that the Constitution is designed to achieve. Although it required almost two hundred years, and immense changes, to achieve its promise, the Constitution has largely – though not fully – met the goals set out in the Preamble.
- By achieving those six aims, and holding together a nation of immensely varied humanity, two of the four conditions of an effective constitution have been met: providing a stable framework for government by channeling conflict into everyday politics and ensuring the peaceful transfer of power.

# 3   Governing Institutions

In America the people are a master who must be indulged to the utmost
possible limits.

De Tocqueville, *Democracy in America* (1996: 64)

...where, outside the occasional academic common-room discussion,
have you heard much in the way of let's-scrap-it-all questioning of the
country's basic constitutional institutions – or, for that matter, the
country's geographic composition? ... We experience these basic US
institutions – the presidency, Congress, and the courts – and this US
geography as fish experience the water. Overwhelmingly, Americans
seize on winning elections, not on overhauling the Constitution, as a
tonic for whatever difficulties come along.

David Mayhew (2017: 6)

## Introduction

The fish are experiencing something distinctly wrong with the water.
America's governing institutions seem chronically dysfunctional.
Presidents "fail" so often that historians label the job "impossible"
(Suri 2017). No matter which party has a majority, Congress wins
minimal public esteem. Even the Supreme Court seems just another
institution staffed by ideologues. According to Gallup, before the
Trump presidency, trust in national leaders was at its lowest ever level
(42 percent); confidence in Congress and the Court plunged record
lows of 7 and 30 percent, respectively, in 2014; and President Obama's
job approval rating over two terms ranked among the lowest recorded
(Newport and Dugan 2017). All this suggests government institutions
no longer fit for purpose, an immobilized democracy, and a Constitution
doubly broken.

First, as a power map, the Constitution misleads. The presidency
has become vastly more powerful than intended. The judiciary acts as
a "super-legislature," more initiating than interpreting laws. Congress,
though retaining its Article I authority, has ceded influence and delegated
powers to executive agencies, independent commissions, and other entities exercising power on its behalf, with limited supervision or oversight.

The constitutional text now reads like an outdated travel guide to a vanished country.

Second, as a mechanism for containing conflict and incentivizing cooperation, the Constitution is under stress. Its adaptive qualities have succumbed to "revolving gridlock" (Brady and Volden 2006). Precluding majority tyranny has been superseded by the tyranny of overlapping minorities: groups employing lobbyists to craft special tax breaks or exemptions to advance their concerns over the national interest. Lobbying "the best Congress money can buy" is the "business of America" because, as the old Washington adage has it, "if you are not at the table you are probably on the menu" (Drutman 2015: 2). Defective institutions have created a crisis of representation and responsiveness.

This chapter examines the institutional dimensions of the case for change: Congress, the presidency, the Court, and the Electoral College. It argues that the Constitution, government, and policy are only as good as those who operate them. If public officials cannot compromise, constitutional barriers cannot be overcome. But that doesn't mean the barriers need weakening.

That case relies on two further questions. First, is the institutional framework the source of problems? Does Congress impede better policy or shirk its responsibilities? Is the presidency too powerful or too weak? Should judges avoid deciding major disputes or intervene more? Good prescription relies on accurate diagnosis. But no consensus exists on what ails America. Second, if the framework *is* flawed, what changes might work? Reform proposals are many, but few are both compelling and feasible. Constitutional engineering, however forensic, cannot overcome the polarization, division, and distrust underpinning political dysfunction.

Reflecting the Founders' suspicion, partisanship is often seen as alien to the Constitution's spirit. Yet partisan conflict dates from America's earliest days and parties traditionally mediated constitutional divides. Despite antagonism, presidents, Congresses, and courts managed crises and crafted policies to assure prosperity and expand rights. The Constitution and partisanship have been constant companions. For those claiming the United States has "never" been so polarized, there is an obvious rebuke: though more a sectional than partisan conflict, the Civil War saw over 600,000 deaths (equivalent to about six million today).

But if the reference point is contemporary, then rarely has politics been so partisan among both elites and the mass public. Once liberals and conservatives "sorted" themselves into, respectively, the Democratic and Republican parties over the past three decades, overlap between the parties withered in Congress. In the 115th Congress (2017–2018), in both the House and Senate, no Democrat was more conservative than the most liberal Republican (as measured by DW-Nominate scores on ideological profiles). Although over one-third of Americans identify as "Independents," the proportion of true independents – with no partisan leanings – is in single digits (Cook 2018). As Figure 3.1 details, in 2017, Pew found partisanship more important than religion, gender, race, ethnicity, or education in shaping the public's political views while the values gap between Republicans and Democrats – on race, government, immigration, national security, and environmental protection – had increased from 15 percent in 1994 to 36. In the thirty-four Senatorial races of 2016, for the first time in American history, the same party whose presidential nominee carried each of thirty-four states also won its Senate contest. Conservative Democrats and liberal Republicans have effectively vanished.

Political scientists disagree about whether polarization is asymmetric or symmetric (has one party moved further away from the center than the other or have both moved equally?) and an elite or mass phenomenon (Abramowitz 2012, 2018; Fiorina 2017). Some depict the parties as distinct cultural entities: Republicans as ideologically driven and Democrats as a coalition of demographic groups with interests served by various forms of government activity (Grossmann and Hopkins 2016). Others claim that party elites help to select preferred congressional candidates in primary elections, shaping the choices offered voters (Hassell 2018).

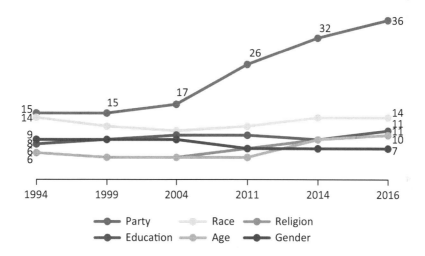

*Figure 3.1* Partisan Values Gap (1994–2017).
Source: Data from Pew Research Center. Survey conducted June 8–18 and June 27–July 9, 2017.

Notes:
Average gap in the share taking a conservative position across ten political values, by key demographics.
Indicates average gap between the share of two groups taking the conservative position across ten values items.
Party = difference between Rep/Lean Rep and Dem/Lean Dem.
Race = white non-Hispanic/black non-Hispanic.
Education = college grad/non-college grad.
Age = 18–49/50+.
Religion = weekly+ religious service attendance/less often.

Intense competition then incentivizes lawmakers to stick together for the sake of party "brand" (Lee 2016). Still others argue that the combination of geography and electoral rules (winner-take-all elections) has helped to bring about a new era "in which a close balance between the Democratic and Republican parties in the nation as a whole contrasts with the reliable electoral dominance of most congressional districts, states, and even entire regions by one party or the other" (Hopkins 2017: 3).

Whatever the causes, "affective polarization" or "negative partisanship" is such that partisans don't merely disagree but dislike and distrust each other. Majorities of both parties' identifiers cite the other party's harmful policies as a major reason for their partisan affiliation, and such negative motivations are even more influential to Independents' choice of which party to "lean" toward (Fingerhut 2018). Such angry tribalism can make even the genteel parts of Washington a rough neighborhood, toxic for governance. The Constitution demands the art of compromise, but partisan politics – fueled by a fragmented media and partisan cable television, radio, and internet news sources – often seems premised on the art of perpetual conflict.

## The Balance of Powers between the Branches of Government

In American political culture, references to democracy are ubiquitous and holding rulers to account is fundamental. Politicians use "America" and "democracy" as synonyms. Many citizens treat as a self-evident truth that "We the People", not politicians, rule. But Dahl's replies to his question – *How Democratic is the US Constitution?* – were "not very" and "not enough" (2003). Even more forcefully, in explaining "why the majority keeps losing," Dionne, Mann and Ornstein (2017) claimed the US is "now a non-majoritarian democracy."

But in key respects, it always has been. The Founders' conception was a minimalist one of government subject to electoral checks:

> We say that to live under democracy is freedom, but democracy enables electoral majorities to beat up on minorities and thus to curtail their freedom. The solution to this problem we call "liberal democracy" – an oxymoron because democracy is illiberal and liberalism non-democratic. (I would prefer to call liberalism the fusion of democracy with legally protected liberty.) We speak of "self-rule", but modern democracy is not self-rule; it is the means by which the electorate decides which officials shall rule.
>
> (Posner 2003: 181)

Majoritarian *and* anti-majoritarian, republican and liberal features coexist in creative tension. The Constitution sliced and diced power within

Washington and the wider federal system. Handing power to the people is balanced by protecting individuals via checks and balances and enumerated rights, frustrating both proponents of illiberal democracy (majoritarianism without rights) and undemocratic liberalism (rights without democracy). The system is not presidential but comprises "separated institutions sharing powers." Vertical separation (federalism), reserving powers to the states and people, is reinforced by horizontal separation. Separation of personnel precludes officials sitting in more than one branch simultaneously. Separation of powers – an executive chosen independently of the legislature – is reinforced by "checks and balances": each branch possessing partial vetoes over the others.

The independence of elected institutions is also protected via fixed terms: a four-year presidency (limited to two terms after ratification of the Twenty-second Amendment); a Senate of two seats for each state, for six-year terms, with staggered elections (with one-third of Senators elected every two years after the Seventeenth Amendment was ratified); and the House of Representatives, with two-year terms (and all 435 members up for election every two years). With variations in constituency size (presidents elected by the nation, albeit indirectly, Senators representing states, and House districts determined every ten years by census), passing legislation demands that divergent ambitions converge. With different constituencies electing different candidates to different offices at different times for different terms, the design institutionalizes multiple veto points.

It is little wonder that government is synonymous with "gridlock." Many nations emulated the Bill of Rights; checks and balances have been an enduring exception to popular US exports. Some might concur with the political philosopher Isaiah Berlin (2013: 165) that the separation of powers was "much too faithfully adopted in the United States, with results not altogether fortunate." But the separation of powers – the absence of which Madison termed "the very definition of tyranny" – is to prevent any individual or institution wielding arbitrary power by controlling all levers of government. Each branch defends its prerogatives because each wants to exercise power. Institutionalizing conflicts of interest has shaped US political development profoundly. To some, it has denied efficient action and set back the republic's advance. To others, by slowing the rate at which change occurs by requiring broad-based support, it has assured political legitimacy and enduing success.

Feared but rapidly embraced, parties have been key to the Constitution, ensuring the system works by bridging what it divides. Parliamentary systems typically see lawmakers sustain the government and pass legislation. But the United States features two sovereign majorities: the presidential one every four years and a congressional one every two years. Prior to recent decades, this seemed a recipe for incoherence. Democrats were internally divided between a largely progressive northern and urban wing and a vehemently conservative and segregationist southern wing.

Republicans, too, were internally riven by a predominantly northeastern liberal and moderate wing and a conservative midwestern and western bloc. In 1950, troubled by the "deadlock" of democracy, an American Political Science Association (APSA) "Committee on Political Parties" report called for sharper disagreements and clearer electoral choices:

> The fundamental requirement of accountability is a two-party system in which the opposition party acts as the critic of the party in power, developing, defining and presenting the policy alternatives which are necessary for a true choice in reaching public decisions.

As Figure 3.2 illustrates, APSA got exactly what it desired and more. With activists participating in primaries and caucuses, the range of views that elected officials held increasingly narrowed. As progressives dragged Democrats to the left, and conservatives pushed Republicans to the right, the center was left increasingly vacant. In terms of values on a range of key issues, not only did the share of Democrats and Republicans who identified as liberal and conservative – respectively – increase, but the share that was consistently so also grew substantially. In Congress, too, the research of Keith Poole, Howard Rosenthal, and others at voteview.com has demonstrated a growing partisan gulf. Competitive elections have increased incentives to stick together rather than cross party lines. That has empowered the fringes: small immoderate groups can hold the majority hostage. Finally, while party cohesion gives more authority to leaders, they still rely on the rank-and-file. In the House, Newt Gingrich,

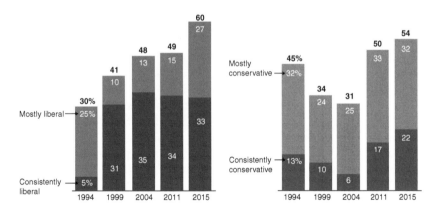

*Figure 3.2* Democrats Are Increasingly Liberal, Republicans Are Increasingly Conservative (1994–2015).

Source: Data from Pew Research Center. Survey conducted August 27–October 5, 2015.

Notes:
- N = 6,004.
- Ideological consistency based on a scale of 10 political values questions.
- Republicans include Republican-leaning independents; Democrats include Democratic-leaning independents.

John Boehner, Nancy Pelosi, and Paul Ryan all faced profound internal party management problems and leadership challenges. In the Senate, coordinating lawmakers has been compared to "herding cats."

Madison was conscious of the need for an important but not overbearing role for public opinion: to balance mass and elite influence on governing institutions. Competition between parties is an essential component of a responsive democracy that addresses citizens' concerns. But the ideological separation of parties has weakened the system of balanced powers, generating "a government of separated institutions competing for shared power" (Jones 1990: 3). That incessant and increasingly zero-sum competition represents the core of what troubles governance.

## Congress

Most Americans regard Congress negatively. Inaction on public priorities seems guaranteed by a slow, cumbersome legislature paralyzed by problems of collective action and achieving supermajorities. With parochial lawmakers attentive to their constituencies, next elections, and donors, Congress is increasingly unable to execute its most basic constitutional duties, such as managing the federal purse, passing spending bills on time and conducting executive oversight:

> Facing low approval ratings after a historically unproductive 112th session and a series of last-minute showdowns over fiscal matters, Congress is now less popular than root canals, NFL replacement referees, head lice, the rock band Nickelback, colonoscopies … traffic jams, cockroaches, Donald Trump, France, Genghis Khan, used-car salesmen and Brussels sprouts.
>
> (Public Policy Polling 2013)

Scholarly opinion is not altogether kinder, though divided. For example, Levinson (2006: 25–77) lamented "our undemocratic legislative process" while Mann and Ornstein described Congress as the "broken" branch, "a supine, reactive body more eager to submit to presidential directives than to assert its own prerogatives" (2008: 16). But Mayhew's (2017) panoramic study suggested important qualifications. Despite their disapproval, Americans consistently believe Congress should make policy and, "Often, when Congress is doing nothing at all, to the despair of partisans, intellectuals, and the media, it is actually responding to an unresolved electorate with a perfect ear" (Mayhew 2017: 107).

What constitutional remedies might improve congressional performance? That requires reconsidering Congress's constitutional setting and supposed deficiencies.

The Constitution accorded Congress primacy in Article I, which takes up more than half the document. For the branches to sustain mutual accountability required a powerful, independent legislature. Congress was given "All legislative powers" and exclusive authority over federal taxing, borrowing, and spending. Article I also established permissible subjects of legislation, confining this to matters of importance to the whole nation. Bicameralism, with distinct forms of election and representation, guaranteed Congress would be responsive both to mass opinion and regional concerns. Legislation could pass only after deliberation and compromise produced broad consensus.

Congress has been essential to America's durability: expanding individual rights and liberties, from drafting the Bill of Rights in the First Congress to passing civil and voting rights in the 1960s; exposing and countering executive misdeeds, from Watergate and Iran-Contra to Russian interference in the 2016 and 2018 elections; and, until the 1960s, exercising fiscal prudence by keeping government operations on a balanced budget, borrowing only for wars, emergencies, and investments (beginning with the Louisiana Purchase in 1803), and paying down the nation's accumulated debts. As a strong assembly, representing the diversity of America more fully than any single president, Congress at its best has weighed voter intensities, blended them into compromise packages, constrained sectarian or overly ambitious executives, and legitimized the system among the public.

But Congress has been in steady if uneven decline. Since the 1960s, Congress has ceded substantial law-making power to the executive. Ambiguous statutes mandate clean air, safe products, and other collective goods, but leave implementation to administrative agencies. When presidents exercise authority unilaterally (as Clinton did in the financial crises of the 1990s, and Bush and Obama did during that of 2008–2009), Congress usually objects but goes along.

Congress has also abandoned fiscal discipline. It transferred most federal spending to "entitlement" programs, and for most of the 2000s and 2010s discontinued annual budgets for remaining "discretionary" programs (such as scientific research, education, and roads, which are all funded year to year through congressional appropriations), instead passing emergency "continuing resolutions" to keep government functioning. Recent congresses borrowed continuously to fund routine operations and income-transfer programs. Spending caps on defense and domestic discretionary programs were imposed after 2011 budget talks broke down between Obama and Republican congressional leaders. Although deals raised the caps in 2013 and 2015, periodic controversy over increasing the federal debt ceiling revealed a growing gulf between congressional revenue and spending decisions.

Congress's chronic inability to follow its own process goes back over forty years. In the four decades since the current system for budgeting and spending tax dollars has been in effect, Congress has managed to pass all its required appropriations measures on time only in fiscal 1977 (the first full fiscal year under the current system), 1989, 1995, and 1997. That said, the scale of the dysfunction is now vastly greater than it was in prior decades.

The Federal Government spent $4.1 trillion in 2018. The Congressional Budget Office projected that annual interest payments on the $20 trillion national debt – the interest on the US credit card – would grow from $307 billion in 2018 to $818 billion in 2027. The deficit, as a share of gross domestic product, hit a twenty-first-century peak of 9.8 percent in 2009, before contracting to 2.4 percent in 2015, and rising again in 2017 to $666 billion, roughly 3 percent. The CBO projected it would hit $1 trillion in 2022, but the tax law and spending bills passed in the 115th Congress promised to take it beyond $1 trillion annually from 2019 through the 2020s.

More generally, Congress is paralyzed by partisanship, parochialism, and "blame avoidance" for tough decisions. Permanent campaigning privileges obsessive fundraising over legislating. On average from 1992 to 2016, 93 percent of House members who sought reelection won. Even in 2010, a year of major turnover when Republicans gained sixty-three seats in the House, the reelection rate fell to "only" 85 percent: 338 of the 396 representatives running retained their seats. The maxim "all politics are local" is increasingly false when elections are nationalized, and partisan incentives encourage legislators accumulating issue positions, not positive policy accomplishments:

> From the perspective of the party that does not hold the White House, major legislation with bipartisan support strengthens the reputation of the President's party, legitimizes the President and leaders of the President's party, and probably disappoints party activists who have to accept less than their ideal outcome. In a highly partisan political environment, uncompromising opposition helps the opposition to minimize its losses and perhaps inflict embarrassing setbacks to the President's party.
>
> (Koger and Lebo 2017: 174)

Rather than embolden lawmakers, incumbency encourages risk aversion, delays, and obstructionism on matters from immigration reform to combating climate change and repairing American infrastructure. A 2017 report found that senior congressional staff lacked confidence in Congress's institutional capacity to do its job. Despite more informational and policy demands, a combination of staff reductions, turnover, modest compensation, and lagging technology limited congressional responsiveness. Only 6 percent of senior staff aides were "very satisfied" that "Members have adequate time and resources to understand, consider and deliberate policy and legislation" (CMF 2017).

## In Defense of Congress

In mitigation, today's lawmakers are at minimum no worse than their predecessors: better educated, less corrupt, and more representative (the 115th Congress, for example, saw a record high of twenty-two female

Senators and eighty-four female lawmakers in the House). Moreover, Congress has never excelled at instant action. During the "Conservative Coalition" era (1933–1981), policy inertia was punctuated by spasms of legislative activism. From Truman's "do nothing" Eightieth Congress (1947–1949) to Jimmy Carter's "malaise" (1977–1981), it was easier to veto than enact change. On civil rights, only massive popular mobilization and large legislative majorities advanced landmark legislation in 1964–1965.

Since the 1980s, the party coalitions have become more internally coherent ideologically (and externally differentiated from each other). The rise of a conservative Republican Party and progressive Democratic Party shrunk the center. Opportunities for bipartisanship are now rare, though Congress can still "do big things," such as health care in 2010 and tax reform in 2017. Presidents can also win bipartisan victories, even under divided party control: Reagan secured major defense increases, spending reductions and tax cuts in 1981; Clinton enacted welfare reform and balanced budgets from 1996 to 2001; and Bush saw tax cuts and education reform passed in 2001–2002. Static pictures are therefore misleading. The separation of powers does not allocate power in a predetermined way but gives each branch tools it can use to battle for power in specific contests (Chafetz 2017). In distinct contexts, the same institutions, under the same Constitution, exhibit different levels of power, influence, and effectiveness. The intervening variable? Partisan politics.

For example, in 1973, the unpopular Vietnam War prompted Democratic congressional majorities to cut off funding, which led to President Nixon withdrawing US forces. But in 2007, when Democratic majorities legislated to force withdrawal of US forces from the unpopular Iraq War, President Bush vetoed legislation and ordered a "surge" of troops that went directly against congressional preferences.

Or take the federal budget. The Constitution requires that: "No money shall be drawn from the Treasury, but in Consequence of Appropriations made by Law." For the Federal Government to spend, Congress must authorize the expenditure. But the constitutional text cannot explain how power works in practice. In 2011, for instance, House Republicans forced Obama and Senate Democrats to make concessions to keep the government open. In 2013, however, the Republican House tried this again and government shut down. But on this occasion, Republicans retreated after a couple of weeks, reopening the government almost entirely on the Democrats' terms. Neither the Constitution nor partisan control had changed in the intervening two years. What had altered were political dynamics. By inflicting major losses on Democrats, the 2010 elections emboldened Republicans in 2011. But the 2012 elections saw Obama reelected and Democrats retain their majority in the Senate. Republicans still controlled the House but with reduced popularity and political capital.

Congress, then, is not broken and can act positively. Even amid partisan conflict, Congress has engaged in serious deliberation, forged consensus, and prevented unwise proposals from becoming law (Connelly, Pitney and Schmitt 2017). On February 8–9, 2018, the Republican Congress voted for a two-year budget deal that included $500 billion increases in military and domestic spending programs, reflecting a major ideological shift for a supposedly conservative party. The deal ended the need for repeated short-term agreements that led to frequent brinkmanship and shutdowns. The Senate voted 71–28 in favor: thirty-three Republicans, thirty-seven Democrats and one Independent voted for the measure, sixteen Republicans and twelve Democrats voted against. The House voted 240–186: 167 Republicans and 73 Democrats approved the measure, 67 Republicans and 119 Democrats voted against. In March, Congress agreed to increase the spending deal to $1.3 trillion, including a $61 billion increase for the Pentagon. Although the longer-term fiscal consequences were arguably unwise, the deal gave hope that bipartisanship is not dead.

If the parties can cooperate, repurposing the legislature through constitutional reform may be redundant. But would constitutional change enhance congressional responsiveness or responsibility? The key problems that are constitutional in origin are twofold: bicameralism and the Senate.

### Bicameralism

Federalism encourages representation of the states in one of two legislative chambers. But although forty-nine of the fifty states are bicameral (apart from Nebraska), bicameralism is comparatively unusual. By the twenty-first century, even federal states like Australia, Germany, and Switzerland did not accord both legislative chambers equal authority. Moreover, the US Senate exercises greater authority than the House, confirming presidential nominations and ratifying treaties. Spending bills need to pass the House with only a majority, but the Senate needs sixty votes. As the 2018 deal showed, spending bills require bipartisan support. To critics, bicameralism hampers efficiency and dilutes popular majorities.

The difficulty here, however, is what alternative would prove better. Dahl (2003: 45) pointed out that democracies such as Norway, Sweden, and Denmark abolished their second chambers. But these are small, homogenous, unitary states, not continental-sized federations. Although some critics (Lazare 1996) endorse it, a unicameral legislature where the House legislated alone would hardly be congenial. With a supportive president, not only would it be able to pass laws without the requirement of supermajorities, but it would also be even more subject to the whims of partisan extremes (imagine the House under

Republican or Democratic control legislating without a Senate, by simple majority vote). Protectionist trade pressures – which increase as the constituency size narrows – would encounter fewer constraints. But, under conditions of divided control, there would be more likelihood of constant presidential vetoes, threats, and overrides. Although the Senate has its problems, a unicameral Congress would hardly remedy the defects.

With three in four Democrats currently serving representing districts in coastal states, the geographic dimensions of partisan polarization would be even starker. And without non-partisan apportionment, the chances of a gerrymandered House exercising unfettered legislative power would be enhanced. That prospect is unattractive. One can maintain that a second branch of the legislature is essential, even while conceding the flaws of equal state representation in the Senate. Levinson (2006: 38) conceded as much in calling for a new convention: "I can well imagine urging its members to retain the general structure of bicameralism even as they engage in the necessary reform of the specifics of our particular version of bicameralism." Feasibility aside, this is a weak argument on which to base a case for constitutional change:

> ...bicameralism, the presidential veto, and judicial review are the bedrock foundation of checks and balances and hence of the Constitution. Here then is at least part of the argument for a bicameral Congress. A unicameral legislature would completely overwhelm the executive and complete the politicization of administration that already is a constant threat to good government.
>
> (Main 2011)

### The US Senate

A much stronger case concerns the Senate which is, as former staffer Ira Shapiro (2018) described it, the institution that has failed the longest and worst: "ground zero for America's political dysfunction." Once a space where Democrats and Republicans worked together to transcend ideological and regional differences to find common ground, its decline has intensified polarization by institutionalizing it at the highest level. That is triply problematic: first, since the Senate has more power than almost any other "upper" house in the world; second, while most US state legislatures' lower houses allow two-year terms, and only five allow representatives to remain in place for four years, no state upper house resembles the Senate in allowing six-year terms; and third, unlike both the Constitution (through amendment and interpretation) and the House (through decennial reapportionment), the Senate lacks the means for its own revision.

Unequal representation is institutionalized. Nowhere is the Constitution more out of sync with democratic sensibilities than in allocating two senators per state regardless of population size. Equal representation was the price paid for political union in 1787. But it makes little sense now. California (2010 population: 37,253,956) has seventy times the population of Wyoming (2010 population: 563,626). A Wyoming Senator represents some 293,000 Americans, a California Senator some 19.5 million. Alaska, Delaware, Montana, North Dakota, South Dakota, Vermont, and Wyoming have greater representation in the Senate, with two members, than in the House, with one "at-large" lawmaker each. The Dakotas send twice the number of senators to Washington as Texas.

The twenty-one smallest states, representing 12 percent of the US population, have forty-two senators, one more than needed to block any legislation. If all fifty senators from the twenty-five smallest states vote for a bill and the vice president casts his deciding vote with them, senators representing only 16 percent of Americans can overrule those representing 84 percent. And if existing trends continue, by 2040, 70 percent of Americans will live in fifteen states and be represented by only 30 of 100 US Senators. In effect, the United States will acquire more and more "rotten boroughs" – relatively depopulated states that nonetheless exercise disproportionate influence in the more powerful of the two legislative chambers and, hence, over congressional outcomes and federal policies and laws. Moreover, although it is mainly the larger states and big cities that provide jobs, opportunities, and progress as the engine of the American economy, they are poorly represented.

Is this defensible? Put bluntly, no. On grounds of basic equity, the system is now profoundly unbalanced. But the main problem is the political feasibility, not the desirability, of change. Some kind of reckoning is likely to occur once sufficient Americans begin to remonstrate about the profound democratic deficit that is institutionalized on Capitol Hill, but its resolution is difficult to envisage as harmonious. Although three considerations offer partial defenses of the existing system, these do not add up to a sufficiently persuasive case.

First, in the constitutional spirit of countervailing powers, some might claim there remains a rationale for state-centered representation to find expression in Washington. The states possess distinct political cultures, traditions, and interests. Their local economies and resource bases should receive some protection in a federal system. Their Senatorial "bonus" is also partially offset by the penalty administered by the Electoral College. That is, the "big states" possess more heft in deciding who is president every four years even if what determines presidential campaigning is not state size but electoral competitiveness.

Second, whatever small state bias exists does not monolithically favor one party. In the 115th Congress, Alaska, South Dakota, and Wyoming each had two Republican Senators. Delaware sent two Democrats. Montana and North Dakota each sent one Democrat and one Republican. Vermont sent one Democrat and one Independent (Bernie Sanders). Thirteen of the fifty states had split-party delegations (in addition to those above, Colorado, Florida, Maine, Missouri, Nevada, Ohio, Pennsylvania, West Virginia, and Wisconsin). Lawmakers representing the same state often vote similarly, but partisanship undercuts this. For example, Democrat Sherrod Brown and Republican Rob Portman represented Ohio in the 114th and 115th Congresses with markedly dissimilar voting records.

Third, if skewed representation is the problem, plurality electoral systems mean this applies to large states as well. For example, in 2016, California elected Democrat Kamala Harris as a US Senator. Harris won with 61 percent of the vote (7.5 million). Her opponent, Loretta Sanchez, lost with 38 percent of the vote (4.7 million). Harris joined fellow Democrat Dianne Feinstein in the Senate. California's Republicans – a declining bloc, but one still more numerous than most small states – had no representation there. Moreover, in 2016, just over 12 of 39 million Californians voted in the Senate election. That reduces but doesn't alter the malapportionment. Any plurality rather than proportional electoral system in single member constituencies risks such results.

Those reasonable points do not outweigh the manifest injustice of a system so malapportioned that, were we asked to design a Senate today, few of us would suggest equal representation for states of 39 million and half a million citizens. The overrepresentation of small and rural states, the conservative bias to policy outcomes, and significant differentials in federal outlays were extensively documented by Lee and Oppenheimer (1999). Although equal representation persists because of historic contingencies 200 years ago, they saw the prospects for reform as "dim" (1999: 15) because of Article V's provision that, "no State, without its Consent, shall be deprived of its equal Suffrage in the Senate." This implied that all states must assent to any constitutional change in Senate apportionment (229).

But it is possible to imagine an amendment abolishing the Senate and creating an entirely new body, with identical powers but a different name and mode of representation. Small states would not then be deprived of "equal suffrage in the Senate" because the Senate no longer existed. Legalistic though this might seem, it suggests that the technical obstacle to solving the problem can be overcome. The question then is one of feasibility. Few turkeys vote for Thanksgiving. Small states are not going to agree to being deprived of their existing influence through such a move, and the partisan dimensions would also kick in. That is, since smaller states are, on balance, more rural and conservative leaning, Republicans in larger states might come to their aid to preserve their influence. Moreover, since most states are overrepresented in the Senate by the one person, one vote standard, "one would not expect majorities within most states to support a change even if a national majority favored it" (Lee and Oppenheimer 1999: 229). Add to this the relative lack of interest in the issue and relative conservatism of Americans toward their political institutions, despite deep dissatisfaction with Washington, and the prospects for change are slight.

Even if such a change was politically feasible, though, do any alternatives promise a better outcome? For bicameral states, a basic dilemma exists: the more proportional the second chamber, the more it is redundant, since it merely replicates the design of the first. Sabato (2007) made several recommendations:

- allow the ten largest population states four senators, and the next fifteen three senators each, for a more representative Senate;
- appoint all former presidents and vice-presidents as "national senators";
- mandate non-partisan redistricting for House elections;
- lengthen the House terms to three years, which, with all Senate terms, would coincide with presidential elections (with the president serving a single six-year term);
- expand the House to 1,000 members, but keep staffing and budget levels the same as present, adjusted for inflation;
- implement (generous) term limits to assure rotation in office.

Some of these amount to what might politely be termed an incomplete approach to reality and raise questions as to whether this represents an improved, and workable, new arrangement. But a reformed Senate along these lines would see: California, Texas, Florida, New York, Illinois, Pennsylvania, Ohio, Georgia, North Carolina, and Michigan with four senators each; New Jersey, Virginia, Washington, Arizona, Massachusetts, Indiana, Tennessee, Missouri, Maryland, Wisconsin, Minnesota, Colorado, South Carolina, Alabama, and Louisiana with three senators each; and the twenty-five remaining states left with their existing two. It is impossible to predict how the partisan breakdown would look, but if it resembled the solid versus split delegation divide noted above, there would be an enhanced Democratic presence in the Senate. The system would have the clear benefit, unlike the House, of being "gerrymander" free. The decennial census would record population shifts, and the 4-3-2 allocations of Senators would be adjusted accordingly.

On the downside, the result would be some seventy-five senators from these states, combined with fifty from those remaining with two each: a total of 125 senators. That would mean that to gain a supermajority of two-thirds, the new requirement would be eighty-three votes rather than sixty-seven. To gain the three-fifths necessary for cloture to end a filibuster, seventy-five rather than sixty votes would be needed. This would represent a change, but more a tremor than an earthquake. In this instance, forty-nine rather than thirty-three senators could block a treaty, appointment, or bill, or sustain a presidential veto, and fifty rather than forty would be needed to keep a filibuster going. In an era of partisan polarization, this would not fundamentally alter the conflictual dynamics shaping Senate politics. But it would not necessarily worsen the current predicament either. A larger Senate would require greater discipline to work without any more chance of clear working majorities or less rampant individualism. But if the Senate were to abolish the filibuster for legislation, the change could induce a greater element of majoritarianism and responsiveness without sacrificing its state-based character of representation or imitating too closely the House.

So, a workable new institution is conceivable, albeit preferably without "national senators." The prospect of a permanent National Senator Carter, Quayle, Gore, Bush, Cheney, Obama, Biden, Trump, and Pence may not warm every American heart. It is a hopeful thought that, with no electorate to be accountable to, these officials would serve in a non-partisan way. But how reliable would that assumption prove? Moreover, since 1913, the notion of allowing important Senate votes to be decided by unelected lawmakers has been repudiated as undermining the principle of democratic election. The institution already contains sufficient Senators who look in the mirror and see a president.

But Sabato's suggestion of a House composed of 1,000 lawmakers would make legislative business close to unmanageable. No democratic legislature comprises so many lawmakers. Party discipline would need to be unimaginably strict. Getting the necessary 501 votes to pass any measure, and 667 to gain a two-thirds majority to overcome a veto, would be a logistical nightmare and demand a level of subservience to centralized authority that lawmakers are unwilling to give. Small groups could hold the majority to ransom even more easily than at present. And, as for operating on the same budget as currently, perhaps only Capitol Hill restaurants, bars and DC lobbying firms would welcome this with enthusiasm. Congress is already overburdened and under-resourced.

Finally, altering term lengths seems an unlikely improvement. Madison justified two-year House terms in *Federalist 52*:

> As it is essential to liberty that the government in general should have a common interest with the people, so it is particularly essential that the branch of it under consideration should have an immediate dependence on, and an intimate sympathy with, the people. Frequent elections are unquestionably the only policy by which this dependence and sympathy can be effectually secured.

But Madison was advocating two-year terms against the annual elections demanded by anti-Federalists and then standard in many state legislatures. Were longer House terms genuinely to result in greater de-liberation and less reelection-focused partisanship, perhaps there would be a case. But the Senate, though marginally less dysfunctional, does not offer a salutary case for longer terms. Moreover, part of the logic of Sabato-style proposals is to induce greater party-oriented voting by synchronizing terms. That, however, is already occurring through in-creasingly nationalized elections, even in midterms, and – to many – is part of the problem with the way Washington doesn't work.

Expansion of the House is an idea whose moment has not arrived. Senate overhaul would be a welcome change, but, politically, its day remains all-too-distant. But reform is no panacea. In 2016, no state with a Senate election chose a senator of one party while giving its electoral votes to the presidential candidate of the other party, the first time this had happened since direct popular election of senators. Not only has split ticket voting decreased, but inside the Senate, the distance between the most conservative Democrat and the most liberal Republican has grown substantially. Moderate Republicans and conservative Democrats are mostly a thing of the past, and no fashion for retro is likely to bring them back anytime soon. To the extent that major legislation happens, it still does so on a bipartisan basis, but forging those coalitions is much harder in an era of polarized parties (the failure of regular attempts at immigration reform is especially illustrative). And with control of the Senate often up for grabs in elections, lawmakers are incentivized to engage in messaging that helps win elections rather than cooperation that helps make laws. Even were it to occur, constitutional reform would make limited impact on such negative partisan dynamics.

### Extra-Constitutional Change

Mann and Ornstein identified two major impediments to a better Congress: "Parliamentary-style parties in a separation-of-powers gov-ernment are a formula for willful obstruction and policy irresolution" (2012: xiii); and a Republican Party that is an "insurgent outlier – ideologically extreme; contemptuous of the inherited social and eco-nomic policy regime; scornful of compromise; un-persuaded by conventional understandings of facts, evidence, and science; and dismis-sive of the legitimacy of its political opposition (2012: xiv)" (a "radical-ization" theme they stressed again after 2016 [Dionne, Ornstein and Mann 2017]). They quoted former Speaker Hastert: "When [you] start making deals where you have to get the Democrats to pass the legisla-tion, you're not in power anymore."

Political scientists dispute how asymmetrical polarization may be, but congressional dysfunction clearly reflects and reinforces partisan polar-ization more broadly. America's separated system has morphed into a quasi-parliamentary system but without the presence of reliable majority rule. Major policy changes usually require bipartisanship, but electoral incentives typically frustrate compromise: the passage of health care reform in 2010 and tax reform in 2017 on narrowly partisan votes were the exceptions that proved the rule. Nor is Congress alone. About half of the states are even more polarized than Congress. Although some are less so (like Louisiana, Delaware, and Rhode Island), they are culturally homogeneous. Most states have polarized, some (Arizona, California and Colorado) more than others.

Again, though, what specifically *constitutional* defects merit change? Reforms need to make institutions more responsive to parties and/or produce less polarized parties.

Some, such as Sabato, recommend term limits, which would require a constitutional amendment. By 5–4, the Supreme Court declared term limits unconstitutional in *US Term Limits, Inc. v. Thornton* (1995), ruling that states could not limit the terms of federal lawmakers. But the public strongly supports them, and legislators have introduced proposals to amend the Constitution to allow them in almost every year since 1943. Advocates claim they would reduce the time lawmakers spend on raising campaign funds, allow them to take unpopular but necessary decisions without fear of electoral defeat, and limit their exposure to special interests in Washington. New blood would not be beholden to established ways and might bring fresh thinking to Congress.

Against that, term limits are by their nature un- and even antidemocratic. They restrict voter choice by barring candidates from the ballot; decrease congressional capacity by reducing the pool of experienced legislators and leaving those remaining with greater say over inexperienced freshmen; limit incentives for gaining policy expertise and increase reliance on interest groups and lobbies for advice; force effective lawmakers into retirement; and speed rather than slow the "revolving door" from Congress to lobbying jobs (Burgat 2018).

Some less onerous non- or extra-constitutional changes could help at the margins. For example, expanding the vote, modernizing registration procedures, moving election day from Tuesday to Saturday, achieving non-partisan redistricting reform, and adopting a system of open primaries might together help temper the more immoderate influences shaping both parties. A complementary institutional measure would explore more ways of organizational innovation, such as the Defense Base Closure and Realignment Commission (BRAC). Between 1988 and 2005, five BRAC rounds produced major reductions and realignments of military installations.

Mann and Ornstein (2012: 129) also made a compelling case that, "Reducing the role of filibusters may be more productive than altering rules of campaign finance." The bulk of money going on attempts to influence public officials is not campaign funding, but lobbying (Drutman 2015). This is not to minimize the role of campaign donations and expenditure. But they represent a relatively small part of the resources that interest groups invest in government relations. Unless the First Amendment is revised or repealed, or the Supreme Court approves campaign finance regulations that its predecessors rejected, reducing the role of money in politics is not going to occur. Governing is about ideas and ideologies as well as incumbents. And the filibuster was one important reason for the failure to enact legislation over 2009–2018 on climate change, gun control, immigration, and entitlement reform. Senate filibuster rules that enable forty-one senators to stymie fifty-nine allow for expressions of asymmetrical intensity. No less than 385 filibusters were initiated between 2007 and 2012, equal to the total number of filibusters between the end of World War I and the final days of the Reagan administration in 1989 (Levitsky and Ziblatt 2018: 163).

But four caveats are worth noting. First, while more than 1,000 of 4,000 administration jobs require Senate confirmation, the filibuster was removed for appointments by Democrats for most federal appointments in 2013, and then by Republicans for Supreme Court and Cabinet appointments in 2017. Second, as Reynolds (2017) details, the Senate can act around filibusters through special rules, or "majoritarian exceptions," that limit floor debate. These allow the majority – even without sixty votes – to legislate. Examples include procedures used to pass budget resolutions, enact budget reconciliation bills, review military base closures, arms sales, trade agreements, and executive regulations. Third, abandoning the filibuster for appointments has weakened the Senate vis-à-vis the executive. Abandoning it for legislation would be a further reduction in legislative power. Fourth, this isn't, ultimately, a constitutional issue but one of Senate rules.

That Congress routinely disappoints is not surprising, but it is unfair to blame Congress for problems not entirely, or even mostly, of its own making. Partisan and ideological polarization, redistricting, and incumbency often cause lawmakers to forget that politics is about addition, not subtraction, and to prefer obstruction and stasis to compromise. The cost is substantial. Negative views of Congress galvanize broader distrust, anti-Washington bias, and an anti-politics "pox on both houses" sentiment that holds Congress as the place where common sense goes to die.

Moreover, it is important to record that, as Drutman (2015: 3) argued, the pervasive presence of business in Washington "guarantees neither influence nor privilege." Campaign contributions may help in corporations and others gaining access, but that is not the same as influence. The bulk of funds spent by those seeking to shape policy goes on lobbying but, even so, policy outcomes are almost always multicausal:

> The policy process is neither a vending machine nor an auction.
> Outcomes cannot be had for reliable prices. Policy does not go to

the highest bidder. Politics is far messier, and far more interesting than such simplistic models might suggest.

(Drutman 2015: 219)

But what the lobbying explosion of recent decades has done is to make policy change even harder in a system that is already biased against it.

Congress, nonetheless, discharges its four functions more fully than its international peers: policy-making; representation; oversight; and legitimation. Its formidable tools, when it chooses to use them, invariably prove effective. Its record has been one neither of partisan subservience nor sustained obstruction. That may not justify what some argue: that with their large memberships, complex information processing structures and resources, modern legislatures merit the primary role in developing constitutional law (Vermeule 2012). But Congress more fully represents the nation than the presidency, a binary institution with which one either agrees or disagrees. Congress is institutionally incapable of the impetuosity that tempts presidents to convert personal whims or gripes into policy. Its job is to represent what Madison called "the cool and deliberate sense of the community." Congress is designed to move slowly to allow public reason to take hold, not to enact major legislation where consensus is missing.

For Congress and the Constitution to function, parties that happily accepted half a loaf – broad, unideological, un-programmatic – appeared better than polarized ones:

> In the post-World War II era, when each party spanned a broad ideological spectrum, passing important legislation meant forming bipartisan coalitions. These coalitions make governing possible, especially when the parties split control of the government. For the United States' constitutional order to function, it seems that either the parties have to become less ideological or the Constitution has to become more parliamentary. The latter path, which requires wholesale constitutional change, is profoundly unlikely. To align with the needs of the US constitutional order, in this argument, the parties somehow have to change.
>
> (Muirhead and Rosenblum 2015: 218)

But those old-style parties expended decades fighting struggles over civil and voting rights, labor laws, and more. Moreover, recent years have shown that elections have consequences. Congress has done "big things." But Congress cannot lead. Without greater compromise, it will continue to rank low in public affection and contribute further to the expansion of the presidency into the kind of institution the Framers rejected.

## The Presidency

The Framers made the legislative and executive branches co-equal. But, to paraphrase Orwell, some branches are more equal than others. If congressional reform is undesirable or unfeasible, might the presidency be a better bet?

The presidency combines the functions of head of state and head of government that most democracies separate. But the regulatory federal state, whose growth places immense power in presidential hands, was never anticipated by the Framers. During the twentieth century, liberals and conservatives vastly empowered the executive. Democrats saw a strong presidency as the only route to push social insurance, welfare, civil, and voting rights through an obstructive "conservative coalition" in Congress. Republicans, once they abandoned isolationism and embraced internationalism during the Cold War, saw a strong presidency as optimal for aggressive anti-communist containment policies.

After Vietnam and Watergate, legislative reforms tried to reassert Congress and rein in presidential power. The War Powers Resolution (WPR) of 1973 aimed to strengthen congressional authority over the use of force. The Budget Act (1974) centralized budgeting to give Congress a stronger voice shaping federal budgets. The Ethics in Government Act (1978) created regulations, and an Office of the Independent Counsel, to deter, detect and deal with executive corruption. But subsequent decades saw these reforms erode and both parties rebuild executive authority. 9/11 proved especially important in an expansion of executive power that weakened Congress' ability to constrain the White House, especially on matters of foreign policy and national security.

Both politics and the Constitution must reckon with the serious problems such an imbalance creates, not least a tendency to grandiosity and to political commentary oscillating between "fears of an imperial presidency on the one hand and of a president fettered by institutional constraints on the other" (Fiorina 2017: 237). Although revisionist scholars claim the presidency was always intended to be powerful (Prakash 2015) and that presidents have exercised restraint in their use of expanded power (Levitsky and Ziblatt 2018: 130), the charge of "imperial" behavior has become a reliable insult against presidents of both parties in relation to their actions at home and abroad (Schmitt, Bessette and Busch 2017). Moreover, the president of the "United" States is now something of a misnomer. Recent presidents have appeared more red or blue champions than purple. Reviling presidents while revering the presidency is now an American tradition as venerable as motherhood and apple pie. The result is that discussion of the presidency occurs on an intellectual fault line: is the institution too powerful or too weak?

Some scholars maintain the presidency is too strong to the point of being unaccountable. Levinson (2006: 79) criticized, "Too-powerful presidents, chosen in an indefensible process, who cannot be displaced even when they are manifestly incompetent." Dahl (2003) rejected the "myth" of the presidential mandate, that by winning a majority of the popular (or electoral) vote, presidents gained authority to implement campaign pledges. Ackerman (2013: 87–119) went furthest, arguing that institutional dynamics have transformed the presidency into a "constitutional battering ram" and potential platform for extremism and lawlessness. Watergate, Iran-Contra, and the War on Terror were symptoms of deeper pathologies that generate profound constitutional crises: the rise of presidential primaries, pollsters and media gurus, centralization of power, politicization of the military, and the manipulation of constitutional doctrine to justify presidential power-grabs.

Clearly, the powers enumerated in Article Two do not tell the full tale. Presidents now command vast areas of domestic and foreign policy with substantial autonomy. Selecting a president is the most expensive global executive search, but running the US government is the most complex executive job. Everything the president does is monitored in minute detail by markets, foreign governments, international competitors, allies, and enemies. As chief executive, commander-in-chief, head diplomat, spokesperson to and for the nation, and consoler-in-chief in time of tragedy, the exhausting duties and pressures are constant.

All this is the result of the presidency acquiring powers through asserting its prerogatives, the expansion of the administrative and security state, and passive acquiescence or active complicity from Congress and the courts. Parties have become predisposed to reflexively support or oppose presidential preferences. This is not so much a decline of "moderates" in Congress as institutionalists. Office-holders in the Cabinet, Congress, and Supreme Court take an oath to the Constitution, not the president. But, with few defenders of congressional prerogative left, the presidency has been empowered as the driving force in American government.

Assessing the presidency is therefore difficult. It is easy to allow individual presidents to obscure arguments about the institutional presidency. In addition, we remain perhaps overly indebted to Neustadt's (1991) paradigm that presidential power is the "power to persuade." Focusing on formal powers, we lose sight of how extra-constitutional influences have empowered the institution and, to critics, marginalized the Constitution. In abstract terms, the presidency is more than a legislative observer, cajoling lawmakers from the other end of Pennsylvania Avenue. In concrete terms, presidents have many peers but no equal. They occupy a central role yet possess limited capacity to influence public views. Evidence that presidential appeals do anything other than fall "on deaf ears" is sparse (Edwards 2003, 2009). Presidents can rarely force others to change their priorities or preferences. What they can do is "facilitate" change: act on an existing opportunity structure they didn't create but can exploit. For "strategic" presidents, given the extent of polarization, exclusive reliance on their own party in Congress is often preferable to futile attempts to lure the other's lawmakers across the aisle. Even then, there is no guarantee of success. Parties remain coalitions, and neither presidents nor congressional leaders can coerce loyalty.

On the other hand, presidents possess a powerful "directive" capacity. Presidents exercise "power without persuasion" (Howell 2003) by ordering executive actions through the administrative state. The president outside the legislative arena possesses formidable authority to exercise presidential unilateralism, with presidents of both parties often turning to this as their primary means of pursuing their goals once legislative efforts have failed. The appeal of such action is especially attractive for being grounded in the Article II clauses: the vesting clause ("the executive Power shall be vested in a President of the United States"); the take-care clause ("he shall take care that the Laws be faithfully executed"); and the pardon clause ("he shall have Power to grant Reprieves and Pardons for Offenses against the United States, except in cases of Impeachment").

Although Congress retains authority to reverse any regulatory powers granted the executive, the White House gets to move first. By declaring policy, presidents challenge other branches to reverse it. Congress finds collective action difficult, especially to mobilize two-thirds supermajorities to override presidential vetoes. The judiciary is often reluctant to overturn elected branches' actions. Lacking democratic legitimacy, courts must choose intervention carefully, to preserve their own authority. Vast areas of the administrative state exist that presidents can command without legislative approval. From desegregation of the armed forces to relaxing environmental regulations, presidents can direct the executive branch to act. That has costs, in that executive actions are not as enduring as legislation and can easily be reversed by subsequent administrations, and it isn't "leadership" in the sense of persuasion. But it gets results, nonetheless.

For example, after Congress failed to pass legislation in his first term protecting around 690,000 children of undocumented immigrants from deportation, President Obama – having previously claimed this was not something presidents could do – issued an executive order in June 2012. This created an administrative program that permitted certain individuals who came to the United States as juveniles to request consideration of deferred action for a period of two years, subject to renewal and eligibility for work authorization. Despite Congress having rejected such a program on multiple occasions, Obama implemented Deferred Action for Childhood Arrivals (DACA) by executive branch memorandum.

This combination of formal and informal authority yields three broad perspectives on presidential power.

For "congressionalists," the presidency has accumulated power unsanctioned by the Constitution. Presidents use unilateral powers extensively and mostly go unchecked by the courts, especially on foreign affairs (Fisher 2017). Moreover, "particularistic" presidents are not national statesmen above politics but, like lawmakers, parochial, narrow-minded and short-sighted – able and willing to routinely allocate federal resources, including disaster aid, to their partisan base and favored electoral constituencies (Kriner and Reeves 2015). As one commentator noted of the Forty-fifth President:

> For all the anger about Trump himself, what Americans have really been awakened to is just how powerful we have allowed the presidency to become at the expense of Congress. When Trump tweeted out one of his provocative statements about North Korea, he dramatized how easy it would be for a reckless president to drag us into a nuclear war. When Trump single-handedly used executive orders to dismantle climate change regulations and international agreements, he showed just how much damage a president can inflict on public policy regardless of what Congress does or does not do.
>
> (Zelizer 2018)

To take one example, since the Supreme Court confirmed their legality in 1942, executive agreements have outnumbered treaties by a ratio of ten to one. The reason? Presidents do not need congressional approval for agreements but require two-thirds of the Senate to ratify treaties. Although only four treaties were rejected between 1945 and 2018, "treaty gridlock" has grown. In 2018, the State Department listed forty-five treaties submitted since 1945 that are still technically awaiting Senate action. Of these, twenty-two were submitted by President Obama, whose rate of treaty ratification was the lowest of any president since Carter (Schultz 2018: 14). Even Obama's one major success – New START in 2010 – was approved by the lowest margin (71–26) of any strategic arms limitation treaty submitted to the Senate for a vote. Getting sixty-seven votes is difficult and the delays and obstructionism that result from polarization serve as a deterrent to seeking treaties and incentive to substitute executive agreements instead. For example, although it had the effect of an international treaty, the Joint Comprehensive Plan of Action (JCPOA) with Iran was not submitted by the Obama administration to the Senate in 2015 (making it easier for the Trump administration to withdraw from the nuclear deal in 2018).

This is not to suggest Congress is marginal, even on foreign affairs. Politics does not "stop at the water's edge," which has always proven more aspiration than reality. Congressional controls over spending, treaties, confirmation powers, and more impose significant constraints on the executive. The derailment of President Reagan's "constructive engagement" with apartheid South Africa by sanctions legislation in 1986, passed over his veto, and the Senate's refusal to ratify the Comprehensive

Test Ban Treaty negotiated by President Clinton in 1999, are cases in point. Congress sometimes defies presidential preferences, such as with the Justice Against Sponsors of Terrorism Act (JASTA) of 2016, which was overwhelmingly passed over Obama's veto, and legislates more assertive measures than the executive prefers, most notably on sanctions policy (albeit usually with presidential waivers attached [Milner and Tingley 2015]). It can also exercise oversight. Kriner and Schickler (2016) identified every congressional investigation of the executive from 1898 to 2014, nearly 12,000 days of investigative hearings: thirty-two years' worth. By highlighting misdeeds, Congress can attract media attention, shape public opinion, and informally constrain presidents. But its willingness to use this power has varied over time: party loyalties have competed with institutional ones and often overcome them (Fowler 2015).

Against "congressionalists" is the "post-Madisonian" argument (Posner and Vermeule 2013). In support of a strong presidency, these scholars agree the presidency has vastly increased in power. But they deny it has become constitutionally unlimited or unaccountable. Instead, the nature of checks and balances has become more political than legal. The federal system reflects a conservative disposition against concentrated power: each branch is jealous of its own power. But across all nations, the greater modern complexity of contemporary problems and state responses to them concentrates power in the executive. This functional expansion transcends partisan changes in control and rarely entertains successful challenge. But the executive-centered state tends to generate political, cultural, and social checks on presidential action that substitute for, and are more effective than, constitutional ones. So, a more powerful presidency exists but this is far from unconstrained.

An illustration of this is international agreements. For the United States to survive in a complex, ever-changing global environment and maintain its leading global power status, it must fulfill international commitments swiftly and confidently. Presidents' preference for executive agreements is not trampling the Constitution underfoot but the result of a symbiotic evolution of the executive and legislative branches. Lawmakers concur that agreements allow each branch to function more efficiently and effectively in relation to the vastly increased activity of the United States since 1945. The House continues to oversee policy areas, and (the JCPOA notwithstanding) presidents still submit most significant international commitments to the Senate as treaties. Executive agreements represent a mutual adaptation of the executive and legislature in a shared power system (Krutz and Peake 2009), albeit at the cost that these may signal weaker political support and, hence, (potentially) less ongoing commitment, to international partners than treaties.

By contrast, a third case depicts the presidency as too weak and argues for a *more* powerful presidency as the solution to an outmoded Constitution. Most clearly articulated by Howell and Moe (2016), this accepts the presidency has grown in strength on foreign and national security issues but claims it is "manifestly underpowered" to address the "vast range of domestic social problems that face the nation" (172). A framework where Congress is still central vests excessive power in a parochial legislature protecting particularistic interests, rendering government ill-equipped to remedy complex, post-industrial problems. Effective governance requires forcing Congress and its pathologies to the periphery of the law-making process by bringing presidents – whose national constituency and legacy-driven ambition cause them to seek coherent policy solutions – to the center. Howell and Moe take "fast track" trade negotiation authority as their model. Presidents negotiate trade agreements with other states and propose these to Congress, which must vote up or down on them with no amendments, within a specified time, on a majoritarian basis (no filibusters allowed). This authority, instead of having to be granted periodically by Congress, should be made permanent and applied to all policies (though Howell and Moe add that if lawmakers fail to address the president's proposal in the specified manner and time, presidential proposals should become law even without Congress's consent [160–161]).

What are we to make of this?

First, most Americans do not want the presidency to be given greater formal power. According to a 2017 survey, 77 percent said it would be too risky "to give US presidents more power to deal directly with many of the country's problems" while only 17 percent said "problems could be dealt with more effectively if presidents didn't have to worry so much about Congress or the courts" (Pew 2017b). How much the results were an artifact of specific concerns about the Trump presidency is unclear, but the results were in line with other survey evidence that points strongly against boosting presidential power.

Second, presidents typically experience reduced power after midterm elections. As Table 3.1 shows, their party usually loses congressional seats in their first midterm (though in "wave" elections – such as 1994, 2006, and 2010 – the close races break in one direction and gains or losses end up being larger than anticipated). That offers something of a reliable electoral check on overly ambitious presidents.

Third, while a "fast track" style proposal sounds appealingly coherent and simple – it would require an amendment but not alter the rest of the Constitution – this is disingenuous. Although Howell and Moe claim Congress could still vote presidential proposals down and legislate independently, the legislature would risk marginalization on domestic and foreign affairs. The presidency would become even more powerful and unchecked, with the president's congressional party reduced to a pliant supportive role and the opposition party ever more obstructionist. Moreover, while a non-partisan presidency might craft sensible proposals to maximize support, the greater likelihood is that a partisan White

*Table 3.1* Presidents and Their First Midterm Elections (1946–2010)

| President and 1st Midterm | Net Presidential Job Approval | House Seats | Senate Seats | Governors |
| --- | --- | --- | --- | --- |
| Truman (1946) | –19 | –55 | –11 | –2 |
| Eisenhower (1954) | +35 | –18 | –2 | –8 |
| Kennedy (1962) | +36 | –5 | +4 | 0 |
| Johnson (1966) | +3 | –47 | –3 | –8 |
| Nixon (1970) | +31 | –12 | +1 | –11 |
| Carter (1978) | +13 | –15 | –3 | –5 |
| Reagan (1982) | –6 | –26 | 0 | –7 |
| GHW Bush (1990) | +26 | –7 | –1 | –1 |
| Clinton (1994) | 0 | –54 | –8 | –10 |
| GW Bush (2002) | +33 | +8 | +2 | –1 |
| Obama (2010) | –3 | –63 | –6 | –6 |

Source: Gallup (Tarrance 2018).

House would submit omnibus measures that packaged multiple items together, forcing lawmakers to vote for measures they disliked to obtain ones they wanted. With the existing lack of transparency over lobbying the executive branch, secrecy and particularism, entrenching presidential power further is problematic.

Elaine Kamarck (2016) argued persuasively that presidents must master three dimensions of their job to succeed: policy, communication, and implementation. In explaining *Why Presidents Fail*, she noted that, "The modern presidency is not impossible, but it does require a reorientation of the presidency itself – toward the complex and boring business of government and away from the preoccupation with communicating"(15). That is sensible advice, albeit unlikely to be closely heeded. Even so, there remains much to commend the status quo:

> American presidents cannot directly introduce bills, may see their legislative ideas amended (except for treaties) or just plain ignored, have no special constitutional advantage in budgeting, lack a line-item veto, cannot do end runs around Congress by calling popular referenda, and, by cross-national standards anyway, pretty much lack decree powers.
>
> (Mayhew 2017: 100)

That said, championing constitutional reform of the presidency depends on which perspective persuades. For Americans on both sides of the partisan divide, it is worth asking whether the benefits of a stronger presidency are worth the potential costs or whether a reinvigoration of the competition between the branches is preferable. For example, Levinson

(2006) advocated abolition of the veto while Sabato (2007) recommended four changes:

- Establish a new six-year presidential term, including a fifth-year extension referendum that could result in an additional two years in the office;
- Replace the unfair Constitutional prohibition against non-natural-born presidents with a requirement that candidates need only have been a US citizen for twenty years;
- Limit some presidential war-making powers and expand Congressional oversight to renew assent to on-going wars at regular intervals;
- Give the president a line-item veto to remove specific items from appropriations bills.

Some of these make sense but not all deliver what they promise.

### *Presidential Term Limits*

King (2012: 128) described presidents being limited to only two terms as an oddly "anti-democratic" feature of the American political system. Although this guarantees rotation in the White House, it also has curious effects. It induces a pattern by which first-term presidents are preoccupied by reelection and, if returned, their "legacy" and place in the history books. In turn, it can hamper legislative productivity. In first terms, presidents usually expect six to nine months during which they can advance key agenda items. Thereafter, attentions turn to midterms and reelection. But with second-term presidents, "lame duck" status typically kicks in quickly. Despite prestige and power, other actors increasingly see the president as exhausted and eye future horizons – the next midterms and the president's successor. Forcing a president to depart after two terms prevents ineffective, tired, and unhealthy figures from outstaying their welcome but it also denies popular and effective presidents the chance to serve longer.

Sabato (2007) recommends a single six-year term, with the option for a Year Five referendum to add two more years, making this the same as currently: eight years. But this seems a convoluted way to fall between two stools. On the one hand, it guarantees a longer term for presidents who may be ineffective, dangerous, or whom many Americans dislike (for Republicans, two more years of Carter, for Democrats, two more years of Trump). On the other, rather than an unpopular president exiting after four years, voters must wait for a fifth to deny the incumbent years 7–8. Although a referendum on a term extension would not formally be another election, it would amount to one, with associated campaigning and cost, and relocate political calculations from Year Four to Five. At least as problematic, it is unclear what meaningful benefits would arise. Lawmakers would still calculate their positions according to their next election. In a hyper-partisan era, this could deepen rather than limit partisan "trench warfare."

An alternative would be to repeal the Twenty-second Amendment and allow presidents an unlimited run. Even without the risk of a Chinese-style permanent president, this could have downsides. Presidents would constantly be thinking of future elections, which could entrench partisan wrangling and gridlock. There would be even less effort to take unpopular decisions or pursue "bold" second-term "legacy" initiatives (Reagan's Soviet diplomacy and "amnesty" for illegal immigrants in 1986, Clinton's diplomacy on Iran, North Korea, and Israeli-Palestinian peace, Bush's Iraq "surge," Obama's Iran deal and Cuba outreach). But a return to pre-1951 practice might rekindle ambition countering ambition within the parties. First-term presidents rarely face serious internal party challenges for renomination. A second-term president thinking of running yet again might encounter such challenges and, more broadly, ending term limits might loosen the shackles of intraparty conformism. On the other hand, the Twenty-second Amendment was enacted because FDR violated what had previously been an unwritten constitutional convention that no president served more than two terms. Abandoning the formal constraint might simply reinstate the informal one.

US practice may be "anti-democratic" but it is not unusual: most nations now have two-term limits for their heads of state, usually of four or five years. After a referendum in 2000, the French presidential term was reduced from seven to five years, and French presidents are limited to no more than two consecutive terms of office. Recent decades have not bestowed America with "great" presidents worthy of renovations to Mount Rushmore (perhaps mercifully, since "great" figures tend only to arise through national crises [Miller 2014]). Term limits merit retention.

### War Powers

When Donald Trump approved sanctions legislation on Russia in 2017, his presidential signing statement asserted, "The Framers of our Constitution put foreign affairs in the hands of the President" (White House 2017). That was plain wrong. The Constitution gives Congress an extensive foreign policy remit, including the power to declare war, ratify treaties, and authority to regulate commerce with foreign nations (Henkin 1996). Why, then, follow Sabato to limit presidential war-making powers and renew assent to ongoing wars at regular intervals?

Congress has exclusive power to declare war while Article II states: "[t]he President shall be Commander in Chief of the Army and Navy of the United States, and of the Militia of the several States, when called into the actual Service of the United States." But Congress last formally declared war in 1942. Since then, it sometimes approved "presidential wars" (Fisher 2004) through permissive Authorizations for the Use of

Military Force (AUMF), such as the Gulf of Tonkin (1964), the post-9/11 AUMF (2001), and the AUMF on Iraq (2002), or more precise resolutions (the 1991 Gulf War). On other occasions, Congress declined to authorize but failed to prohibit the use of force by presidents (Grenada [1983], Libya [1986] Panama [1989], Haiti [1994], Bosnia [1995], Kosovo [1999], Libya [2011], and Syria [2017, 2018]). Moreover, despite criticism of Bush "war on terror" policies, Congress largely acquiesced through laws such as the Military Commissions Act (2006), Protect America Act (2007) and amendments to the Foreign Intelligence Surveillance Act in 2008.

Two factors explain the constitutional imbalance. First, the WPR was ineffective in constraining military adventurism, not least by legalizing presidential war making for ninety days (Haas 2017). Presidents have used force and interpreted congressional failure to act as "acquiescence," if not "ratification." Presidents have resisted "micromanagement" and recognized neither the WPR's constitutionality nor applicability, even as they sent notifications to Congress "consistent" with, though not "pursuant to," its provisions. Second, partisanship plays a key role. Presidents can normally rely on strong support from their own party on questions of military force (Howell and Pevehouse 2007). Moreover, if the political class is not strongly divided, the public is unlikely to oppose such action (Berinsky 2009). But polarization again has intervened with adverse effects, substantially raising the political risks of military action: after 1990 bipartisanship on using force broke down with striking consistency, and only the 2001 AUMF in Afghanistan won solid majority support from both parties (Schultz 2018: 12).

Enacting a formal amendment on war is therefore unwise and unnecessary. Outside self-defense, where the president can legitimately use the armed forces without prior legislative approval, Congress can and should decide whether and when the nation will fight. But if Congress wants to legislate to limit, or stop, military action, it can already do so. Congress possesses authority to restrict the president through funding cut-offs (as occurred in 1973 over Vietnam) and prohibitions on foreign adventures (such as the Boland Amendments from 1982 to 1984 over Nicaragua). But the congressional record for institutional responsibility has been unimpressive. Defense Secretary James Mattis even testified in February 2018 that:

> no enemy in the field has done more to harm the readiness of the US military than the combined impact of the Budget Control Act's defense spending caps, worsened by operating in 10 of the last 11 years under continuing resolutions of varied and unpredictable duration.
> (House of Representatives Armed Services Committee 2018)

The problems here are threefold, as the *National War Powers Commission Report* – co-chaired by former Secretaries of States James Baker and Warren Christopher – concluded (Miller Center of Public Affairs 2008).

First, the elected branches strongly contest the scope of their respective powers. Presidents claim Article II authority as Commander-in-Chief, reference their ninety-day legal right under the WPR, and invoke authorizations when delegated the use of force. As Henkin (1996: 68) noted, "issues of War Power have become issues of conflict and cooperation in a 'twilight zone' of uncertain or perhaps concurrent power." Even on nuclear war, the Cold War's legacy and development of an enormous nuclear weapons arsenal at the presidency's disposal unbalanced the Constitution. As Vice-President Cheney explained:

> The President of the United States now for fifty years is followed at all times, twenty-four hours a day, by a military aid carrying a football that contains the nuclear codes that he would use, and be authorized to use, in the event of a nuclear attack on the United States. He could launch the kind of devastating attack the world has never seen. He doesn't have to check with anybody, he doesn't have to call Congress, he doesn't have to check with the courts.
>
> (Wills 2010: 3–4)

This was not merely a matter of responding to an attack against the United States with a retaliatory second strike. It also included presidents making first use of nuclear weapons in preventive or preemptive acts of war. Although the Senate held hearings on the president's nuclear authority in 2017 (for the first time in forty-one years), and a bill was introduced in the 115th Congress to make presidential first-use contingent on a prior law authorizing this in a war declaration, no action was taken. The ultimate presidential power remains unchecked and unbalanced (Singh 2018).

Second, the courts have been petitioned to adjudicate over war powers, but refused, citing lack of policy expertise to declare this a "nonjusticiable" or "political question" for elected branches to resolve (Fisher 2017). Beyond this, scholars disagree about the constitutionality of "presidential wars" (Fisher 2004; Griffin 2013). Constitutional constraints on presidents are broader than war powers alone (Zeisberg 2013) but, as Milner and Tingley (2015) show, presidents typically select policy instruments over which they have more control – such as the military – while Congress seeks to dominate areas that its domestic constituents and interest groups have material interests in (trade, foreign aid, immigration). In short, political incentives routinely differ.

Third, as Burns (2017) argued, the constitutional imbalance has occurred as much from congressional irresponsibility and irresolution as presidential usurpation. As risk transferors rather than risk takers, lawmakers have irresponsibly avoided asserting their institutional prerogatives because they have not wished to pay for the rope that hangs them. Although, for example, Congress authorized the "war on terror," sixteen years later, the United States was fighting new groups in new nations under the same AUMF. In September 2017, the Senate voted down (by 61–36) a measure to amend the National Defense Authorization Act to attach a six-month sunset to the 2001 and 2002 AUMFs and establish exactly what powers the presidency possessed to combat transnational terrorist groups (Carney 2017). The Democrats wanted a restrictive resolution, Republicans (other than noninterventionists such as Rand Paul [R-KY]) a more permissive one.

Again, partisanship rather than constitutional formalism is ultimately the issue. Posner and Vermeule's case has notable force. If the primary function of legal restrictions is to raise the political costs of war, presidents who genuinely perceive national security to be endangered will nonetheless act. Legal constraints will not prevent their acting to defend the United States, since, whatever else it may be, the Constitution is not a suicide pact (Posner 2006). Even threats of impeachment face the political problem that it requires two-thirds of the Senate to vote to convict. A president with thirty-four Senators in his corner will survive. International diplomacy is a "two-level" game (Putnam 1988) and presidents and lawmakers alike recognize that legislative action can on occasion be a hindrance as much as a help to securing national interests.

Constitutional reform is neither necessary nor sufficient to restrain presidential war-making. What is required is political will. As Fowler (2015: 184, 187) noted:

> Imperial presidents cannot rule without the collaboration of complicit lawmakers ... The challenge for Congress is inadequate capacity to generate credible information in a timely manner and to sustain a serious review of the president's proposals for more than a day.

Multiple factors determine how far Congress adopts a supportive, strategic, competitive, or disengaged orientation to foreign policy, including military force (Carter and Scott 2012). But, as Mayhew (2017: 51) documented:

> From Jefferson's First Barbary War to Obama's use of drones, the White House has bent, at least relatively, toward international action and commitment. Congress has bent toward insularity – not always, but recurrently. This distinction is not a surprise given the differing assignments of legislative and executive authority in the Constitution. Across history, the making of foreign policy has brought a kind of competitive channelling – the White House toward matching the British Empire or even Prussia in style and aims, Congress more comfortable with emulating something akin to a large Switzerland.

As Justice Jackson cautioned in *The Steel Seizure Cases* (*Youngstown* 1952), "[O]nly Congress itself can prevent power from slipping through its fingers."

## Presidential Veto Powers

Should presidents be able to veto laws passed by Congress? As Table 3.2 shows, the number of vetoes varies dramatically, as do their overrides by Congress. Whereas almost one in five of Ford's vetoes were overturned by Congress, there was but a single instance under Obama.

Levinson and others criticize the veto as denying legislative majorities their will, on policy rather than constitutional grounds (the South African president, by contrast, can only veto bills on constitutional grounds, subject to judicial review). Congress and the presidency both have national mandates. That said, though, it is curious to highlight so many congressional failings and then argue that presidents' ability to veto unwise legislation is problematic. Instead, it offers a necessary safeguard, even if it is one that is open to partisanship. Similarly, when Levinson (2006: 38–49) notes the remarkable number of vetoes that presidents used to make in the past compared to recent decades, this would appear "progress."

Admittedly, it is also a function of two influences: most notably, increasing polarization, since presidents have less reason to veto laws enacted by their own party; and secondarily, but importantly, increasing use by presidents of "signing statements" that seek to impose their own imprint on the purported meaning of new laws. For example, President George W. Bush issued a signing statement on December 30, 2005 to the Detainee Treatment Act, offered as an amendment to a supplemental defense spending bill, that indicated that he intended to ignore the provisions – proposed by Senator John McCain (R-AZ) – relating to enemy detainee treatment and enhanced interrogation techniques that many viewed as torture ("The executive branch shall construe Title X in

*Table 3.2* Presidential Vetoes and Congressional Overrides (1932–2017)

| President | Regular Vetoes | Pocket Vetoes | Total Vetoes | Veto Overrides | Percentage Overridden |
|---|---|---|---|---|---|
| Roosevelt | 372 | 263 | 635 | 9 | 1 |
| Truman | 180 | 70 | 250 | 12 | 5 |
| Eisenhower | 73 | 108 | 181 | 2 | 1 |
| Kennedy | 12 | 9 | 21 | 0 | 0 |
| Johnson | 16 | 14 | 30 | 0 | 0 |
| Nixon | 27 | 17 | 43 | 7 | 16 |
| Ford | 48 | 18 | 66 | 12 | 18 |
| Carter | 13 | 18 | 31 | 2 | 6 |
| Reagan | 39 | 39 | 78 | 9 | 12 |
| Bush | 29 | 15 | 44 | 1 | 2 |
| Clinton | 36 | 1 | 37 | 2 | 6 |
| Bush | 12 | 0 | 12 | 4 | 33 |
| Obama | 12 | 0 | 12 | 1 | 8 |

Source: Sollenberger 2004; US House of Representatives http://history.house.gov/Institution/Presidential-Vetoes/Presidential-Vetoes/.

Division A of the Act, relating to detainees, in a manner consistent with the constitutional authority of the President to supervise the unitary executive branch and as Commander in Chief and consistent with the constitutional limitations on the judicial power, which will assist in achieving the shared objective of the Congress and the President, evidenced in Title X, of protecting the American people from further terrorist attacks."). Such signing statements represent an underappreciated but important aspect of the extraconstitutional expansion of presidential power as an attempt to modify the meaning of statutes passed by Congress.

But it is worth qualifying the veto controversy. The most definitive veto is the "pocket veto," whereby a president refuses to sign a bill. Since it cannot be overridden, this is also a wholly negative power. The partial, or line-item, veto is an active power that presidents most desire, even though it can be overridden, and offers a means of countering congressional pork-barreling (albeit with the potential for partisan bias). Although passed in 1996, the line-item veto was ruled unconstitutional in *Clinton v. City of New York* (1998). The Supreme Court stated that it violated the Presentment Clause, which prohibits presidents from unilaterally amending or repealing legislation passed by Congress. Although presidents therefore retain the "package veto" to reject a bill in its entirety, this is the least effective veto power. It can be overridden, and presidents are cornered into either giving up or accepting the whole bill (Sartori 1994: 163).

Doing away with the veto seems imprudent. In the context of highly polarized politics and competitive elections, the chances that a Congress with narrow majorities can enact laws with limited support cannot be discounted. No Republicans voted for the 2010 health care reform; no Democrats voted for the 2017 tax reform. A veto potentially can preserve the national interest from partisan excess. Equally, a measure that commands serious support should secure the two-thirds supermajorities to overcome a veto motivated by partisan, ideological, or policy concerns (such as the override of Obama's JASTA veto in 2016).

Since the line-item veto has been ruled unconstitutional already, this would require a constitutional amendment to enact. But while it seems an attractive weapon in the presidential armory, its benefits are mixed. It is probably insufficient to make a serious dent in the irresponsibility that characterizes congressional budgeting. It could also be used more as a partisan than institutional instrument. That said, it would assist in negotiations – even the threat of its use might help induce more responsibility or advance a deal. The problem with the full veto is that it has an all-or-nothing quality. To that extent, a line-item veto would probably do limited damage and could be of modest benefit.

### Eligibility: Who Can Be President?

The Constitution sets three eligibility requirements to be President in Article II, Section I: age (thirty-five years or above), residency "within the United States" for fourteen years, and being a "natural born Citizen." No Supreme Court case has ruled specifically on the age and residency requirements (though several have addressed the term "natural born" citizen). But there is a compelling logic to relaxing these.

Given the incredible demands of a unique office, it makes sense to maximize, not limit, the candidate pool. For a nation of millions, recent elections have hardly winnowed out the best America can offer. Requiring a candidate to have resided in the United States for fourteen years seems excessive, especially in an era when many Americans live and work abroad for some period of their lives. And the danger of a "non-naturalized" citizen serving as a foreign agent or exchanging influence for gifts or personal enrichment now looks more than a little ironic.

Whether the age requirement should also be relaxed is less clear. Most nations have minimum age requirements to run for elective office but make no distinction between the levels. Some might find a maximum age limit more attractive than a minimum. That said, thirty-five years does not seem to deny too many obviously compelling youthful politicians the opportunity to age prematurely in the White House.

## The Supreme Court

The third governing institution attracting reform proposals is the federal judiciary. For some presidents, their greatest legacy is judicial appointments and reshaping constitutional law. President Trump advanced an aggressive appointment strategy in his first year. In addition to Supreme Court Justice Neil M. Gorsuch, the Senate confirmed twelve federal circuit court (and ten federal district court) judges, the largest number in history, though eight of these joined courts with already-strong majorities of Republican appointees (JFK and Nixon each appointed eleven circuit court judges in their first years, and Carter, ten [Wheeler 2018]).

Appointments are now a political circus. 2017 was the first year since 2006 in which Republicans controlled the presidency and Senate, presenting a prime opportunity to fill lifetime appointments to almost 150 federal vacancies. Senate Republicans confirmed fewer judges in Obama's last two years (22) than in any two-year period since 1951–1952. In 2013, Senate Democrats eliminated the filibuster for lower-court nominees, allowing a simple majority vote rather than the filibuster-proof supermajority of sixty previously required. The Republicans then removed this for Supreme Court nominees in 2017. By relying on the conservative Federalist Society for conservative nominees and prioritizing candidates in their thirties and forties – judicial spring chickens – Trump appointees will remain on the bench for decades. As Table 3.3 shows, the favorable response among Republicans accounted for the overall uptick in trust in the federal judiciary from 2016 to 2017.

*Table 3.3* Trust in the Federal Judiciary, by Political Party (2016–2017)

|  | 2016 (%) | 2017 (%) | Change (%) |
|---|---|---|---|
| All US adults | 61 | 68 | +7 |
| Republicans | 48 | 79 | +31 |
| Independents | 62 | 65 | +3 |
| Democrats | 74 | 62 | –12 |

*Note:* Trust measured by those expressing "a great deal" or "fair amount" of trust.

Source: Gallup (Jones 2017).

The Supreme Court sits at the apex of a broader judicial edifice where law and politics meet. Although not expressly granted by the Constitution, its exercise of constitutional judicial review since *Marbury v. Madison* (1803) has been as essential to the republic's evolution as any election. Scholars still debate the soundness of Marshall's reasoning in *Marbury*, but the power to strike down laws and executive actions as unconstitutional has become an enduring norm. The Constitution's rigidity – the difficulty of amendment – imposes on the judiciary a heavy responsibility that mandates creativity and generates controversy. The testaments to its influence are the common but contradictory charges that it is imperial and impotent, which suggest a more complex reality.

The "counter-majoritarian difficulty" concerns the tension between according the power to make policy decisions affecting millions to an unelected body of nine – in effect, five – justices. A democratic state requires a supreme court with authority to review the constitutionality of legislative and administrative enactments, whether (in a federal system) states have exceeded their proper bounds, and whether fundamental rights and liberties have been infringed. But, as Dahl (2003) noted, the more courts move outside the realm of fundamental rights, the more they resemble unelected legislatures, and the more dubious their authority becomes:

> In the guise of interpreting the Constitution – or, even more questionable, divining the obscure and often unknowable intentions of the Framers – the high court enacts important laws and policies that are the proper province of elected officials.

(2003: 154)

As Table 3.4 shows, confidence in the judiciary globally was mostly split in 2013. In the United States, what is wrong with courts is in the eye of the beholder. To some, the Supreme Court exceeds its authority by effectively annulling election results. Zirin (2016) argued it has become "supremely partisan." To others, judicial supremacy has more often been "established

*Table 3.4* Global Confidence in Judicial Systems and Courts (2013)

|  | Yes (%) | No (%) | Don't Know/ Refused (%) |
|---|---|---|---|
| Asia | 65 | 25 | 10 |
| Europe | 49 | 45 | 6 |
| Sub-Saharan Africa | 48 | 45 | 7 |
| Middle East and North Africa | 47 | 38 | 15 |
| Northern America | 47 | 52 | 0 |
| Latin America and the Caribbean | 35 | 59 | 6 |
| Former Soviet Union | 28 | 55 | 17 |

Source: Gallup (Rochelle and Loschky 2014).

by political invitation [than] by judicial putsch" (Whittington 2007: 294) with lawmakers and presidents repeatedly inviting judges to resolve divisive policy conflicts. For still others, a lack of enforcement tools and political will undercuts claims of judicial supremacy. For example, Chemerinsky (2014) argues the Court has not fulfilled its celebrated role as protector of minority rights, but instead more frequently acts as an instrument than opponent of majoritarianism. Similarly, Klarman (2004) and Rosenberg (1991) emphasize that without broad public support, rulings tend to be ignored or successfully resisted.

Three striking features overlap. First, as Keck (2014: 251) noted, on some controversial issues, "…in the absence of independent judges and mobilized rights advocates, the policy landscape on abortion, affirmative action, and gay rights would be substantially different today, and the policy landscape on gun rights would likely differ at the margins." Second, the courts' political role is well recognized. 2016 exit polls showed 21 percent of voters saying the Supreme Court was "the most important" factor in their decision, with most favoring Donald Trump (Berenson 2018). Third, public esteem for the judiciary is volatile and shaped by partisanship, endangering its legitimacy. The Court has become part of the problem with "Washington."

Judges like to employ the metaphor of an umpire or referee: neutral, impartial, calling plays honestly according to the rules. But it is not necessary to be a Harvard law professor to doubt the claim. In this, the Court has been both a victim of and vehicle for polarization. Instead of standing above the fray, the Justices are active in the melee. Some interventions – from Justice Alito mouthing "not true" during Obama's 2010 State of the Union to Justice Ginsberg's anti-Trump comments in 2016 – gave credence to charges that Justices are merely "politicians in robes." While politically shrewd, Senate Republicans' refusal to move action on Obama's nominee, Merrick Garland, in 2016 breached constitutional norms and was another instance of overt, unapologetic politicization.

Since the liberal Warren Court (1953–1969), conservatives have condemned "judicial activists" overturning precedent and reading into the Constitution rights not expressly there. In refusing to defer to elected branches and interpreting constitutional clauses expansively rather than narrowly, unelected judges illegitimately impose their values in place of the Framers, Congress, and the president. In recent years, the Roberts Court has antagonized both left and right by providing "uncertain justice" (Tribe and Matz 2014). In 2008 and 2010, respectively, rulings on gun control and campaign finance prompted outrage among progressives, with the supposedly conservative court engaging in judicial "activism." Yet rulings on health care and marriage equality in 2015 enraged many on the right, with cries of betrayal targeting the Chief Justice for siding with the Court's liberals.

As Table 3.5 shows, judicial nominations are important opportunities for the exercise of presidential power but rely on the "advice and consent" of the Senate to become appointments. Although Levinson devoted modest attention to the Court, he asked, "Do you really want justices on the Supreme Court to serve up to four decades and, among other things, to be able to time their resignations to mesh with their own political preferences as to their successors?" (2006: 7). Sabato (2007) proposed three reforms to address this: replacing life tenure with a single, nonrenewable term of fifteen years for all federal judges; granting Congress the power to set a mandatory retirement age; and expanding the Court from nine to twelve members. Would these remedy existing problems at an acceptable price? Partially, but not entirely – the first two, though, seem sensible steps to adopt.

Under Article III, judges "hold their offices during good behavior." Federal judges, having life tenure, can be removed only by impeachment. But when the Constitution was written, life expectancy was forty; it is now double that. Supreme Court Justices serve longer on average than at any point in US history. Life tenure supposedly guarantees judicial independence and frees justices from having to secure reappointment, being fired for unpopular rulings, or running for reelection. It enables judges to administer justice without fear or favor and provide necessary checks on other branches. In the 2014–2015 term, for example, such independence was evident among the conservative bloc, as Roberts voted to save Obamacare (*King v. Burwell* 2015), Thomas voted to permit Texas to refuse to print Confederate flags on license plates (*Walker v. Sons of Confederate Veterans* 2015), and Alito defended the rights of pregnant women in the workplace (*Young v. UPS* 2015).

But the flip side is that tenure also ensures unaccountability. Hamilton claimed in *Federalist* 79 that the "danger of a superannuated bench" is "imaginary." But in recent years unexpected deaths among elderly Justices (William Rehnquist in 2005, Antonin Scalia in 2016) as well as retirements created vacancies. Moreover, many justices are

Table 3.5 Presidential Nominations to the US Supreme Court (1946–2018)

| Republican President | | Democratic President | |
| --- | --- | --- | --- |
| Democratic Senate | Republican Senate | Democratic Senate | Republican Senate |
| (15) | (9) | (13) | (1) |
| 1955 Eisenhower (Harlan) | 1954 Eisenhower (Warren) | 1946 Truman (Vinson) | 2016 Obama (Garland) |
| 1957 Eisenhower Brennan | 1981 Reagan (O'Connor) | 1949 Truman (Clark) | – |
| 1957 Eisenhower (Whittaker) | 1986 Reagan (Rehnquist) | 1949 Truman (Minton) | – |
| 1959 Eisenhower (Stewart) | 1986 Reagan (Scalia) | 1962 Kennedy (White) | – |
| 1969 Nixon (Burger) | 2005 Bush, GW (Roberts) | 1962 Kennedy (Goldberg) | – |
| 1969 Nixon (Haynsworth) | 2005 Bush, GW (Miers) | 1965 (Johnson (Fortas) | – |
| 1970 Nixon (Carswell) | 2005 Bush (Alito) | 1967 Johnson (Marshall) | – |
| 1970 Nixon (Blackmun) | 2017 Trump (Gorsuch) | 1968 Johnson (Fortas) | – |
| 1971 Nixon (Powell) | 2018 Trump (Kavanaugh) | 1968 Johnson (Thornberry) | – |
| 1971 Nixon (Rehnquist) | – | 1993 Clinton (Ginsburg) | – |
| 1975 Ford (Stevens) | – | 1994 Clinton (Breyer) | – |
| 1987 Reagan (Bork) | – | 2009 Obama (Sotomayor) | – |
| 1987 Reagan (Kennedy) | – | 2010 Obama (Kagan) | – |
| 1990 Bush, GHW (Souter) | – | – | – |
| 1991 Bush, GHW (Thomas) | – | – | – |

Source: Adapted from Congressional Research Service, 2016 (www.fas.org/sgp/crs/misc/IN10458.pdf).

Notes:
- Haynsworth, Carswell, and Bork were rejected by the Senate.
- Fortas (for Chief Justice in 1967), Thornberry, and Miers were withdrawn.
- Rehnquist's 1986 nomination was for Chief Justice.

more predictable than independent. Political scientists disagree between different models of judicial decision-making: *legal* ones, where the law, precedent, and facts of the case dominate; *attitudinal* ones, where values predominate and, in essence, conservatives rule for conservative policy outcomes, progressives for left leaning ones; and *strategic* models, where small group interaction, "winning" and reputations count most (many judges worry about being reversed or overruled, criticism, colleagues, media and the legal profession). Although no single-cause explanation adequately explains judicial decision-making (Pacelle, Curry and Marshall 2011), incumbents do determine their retirement with politics in mind, to allow a "friendly" president to nominate a successor of similar leanings. Exploiting this, Bush, Obama, and Trump all nominated "younger" candidates to courts, knowing their influence would last long after they had departed Washington.

A few scholars favor non-renewable eighteen-year terms, which would see a new justice nominated every other year. Every president would get to nominate two justices per term. (If a justice died in office, her seat could be filled by a lower-court judge or retired justice.) Eighteen years is long enough to master the job but not so long as to risk a Court that reflects political choices from decades earlier. A fixed term would offer attractive benefits. It would guarantee turnover. In conjunction with a mandatory retirement age, it would limit politicized retirements and preclude a Court comprising Justices in their seventies and eighties, sometimes mentally or physically impaired and close to death. But it would not eliminate politicization. More turnover would mean more nomination battles and could risk recasting the judicial role to reflect presidents' political views. It would also deny the Court the extended service of potentially great jurists by forcing premature departures. And greater proximity in time to prevailing opinion would also mean less likelihood of standing apart and taking unpopular but necessary steps to stand up for minority rights.

Almost fifty states have rejected the model of judges nominated by the president and confirmed by the Senate. Most state judges are electorally accountable and almost all must retire at a given age (over thirty states either elect or confirm many or all state judges). Many states have also adopted independent commissions to limit politicization of the appointment process. At federal level, the last thing that the United States needs is more elections, campaigns, funding, and lobbies that would cloud judicial politics. But a mandatory retirement age is a sensible step that would echo practice in the states. In New York, for example, a mandatory retirement at age seventy exists for the state's highest court (a referendum to increase that to eighty was defeated in 2013). In 2016, while Pennsylvania voters narrowly agreed to raise the age limit for judges from seventy to seventy-five, Oregon voters defeated a proposal to repeal it entirely, to keep it at seventy-five. For the Supreme Court,

Congress could set seventy-five or eighty and require that the age could not be changed without a supermajority vote.

Expanding the Court from nine to twelve could enable the body to deal more easily with a heavy workload and encourage the Court to take more cases and administrate justice more speedily. But that could be accomplished by an expanded professional staff. Whether an enlarged bench would lead to fewer "knife-edge" rulings would depend on how far appointees reflected a divided governing coalition. Although 5–4 decisions being "polarized" is not the same as "partisan," enlarging the Court would exacerbate the problem of politicized nominations. Each appointment would not be as momentous, but they would remain crucial opportunities for presidents to advance their agendas.

A variant, proposed by Levinson (2012), is a supermajority. It might be possible at the federal level to emulate what occurs in, for example, North Dakota and Nebraska, which require supermajorities of their courts to invalidate state legislation. It could be reasonable to require seven of the nine justices to overturn national legislation (and thereby deny a single Justice disproportionate influence). The difficulties here are, however, notable. For one, it would seem odd to decry the existence of supermajorities as frustrating democratic policy-making in Congress while echoing them with supermajorities on the Court. Even if that inconsistency were not so serious, it is unclear how a new Court majority might avoid the problem of one or more "swing" Justices deciding constitutional law. This is largely a function less of numbers than the balance of power between the elected branches, a result of democratic elections. That is, the Court's composition reflects, with a lag, the nation's direction in choosing the White House and Senate. Sandra Day O'Connor (1981–2006) and Anthony Kennedy's (1988–2018) influence as "swing" votes partly reflected divided government after 1968 but also expressed the judicial independence questioned by academics but lamented by presidents.

Judges are supposedly above party politics. But they are appointed by politicians and adjudicate disputes that sway elections. Even if one disagrees with his advocacy of "bipartisan judicial activism," Keck (2014) persuasively refutes claims that judicial review amounts to a systematic disenfranchisement of democratic majorities. Judicial decisions are neither final nor infallible. Many are popular. And rather than thwarting public preferences, they form part of constitutional democracy. Policy emerges from courts, legislatures, and executives interacting. That is more responsive than a hypothetical system of elected institutions acting alone would be. And partisanship is nothing new. During the *Lochner* era from 1905 to 1937, the Court routinely struck down legislation to improve worker health and safety and extricate America from the Depression. When FDR tried to pack it to approve New Deal measures – proposing on February 5, 1937 to add up to six additional members, one for every seventy-year-old Justice who refused to retire – the results were stark. Although Americans were evenly divided (47 percent for, 53 percent against), 70 percent of Democrats supported the plan, while 92 percent of Republicans opposed it (Saad 2016). The danger in a hyperpolarized system is less counter-majoritarianism than partisan capture (Keck 2014: 256). But courts – whose function of conflict resolution incentivizes judges to seek compromise – may be advantageously placed to resolve conflicts that parties cannot.

## The Electoral College

The Constitution provides the framework for democracy. Might the shortcomings of politics be ameliorated by changes here?

The United States is doubly unique in how it chooses its head of state and government. First, only America employs the arcane device of an Electoral College (EC). Second, only the United States institutionalizes this form of indirect democracy and holds presidential primaries and caucuses. The system can yield curious outcomes. In 2016, for example, Trump lost the election to Clinton by over 2.8 million votes but won the EC by seventy-seven votes. Trump received 46.09 percent of the popular vote (62,984,825 votes), while Clinton received 48.18 percent (65,853,516 votes). On December 19, 2016, electors in each state met and, of 538 EC votes, Trump received 304, Clinton 227, three went to Colin Powell, and one each to John Kasich, Ron Paul, Bernie Sanders, and "Faith Spotted Eagle." On December 22, 2016, the fifty states certified the outcome. On January 6, 2017, a joint session of Congress certified the results and Vice President Joe Biden, as President of the Senate, read the final vote tally.

Predictably, this system has attracted immense criticism. Concern at democracy by one remove is understandable and many question its fitness for purpose. Dahl (2003: 88) declared the EC an "undemocratic blemish on the American constitutional system." Levinson (2006: 82–83) viewed it as "perverse" and "embarrassing." Edwards (2011) argued the EC is "bad for America." And Barone (2016) contended that, "Our presidential nominating system is the weakest part of our political system and, even after major reform and minor tinkering, there seems to be no entirely satisfactory way to structure it." Congress has considered but rejected literally hundreds of constitutional amendments to transform it (Keyssar 2018).

Critics typically identify multiple flaws: the candidate losing the popular vote winning the election, lack of proportionality, overrepresentation of smaller states, and the disproportionate influence of swing states. In 1956, when a voter told the Democratic presidential candidate, Adlai Stevenson, that he had the vote of "every thinking person in America," Stevenson quipped that "Madam, that is not enough, I need a majority." Ironically enough, he was wrong: Winning 50 percent of votes in presidential elections is an aspiration, not a requirement. But some contend that although the EC is an odd institution, "it is not a sufficiently un-democratic institution to upset most Americans" (King 2012: 167).

The US commitment to democracy is neither absolute nor unlimited. In *Federalist 10*, Madison identified the Constitution with "popular government" but this did not mean unimpeded majority rule. The Founders created an enlightened, not unbridled, democracy, and a compound republic in which states were more than organized departments of a centralized government. With some prescience, they worried that pure democracy could result in the election of a demagogue, charismatic autocrat, or someone under foreign influence. In *Federalist 68*, Hamilton wrote that, "The process of election affords a moral certainty that the office of President will never fall to the lot of any man who is not in an eminent degree endowed with the requisite qualifications." Electors would use their judgment to prevent the "tumult and disorder" that would result from the "mischief" of candidates exploiting "talents for low intrigue, and the little arts of popularity."

That hope has not been fully realized, partly because democratizing impulses changed the EC's character. The Framers never intended electors to be chosen by popular vote. Direct popular election was proposed but rejected at the Constitutional Convention in 1787. The EC was a compromise among delegates who had no previous experience electing a chief executive. The Founders envisioned it as a council of qualified experts, chosen by individual state governments. The EC was a hedge against a national majority having too much power over the states. Its rationale was to guard against an uninformed electorate while preventing larger states from becoming too dominant. "Electors" would add additional checks to prevent a radical mobocracy gaining control. Article II, Section I gave the states exclusive control over awarding their electoral votes: "Each State shall appoint, in such Manner as the Legislature thereof may direct, a Number of Electors...". But early elections and the rise of party politics transformed electors from independents into party agents. And over time, states granted the power over their delegates to a popular vote.

With weak parties and a communications revolution, 2016 confirmed to some that Lincoln's promise of government of, for and by the people could yield to Hamilton's nightmare that popular elections would produce demagogues who paid an "obsequious court to the people," appealing to passions and prejudices rather than reason (Mezey 2017). But this was more a problem of the "invisible primary" and the parties than the EC. Flawed though it is in four respects, it retains strengths that commend retention, and reform, rather than abolition.

First, democracy means the candidate winning the most votes wins the election. But the EC requires a candidate to win 270 of 538 electoral, not popular, votes. Amid deeply polarized electorates, the national popular vote loser has won the EC vote five times (1824, 1876, 1888, 2000, and 2016) in fifty-eight presidential elections. In 2000, George W. Bush received over half a million fewer votes than Al Gore but – thanks to the Supreme Court's *Bush v. Gore* ruling that decided Florida's votes – won 271 to 266 in the EC. In 2016, Clinton's was the largest popular-vote lead in history for a candidate who lost the election.

In context, however, these are anomalous. Over 90 percent of the time, the system produces the same electoral as popular vote winner. Typically, the EC also provides a winner with more than 50 percent of the popular vote. In eighteen of twenty-five elections from 1920–2016, the winner received an absolute majority. In three of the remaining seven, the winner fell less than 1 percent short. Just four elections saw the winner fall well below 50 percent: 1968 (Nixon), 1992 (Clinton), 2000 (Bush), and 2016 (Trump). In fifty-two of fifty-eight presidential elections from 1788 to 2016, the College elected the popular vote winner. Its misfiring in 1876 and 1888 was followed by 112 years of successful operation. The overall record is not poor. Moreover, for those who favor parliamentary systems, it is rare that a governing party wins 50 percent of the vote. In the United Kingdom, for example, no general election from 1945 to 2017 saw a single instance of the victorious party winning 50 percent of the vote (the Conservatives came closest with 49 percent in 1955 and 1959).

Second, the College violates political equality: "one person, one vote." The EC guarantees that populous states cannot dominate an election. Yet it also sets up a disparity in representation. A state's electoral votes equal its number of representatives and senators. While California has one electoral vote per 712,000 people, Wyoming has one per 195,000. But the College performs what the Framers desired by preserving the voice of smaller states. Any alternative would lead to elections dominated by California, New York, Texas, and Florida. The twenty-five least-populated states total only 116 electoral votes, or 21 percent of 538 electors, while the ten most-populated states have over double that (256 electoral votes, about 50 percent of the electors). The 2016 election revolved around a handful of states that reflected regional diversity: in the Northeast, New Hampshire and Pennsylvania; in the Midwest, Iowa, Michigan, Ohio, and Wisconsin; in the South, Florida and North Carolina; and in the West, Colorado and Nevada.

Third, the EC produces a democratic deficit and wasted votes. In 2016, for example, Clinton defeated Trump in California by a margin of 62–33 percent in the popular vote, 29 percent more than she required to take all the state's electoral votes. By contrast, Trump won five of six swing states by slender margins: 48.6 in Florida, 49.9 in North Carolina, 48.2 in Pennsylvania, 51.3 in Ohio, and 47.3 in Michigan. But 2016 demonstrated the importance of individual states. Few observers – especially in the Clinton camp – anticipated so many competitive races. The failing was not really of vote allocation but campaign strategy.

Democracy should be representative of the nation. But in 2016, had a more direct form of popular election prevailed, Clinton would have become president after winning only twenty states. Her popular vote margins came mainly from California and New York, in millions, yet those two states do not fully reflect the wider United States or other states' values and aspirations. In 2016, California was the most misrepresented state; home to 12 percent of Americans but 10 percent of EC votes. But since 1960, California has gained twenty-three electoral votes, more than any state. Even though the Golden State's population is underrepresented, its vote gain has kept this gap relatively modest.

Fourth, there is campaigning "bias." For example, two-thirds of 2012 general election campaign events (176 of 253) took place in Ohio, Florida, Virginia, and Iowa. In 2016, over nine in ten campaign stops occurred in eleven "battleground" states, and two-thirds in Florida, Pennsylvania, Ohio, and North Carolina. Combined with intense advertising blitzes, certain states – and issues they care about – receive special attention. But visits, ads, and concerts with Beyoncé and Jay-Z are unlikely to sway elections. Especially in an intensely polarized era, partisans – regardless of where they vote – are rarely influenced by the flattery of local "meet-and-greets." Elections are not so much swayed by a handful of lucky, unrepresentative states as electoral math: since most states are safely partisan, candidates go hunting where the ducks are.

But what if such rebuttals do not persuade? Three possible alternatives are a direct popular vote or national runoff, an "interstate compact" and an end to "winner-takes-all." None are foolproof.

A direct popular vote sounds appealing. The danger of a candidate who lost the popular vote but prevailed in the EC would be removed. The election would hinge less on "battleground" states. Voters across all fifty states would know their vote mattered. And the problem of "faithless electors" would end (in six presidential elections from 1980 to 2016, there was at least one faithless elector). This looks a promising change and is one that the American public has long supported.

But how would a direct election work? A straight popular vote with a plurality rule (whoever gets most votes wins) would be dangerous. A contest that allowed multiple candidates to run could be decided by a mere 10 percent of the vote. A multi-candidate, or multi-party, system could make a mockery of democracy. So, a sensible minimum threshold would be required: perhaps 40 or 50 percent. But if a candidate failed to meet that threshold, a further election would be necessary: a national run-off.

One national run-off option might be the "second ballot" system, used in France. If no candidate reaches the threshold on the first ballot, the two leading candidates advance to a second election, two weeks later. Rather than making a positive vote, the election forces voters to choose the "least bad" candidate. But this system encourages multiple candidacies, fragmenting party unity. It is also entirely feasible that two immoderate or sectional candidates garner the top positions in a crowded first ballot field, with voters then having to select between intolerable choices for president on the second ballot. As French experience has shown, this is no abstract possibility. In 2005 and 2017, a far-right candidate emerged as one of the leading two candidates on the first ballot (the National Front's Jean-Marie Le Pen and his daughter, Marine, respectively). Even a majority victory would be risky without some requirement to spread the winner's geographical support to avoid sectionalism. Add to this the heightened expense and duration of a nationwide campaign, and the risks of narrow victory margins, fraud allegations, recounts, and litigation, and a direct election looks positively risk-laden.

The post-election consequences also merit consideration. At present, narrow popular vote victories or minority votes translate into decisive EC wins. This lends a legitimacy to govern that would otherwise be missing. Winning less than a popular vote majority did not impair the administrations of Wilson (1912, 1916), Truman (1948), Kennedy (1960), Nixon (1968), Clinton (1992, 1996), Bush (2000), and Trump (2016). (Although Trump's popular vote loss seemed to cause him angst about his own legitimacy.) It might also be that a successful candidate owed victory to a sectional base, within a region or demographic group. At present, these are avoided through the necessity of forging a coalition sufficiently broad to reach 270 EC votes. Imagine instead a popular election decided by forty votes cast out of 140 million. The losing side would be unlikely to view the president as legitimate. Moreover, the existing EC has the benefits of not requiring national recounts in contested results and minimizing attempts at fraud or manipulation (at least from within the United States). Even William Daley (2016) – Gore's losing campaign chair in 2000 – rejected abolishing the EC as a "bad idea."

The second option is the "interstate compact." This would guarantee the presidency to the candidate receiving the most popular votes nationwide. The compact would not take effect until enacted by states with 270 of 538 electoral votes. Under its terms, when the EC meets in mid-December, the national popular vote winner of the November election would receive all the electoral votes of the enacting states. This preserves the EC and state control of elections but offers an indirect route to direct popular election. By early 2018, it had been adopted by ten states and the District of Columbia, holding 165 EC votes (30.7 percent of the total EC and 61.1 percent of the EC votes needed to give the compact legal force).

Should this be implemented, it may provide the "modernization" critics seek. But serious problems remain. Congress must assent to the compact and certify the results. Faithless electors may still exercise discretion, and some state legislatures' delegates may not adhere to the compact, turning faithless electors into faithless states. Would a state's electors truly disregard their own voters' choice? That is, if for example, a Republican won nationwide in 2020 or 2024, would the electors of New York cast their ballots for that candidate if New Yorkers had voted for the Democrat? The national election, being genuinely national, would also be far more expensive than currently. Candidates would logically invest in the major media markets centered on New York, Los Angeles, Chicago, and Dallas. Smaller states will lose attention in such a contest. The danger of voter fraud and nationwide recounts would increase. One can easily envisage endless litigation at the state and federal levels that might make the thirty-six days of hiatus in 2000 look like a picnic. Moreover, there is no guarantee that the eventual winner would gain legitimacy. The compact's promise is to rebalance the EC in favor of larger states. But it represents something of an end-run around the Constitution and no guarantee of future proofing presidential contests against controversy.

For those who believe the EC merits mending, not ending, a third possibility is abolishing "winner-takes-all" rules. Maine and Nebraska, for example, allocate EC votes by congressional district, with a two-vote top-up bonus going to the statewide popular winner. Were more states to adopt this system – an action requiring state law changes, not amending the US Constitution – the election would likely become more competitive, less focused on battlegrounds, and with higher turnout. But this would encourage even more partisan gerrymandering, to maximize the presidential vote. Moreover, for Democrats at least, the move would be doubly unattractive, because states like California would then hand the Republican candidate a sum of EC votes equivalent to those of Ohio and because the current congressional vote distribution benefits Republicans (the GOP base is scattered across districts whereas the Democratic one tends to be more concentrated in urban centers). Had this operated in 2012, Mitt Romney would have prevailed, despite winning 5 million fewer votes nationally than Obama (Romney won in 226 House districts to Obama's 209). In 2016, Trump would also have beaten Clinton decisively (230 to 205 districts).

But this would at least seem to be a case of not throwing the baby out with the bathwater – retaining the current system's strengths but reinforcing elements of choice, competition, and balance. Although unlikely to be embraced, a proportional rather than plurality system of allocating the EC votes would also do away with the gerrymandering issue entirely. That is, based on the statewide vote, a state's electoral votes would be allocated accordingly: if the Democrat won 60 percent and the Republican took 40 percent in Pennsylvania, twelve of the state's twenty electoral votes would go to the Democrat and eight to the Republican. This would retain the state-by-state feature of the EC, make elections more competitive, and dispense with the "winner-take-all" aspect that discourages candidates campaigning in states where their party's votes are "wasted." This seems the optimal route to a better selection system. That said, the history of "modern" (post-1968) presidential selection has not produced uniformly poor presidents and the pre-1968 system did not preclude "duds."

### Gerrymanders and Referenda

If the method of electing presidents appears unripe for alteration, perhaps that of Congress might prove more fruitful. Partisan gerrymandering is often seen as what is wrong with current politics, from the lack of competitive districts to the rise of ideological extremes and the ensuing gridlock in Washington. Most Americans recoil at the contorted shape of some districts. Redistricting is inherently a political process, and in most states, it remains in the hands of politicians. Democratic voters are far more clustered in and around urban areas than are Republicans, making it easier to pack them into districts. Republicans are more spread out. This geography of politics favors Republicans in the construction of congressional districts. In 2016, Trump lost the national popular vote by 2.1 percent but Republicans won the median House seat by 3.4 points and the median Senate seat by 3.6 points. Another factor is the role of the Voting Rights Act. Democrats can't maneuver their voters into districts so easily because that could reduce the number of majority-minority districts.

Three points are worth making.

First, Senate boundaries are not redrawn every ten years, but like the House, polarization has sharply increased there. Something more than drawing boundaries fuels the party divide: division among the public.

Second, lack of competitiveness in House districts has come gradually, not simply from partisan gerrymandering. "The Gerrymandering Project" by FiveThirtyEight and the Cook Political Report (http://fivethirtyeight.com/tag/the-gerrymandering-project/) rejected the idea that there is a straightforward solution to partisan gerrymandering. The number of competitive districts declined from 164 after the 1996 election to just 72 after 2016, but less than a fifth of that decline was caused by redistricting. One factor reducing the number of competitive House districts was that fewer counties are balanced politically. In 1996, 1,111 counties – one third of the national total – were decided by margins of 10 percent or fewer. In 2016, that number was just 310. That makes it even more difficult to produce competitive districts without trampling on the goal of keeping counties and communities as intact as possible. Although few would disagree that voters should select their lawmakers rather than lawmakers choose their voters, gerrymandering is easy to condemn but complex to solve. Just as there are no permanent majorities in politics, so there is no perfect map.

Third, the judiciary is intervening, as it did in prior decades, on the issue. For example, in February 2018, the Pennsylvania Supreme Court drew a new congressional district map for the state after finding that the previous map, drawn by Republicans following the 2010 Census, was an illegal gerrymander that deprived the state's voters of their right to participate in free and equal elections. One of the criteria used by the court in drawing the new districts was "compactness": that wherever possible districts should avoid the sprawling, inkblot-like shapes of the old map, and gerrymandered maps in several other states, as well. Although the Supreme Court has not held partisan fairness as a requirement, its 2018 term featured two redistricting cases – *Gill v. Whitford* and *Benisek v. Lamone* that – directly addressed the issue of whether some form of partisan fairness is a requirement. A court ruling that ruled partisan gerrymandering unconstitutional would obviate the need for a constitutional amendment mandating nonpartisan redistricting, as recommended by Sabato. But the Constitution already gives state legislatures authority to draw such districts and a few have in turn legitimately given that authority to independent commissions. The result has been the drawing of more sensible, contiguous district boundaries.

One final possibility that scholars such as Levinson endorse would be greater direct democracy via national referenda. Referenda are a prominent part of American political life at the state level for all states bar Delaware. For example, California allows constitutional amendment at the ballot box. Maine allows its citizenry to override legislation its citizens deem objectionable. Might the United States not be better off with national referendums on taxes, gun control, or immigration reform?

There is an abstract case for referenda that is coherent and appealing. On issues that have national salience, why not allow the people to decide directly? A nationwide campaign could concentrate popular minds on an issue. It might be a partial antidote to partisanship, allowing Democrats and Republicans to choose whichever side of the debate they felt most comfortable on, without electoral penalties. Nonpartisans could participate. Turnout might benefit from the novelty of a continent-wide referendum on a discrete issue. And polls suggest the public appears supportive of the national referenda option, across party lines.

Ultimately, however, the same issues that complicate federal elections surround referenda: who finances them? Are there limits on the campaigns in terms of spending and adverts? Would an informed electorate vote on the merits or, as in referenda from Europe, vote to express an opinion about the government? In the United Kingdom, referendums on Welsh devolution, Scottish independence, voting reform, and EU membership occurred between 2011 and 2016. But their conduct revealed glaring democratic deficiencies, from people feeling as ill-informed by the end as the start of campaigns, unengaged voters, and rival campaigns telling outright lies to win.

Referenda would also undermine the job of lawmakers and exculpate them from their responsibilities. But perhaps most telling, would Americans be content to decide an important, contentious national issue by a single vote? Thresholds could be built in, but the greater the threshold, the less "democratic" the outcome. National referenda fit awkwardly into the American constitutional universe. A referendum is a moment and moments mislead. As was once said of opinion polling, "Although you can take a nation's pulse, you can't be sure that the nation hasn't just run up a flight of stairs." Checks and balances exist precisely to modify such pulse-taking. Referenda are open to abuse and do violence to the constitutional spirit. Plebiscites have a place at state and local level but not for the nation. As King (2012: 160–161) notes, national referenda would:

> admit of no compromise or delay, would be hideously expensive to organize, would almost certainly be deeply divisive and would inevitably have the effect of creating an enormous body of losers, many of whom, especially in an era of cultural conflict in America, might well feel deeply aggrieved.

## Conclusion

To return to Mayhew's analogy that began this chapter: can the fish in America refresh their water without replacing the ocean?

Profound concern for the limits of human reason, virtue, and wisdom led the Framers to place a high premium on checks and balances. Although, in *Federalist 22*, Hamilton wrote, "The fundamental maxim of republican government … requires that the sense of the majority should prevail," Madison countered in *Federalist 51* that the separation of powers is "essential to the preservation of liberty." Institutions matter. But so, too, do the individuals who populate them as temporary custodians of public trust. In recent decades, the Shakespearian cast of characters who each enjoyed a temporary lease on 1,600 Pennsylvania Avenue – Clinton, Bush, Obama, and Trump – all proved consequential, in very different ways and with markedly distinct results.

Judging constitutional design implicates ideological viewpoints. The separation of powers results in a smaller government and welfare state than would likely otherwise obtain. If one is in favor of a larger government, that is a problem; less so, if not. One can make a case for either preference. But democracy is government by persuasion: winning through the force of argument, not by the argument of force. The business of politics is trade-offs: conciliating differing interests. Democratic politics presumes ways of living, working, and progressing despite differences and disagreement, and serious politicians who can put pragmatism over purity and accentuate the positive.

But that is difficult in an era of "negative partisanship" (Abramowitz and Webster 2016). As partisan identities have become more closely aligned with social, cultural, and ideological divisions in society, party supporters – including nominal "Independents" – have developed increasingly negative feelings about the opposing party and its candidates. This has fed dramatic increases in party loyalty and straight-ticket voting, a steep decline in the advantage of incumbency and growing consistency between the results of presidential elections and those of House, Senate and even state legislative elections. In terms of electoral competition, democratic representation and governance, the rise of negative partisanship and polarization is not an illusion but unique in American history, reflecting an unprecedented alignment of racial, ethnic, religious, geographic, and ideological divides (Abramowitz 2018). Party affiliation is increasingly an aspect of self-identity, while parties have increasingly abandoned their "gatekeeping" role – exercising peer review to filter out unsuitable candidates for office – for a hyperpoliticized, win-at-all-costs politics of persistent messaging and total opposition.

On balance, constitutional change, no matter how granular, cannot remedy this kind of deep division and the sometimes toxically tribal-style politics to which it gives rise. One irony of Sabato's comprehensive reform agenda was that, by his own polling evidence, public support was lacking. With only a few exceptions, Americans were either divided or mostly opposed to his recommendations. (For example, although 24 percent either strongly or somewhat favored a more representative Senate, 74 percent did not [58 percent strongly opposed this]; 52 percent also strongly opposed a new Constitutional Convention.) Enlarging the Congress and Court, or abolishing the Electoral College, will exacerbate rather than cure existing maladies. But some changes would make sense while expressing fidelity to the constitutional structure and values. Politically unfeasible as it is, an end to equal state representation in the Senate, alongside relaxed eligibility requirements for president, judicial term limits, and a proportional state system for allocating electoral votes would remedy some of the existing inequities. But constitutional reform cannot resolve policy differences from climate change to health care. Only politics can achieve that.

To address the sources of disagreement, the parties require relearning the art of compromise that is the soul of the Madisonian order. To get there requires leaders facing down more intemperate elements in their coalitions and a return to deal-making in the public interest. Otherwise, no rational politics will reemerge unless forced on the nation by an external shock that no American would wish their nation to suffer. But while division in Washington reflects a much broader divide in American society at large, hopes of making bipartisanship great again are likely to remain forlorn. As Tocqueville noted, imperfect though American democracy is, the people tend to receive maximum indulgence.

Flawed as they are, the governing institutions mostly merit a stay of execution and meet the third condition of an effective constitution: allowing the expression of the majority will while protecting the rights of minorities. It is to the fourth condition – the means of its own revision – that we turn next.

## Summary

- Congress, the presidency, the Federal Judiciary, and the electoral system have all attracted strong criticism and multiple constitutional reform proposals. Some proposals are desirable but politically unfeasible – such as ending equal representation in the US Senate – while others are feasible but undesirable (such as a six-year presidential term and abolition of the Electoral College).
- On balance, those constitutional changes that are both desirable and feasible – including the line-item veto, judicial terms limits, and a mandatory retirement age – would improve American government and politics at the margins, but would not address the underlying cause of political dysfunction: partisan and ideological polarization.
- Since the 1990s, a new party system has emerged that features resurgent party loyalty in the electorate, closely balanced competition in presidential and congressional elections, and secure regional partisan strongholds for both parties. Small electoral shifts are magnified into changes of partisan control in Washington while being a Democrat or Republican has become not only an affiliation but an identity.
- With the same party in control of the White House and Congress, polarization can overcome stasis through more coherent if contingent party government, but polarization tends to yield gridlock under conditions of divided party control.
- For all its faults, the interplay of governing institutions under the existing arrangements meets the third condition of an effective constitution: reconciling majoritarianism with the protection of minority rights and liberties.

# 4 Amendments and Interpretations

American politics has its share of odd symbols, practices, and ortho-doxies, but surely the most peculiar is the constant reference to the nation's Founders in contemporary debate. Everyone cites the Founders. Constitutional originalists consult the Founders' papers to decide original meaning. Proponents of a living and evolving Constitution turn to the Founders as the font of ideas that have grown over time ... But, in fact, the Founders disagreed with each other.

David Sehat (2015: 1)

...the central fact remains that at no time since the Constitution was ratified at the end of the eighteenth century has there ever been a serious, organized movement to revoke it and replace it with something com-pletely different. That one non-event in American political history is at least as significant as any event that has actually taken place.

Anthony King (2012: 66)

## Introduction

Beyond its governing institutions, the Constitution has survived through two principal mechanisms: the amendment process and constitutional interpretation. This chapter examines both as integral, though distinct, parts of a healthy constitutional ecosystem ensuring the means of its own adaptation.

The twenty-seven amendments have predominantly concerned the framework of government, citizenship, and the relationship between political liberty and equality. Most have expanded the political com-munity, protected individual rights, and helped to secure due process and equality before the law. Some of these literally "made amends" for excluding women, African Americans, and young Americans from cit-izenship. Thanks partly to their protections, state laws that punished particular groups and were once taken for granted – enforcing racial apartheid, permitting sterilization, criminalizing abortions – were ruled unconstitutional. Even when amendments failed, they mobilized action and reframed debates (Hartley 2017). The amendment process offers a key avenue to seek change. Not just presidents, lawmakers and judges, but numerous social forces – revolutionaries and abolitionists, suffragists and teetotalers, peace activists and students – helped revise the founding design to realize a more perfect union.

Since the requirements are so demanding, some imagine that ratifying an amendment ends the story for constitutional change. But in many ways, it represents only the end of the beginning. An ongoing convention in the courts continually reinterprets constitutional meaning, reapplying old values to new circumstances. Articles, sections, and clauses – including amendments – are tested anew by novel controversies where the law is unclear or important rights collide. Although the Constitution can at points be embarrassingly precise – such as the Seventh Amendment, requiring jury trials in civil cases where the value at stake exceeds twenty dollars – many provisions are deliberately vague and ambiguous.

That requires interpretation and adjudication. Indeed, there is a strong case that the evolution of common law, precedents, norms, and traditions are more important than formal amendments in altering constitutional meaning. As Lepore (2011) noted:

> A great deal of what many Americans hold dear is nowhere written on those four pages of parchment, or in any of the amendments. What has made the Constitution durable is the same as what makes it demanding: the fact that so much was left out.

The Constitution does not expressly identify all rules, rights, principles, and procedures governing America. It makes no mention of democracy, separation of powers, or privacy. In this regard, interpretation must rely on more than the text alone: precedents, norms, and shared values. These supply insights into the Constitution, supplementing but not supplanting its central role. As Burns (1990) argued, the Constitution has been altered, and strengthened, by the creation of rights not enshrined in the document but essential to it. And norms of mutual toleration (rival parties accepting each other as legitimate) and forbearance (exercising restraint in the use power) have been integral to making the Constitution work (Levitsky and Ziblatt 2018).

American constitutionalism is multidimensional: Congress, presidents, and the people voice their own views about what is constitutional. Moreover, by their behavior (for example, allowing use of the military through congressional authorization), they effectively rewrite constitutional practice without altering the text. Interpretation is a continual dialogue between the branches. Nonetheless, matters that elsewhere would be addressed by elected branches are typically left in the United States for courts to decide in a culture where rights are capacious and expansive. That enhanced role, together with the prevalence of "rights talk," conflicts between group rights and individual liberties, and courts exercising judicial review so fully makes interpretation integral to constitutional order.

But that also makes interpretation controversial. Constitutional decisions are, in principle, anti-democratic: they can reject the actions of elected officials, denying them the policy fruits of political victories. For progressives, that is often appropriate, since the "living" constitution is not synonymous with the text alone. Too close an adherence to the latter threatens to make the Constitution outdated and freeze America in an eighteenth-century straitjacket via an inflexible supreme law. For many conservatives, however, granting judges an expansive license to reinterpret the Constitution is politically illegitimate. Allowing the invention of rights not expressly enumerated elevates unelected officials over the public and its representatives. It threatens to transform the Bill of Rights from a barrier *against* into an instrument *of* majoritarianism, if its protections are interpreted according to what public opinion prefers.

The avenues for constitutional change provoke heated conflict but also ensure that government remains responsive to citizen demands, balancing majoritarianism with minority rights and liberties. As Keith Whittington (1999) argued, the Constitution is dualistic. It constrains and empowers officials. Legal scholars focus on interpretation: how binding rules that can be neutrally interpreted are applied by courts against government. But the Constitution also guides officials making policies. It relies on them to formulate authoritative requirements and enforce agreed settlements. Constitutional meaning is shaped within politics as the Constitution shapes politics, a process of construction rather than interpretation. Textual ambiguities and political incentives encourage officials to construct their own understandings. But they also allow citizen groups to reshape constitutional law from the ground up on matters from marriage equality to firearms regulation (Cole 2016).

## Constitutional Continuity and Change

The Constitution represents one of the greatest expressions of liberty and law ever conceived. But it has only survived America's transformation, from a minor power on the edge of the modern world to a hyperpower with unprecedented global influence and reach, through accommodating immense change. The outer façade suggests continuity. But its substantive content has facilitated, and adapted to, America's transformation from a predominantly agrarian, insular, and weak confederation of thirteen states to the most powerful, technologically advanced, and prosperous nation-state. Reconciling these seemingly contradictory phenomena – a constitution crafted in and for the eighteenth century, and a twenty-first century America where disruptive change seems the only constant – is integral to its continuing viability.

As Chapter 1 noted, the Framers were divided over constitutional veneration. But they all understood that no constitution can anticipate every future contingency. To remain relevant, every functional constitution requires a provision by which it can be amended and the means for its interpretation. The combination is necessary, if insufficient, to fuse democracy with legally protected liberty. Two of the most important structural features ensuring the Constitution's survival – beyond the separation of powers and federalism – have been Article V and the Bill of Rights.

Article V established the amendment provisions:

> The Congress, whenever two thirds of both Houses shall deem it necessary, shall propose Amendments to this Constitution, or, on the application of the Legislatures of two thirds of the several States, shall call a Convention for proposing amendments, which in either Case, shall be valid to all Intents and Purposes, as Part of this Constitution, when ratified by the Legislatures of three fourths of the several States, or by Conventions in three fourths thereof, as one or the other Mode of Ratification may be proposed by the Congress.

A principal impediment to constitutional change is the rigidity of the process. Among constitutions, the United States is the single most difficult to amend. Formal revision can seem like one of the labors of Hercules. The standard provision for amendment is demanding, requiring supermajorities at federal and state level: two-thirds of both houses of Congress and three-quarters of state legislatures must approve an amendment proposal. Amendments require a broad political consensus typically in short supply, even is less polarized times. Since many proposed amendments also have a partisan source or purpose, securing the necessary supermajorities is even tougher. Among those that failed despite substantial support were the Equal Rights Amendment and proposals to outlaw abortion and flag desecration.

Of nearly 12,000 amendments proposed since 1787, only thirty-three have gone to the states for ratification. Of these, twenty-seven succeeded. Moreover, since the first ten amendments were ratified in 1791, a mere seventeen have been enacted in more than 200 years. Only Australia is comparably resistant to change. From 1906 to 2017, nineteen national referendums were held, in which forty-four proposals to change the Australian Constitution were put to the people, but only eight were approved. By contrast, India – the world's most populous democracy – adopted its postcolonial Constitution in 1949 and amended it 101 times over the following seventy years.

Like Article V, the Bill of Rights was also a compromise to make the Constitution operational. Madison and the Federalists conceded the further checks against tyrannical government demanded by opponents of the original Constitution, who feared that empowering the Federal Government endangered liberty. During the ratification debates, supporters of the Constitution argued that a list of specially protected rights was unnecessary. No significant distinction existed between the government and the people. Those elected to positions of power, the Framers believed, would represent the people's interests. But Anti-Federalists were unpersuaded that government would respect popular rights. Placing some aspects of life beyond government intrusion as strictly no-go areas was required. So, too – after George Mason of Virginia argued the power to convene a constitutional convention should not be exclusively in the hand of Congress, in case the Federal Government became tyrannical – was a revised Article V, that allowed two-thirds of state legislatures to call for a convention independently of congressional lawmakers.

Madison, in the first Congress, drew up the Bill of Rights. Originally, the House passed seventeen amendments with new protections, which the Senate consolidated to twelve. Ten were ratified by the states. Of the two "lesser" proposals that were not, one – calculating population size for representation in the House – lapsed. So, for a long time, did the other, on congressional pay, which prohibited lawmakers awarding themselves a pay raise until an intervening election had occurred. Proposed by Madison, this languished until resurrected in the 1980s. From being submitted to the states for ratification on September 25, 1789 to ratification on May 7, 1992 the Twenty-seventh Amendment took no less than 202 years, seven months and twelve days to be enacted.

Nowhere is the Constitution more a battlefield for warring parties than in efforts to prevent its erosion or extend its guarantees. The Bill of Rights, though formally listing ten protections against the *Federal* Government, facilitated – through judicial interpretation – the extension of those rights to all fifty states and the people. Rights now taken for granted were institutionalized by judicial rulings that the other branches, and the people, came to respect. Although each individual amendment is self-contained, like a portrait on a postage stamp, it offers immense details within a small space, magnified to cover the entire nation.

In listing the most important citizenship rights, the Bill of Rights represents the chief expression of American individualism and core liberal contribution to republican government. Two analogies are illustrative. First, the rights act as trump cards for every citizen against the state. Second, the structure of government resembles a ship. Sturdy and unlikely to sink, lifeboats are vital additions, just in case. The constitutional structure, with its fragmentation of state power, *should* safeguard individual rights against government. But the Bill of Rights provides additional guarantees. And rights-based appeals are powerful in an era when important elements of both the left and right emphasize choice and autonomy, from right-to-die laws to marijuana legalization.

That said, the widespread veneration of rights as a constraining force against the state is a relatively recent development. As Magliocca (2018) details, until the twentieth century, few Americans called the first ten amendments "the Bill of Rights." When people started doing so between the Spanish-American War and World War II, the Bill of Rights was usually invoked to justify *increasing* rather than restricting the Federal Government's authority. President Franklin D. Roosevelt played a key role by using the Bill of Rights to justify expanded national regulation under the New Deal, and then transforming it into a patriotic rallying cry against Nazi Germany. Only after the Cold War began did its modern form take shape as a powerful symbol of limits on government power. Its guarantees required hundreds of years to apply nationwide.

## Constitutional Amendments

The US Constitution pioneered the "do-over": amendments instigated by popular will. In his first inaugural address as president on March 4, 1861, Abraham Lincoln declared that, "This country, with its institutions, belongs to the people who inhabit it. Whenever they shall grow weary of the existing government, they can exercise their constitutional right of amending it, or their revolutionary right to dismember or overthrow it." Amending is not "anti-constitutional" but part of constitutionalism.

As Figure 4.1 illustrates, the US Constitution resembles many state ones, in that it can be amended in more than one way. In practice, however, it is much less detailed than state constitutions, many of which prescribe matters such as taxation policy. Moreover, every state except Delaware

---

The US Constitution and the Florida Constitution are "living documents" because both detail the process by which they can be altered. But the amendment process is very different. In Florida, voters must agree to amend the Florida Constitution. Amendments are included on Election Day ballots. Voters vote "yes" or "no" to proposed amendments. An amendment can only be added to the Florida Constitution if 60% or more of those voting vote "yes". Proposing an amendment to the Florida Constitution can occur in five ways:

• *Ballot Initiative Process*: A set number of registered voters representing 8% of the votes cast in the most recent presidential election must sign a petition supporting an amendment being placed on an Election Day ballot.

• *Constitutional Convention*: A set number of registered voters representing 15% of the votes cast in the most recent presidential election may call for a constitutional convention. Amendments may be proposed at the convention.

• *Constitutional Revision Commission*: The Constitutional Revision Committee meets every 20 years (the most recent was 2017) and proposes amendments to the state constitution.

• *Legislative Joint Resolution*: Three-fifths (60%) of each house of the Florida Legislature can pass a joint resolution proposing an amendment to be placed on an Election Day ballot.

• *Taxation and Budget Reform Commission*: The Taxation and Budget Reform Commission proposes amendments to the state constitution. This meets every 20 years (the last occasion was in 2007).

---

*Figure 4.1* Amending the US Constitution and Florida State Constitution.

requires proposed amendments to the state constitution to be put to the people in a referendum. Although no provision exists for national referenda, 26 of 27 amendments to the Federal Constitution were enacted by a two-thirds vote of both houses of Congress and ratification by three-quarters of state legislatures (currently thirty-eight states). (The Twenty-first, repealing Prohibition, was ratified by state conventions.)

America's democratic peers operate differently. For example, Article 89 of the French Constitution stipulates that a bill must be approved by both houses of Parliament and then by a Congress, in a special joint session of both houses, or by the people in a national referendum. Section 128 of Australia's Constitution states that a proposed change must be approved in a bill by the Federal Parliament. It then goes to a national referendum, where a "double majority" is required: a majority of Australians in a majority of states *and* a majority of people across the nation must vote "yes," otherwise the Constitution remains unchanged. Canada operates similarly: proposed amendments must pass the bicameral national legislature – the House of Commons and Senate – and then win approval in two-thirds of the provincial legislatures with at least 50 percent of the total Canadian population.

Despite their unhappiness with politics, Americans show only limited support for changes to their political system. But while politicians express constant admiration for the Constitution, every year they seem keen to rewrite it. Neither modest public demand nor difficult odds of success has discouraged lawmakers. As Table 4.1 shows, from 1789 through the start of 2017, over 11,000 amendments were introduced to Congress. As Table 4.2 records, from 1999 to 2017, 739 proposals were

*Table 4.1* Proposed Constitutional Amendments (1789–2017)

| Congress | Date | Number Proposed |
|----------|------|-----------------|
| 1st–101st | 1789–1990 | 10,431 |
| 102nd | 1991–1993 | 153 |
| 103rd | 1993–1995 | 155 |
| 104th | 1995–1997 | 152 |
| 105th | 1997–1999 | 118 |
| 106th | 1999–2001 | 71 |
| 107th | 2001–2003 | 77 |
| 108th | 2003–2005 | 77 |
| 109th | 2005–2007 | 72 |
| 110th | 2007–2009 | 66 |
| 111th | 2009–2011 | 75 |
| 112th | 2011–2013 | 92 |
| 113th | 2013–2015 | 84 |
| 114th | 2015–2017 | 76 |
| Total |  | 11,699 |

Source: US Senate, www.senate.gov/pagelayout/reference/three_column_table/measures_proposed_to_amend_constitution.htm.

*Table 4.2* Proposed Constitutional Amendments, by Party (1999–2017)

| Congress | Democratic Amendments | Republican Amendments | Total |
|---|---|---|---|
| 106th (1999–2001) | 23 | 46 | 69 |
| 107th (2001–2003) | 38 | 34 | 72 |
| 108th (2003–2005) | 36 | 42 | 78 |
| 109th (2005–2007) | 33 | 39 | 72 |
| 110th (2007–2009) | 29 | 37 | 66 |
| 111th (2009–2011) | 29 | 46 | 75 |
| 112th (2011–2013) | 35 | 56 | 91 |
| 113th (2013–2015) | 26 | 56 | 82 |
| 114th (2015–2017) | 26 | 49 | 75 |
| 115th (2017–2019) | 22 | 37 | 59 |
| Total | 297 | 442 | 739 |

Source: Data from Pew Research Center, "A look at proposed constitutional amendments and how they seldom go anywhere," September 15, 2017 www. pewresearch.org/fact-tank/2017/09/15/a-look-at-proposed-constitutional-amendments-and-how-seldom-they-go-anywhere/.

introduced (the decline in the numbers each session was accounted for mostly by growing partisanship). These proposals comprised lengthening the terms of the House of Representatives to prohibiting efforts to replace the dollar with a global currency. Proposals in the 115th Congress (2017–2019) included reintroduction of the Equal Rights Amendment (which fell three states short of ratification in 1982) to specifying that presidents cannot pardon themselves for criminal behavior.

Since the Twenty-seventh Amendment was ratified in 1992, and despite the frequency of proposals, none has succeeded. Instead, amendments typically die in committee. From 1999 to 2017, proposals have been voted on by the full House or Senate on just twenty occasions. Only a proposed ban on desecration of the Stars and Stripes came close to passing. Each congressional term, from 1999 to 2006, the House approved an amendment prohibiting flag desecration, which then failed in the Senate (although by only one vote short of the two-thirds requirement in 2006). However, as Table 4.3 shows, easily the most frequently proposed amendment is to require that the federal budget be balanced (so revenues meet expenditures, without allowing a deficit).

The rise and fall of amendments usually reflects an issue's public salience or a response to Supreme Court rulings. For example, proposals related to campaign finance sharply increased after the *Citizens United* ruling in 2010 that federal law cannot prohibit corporate election spending. In response, some amendment proposals tried to limit constitutional rights to "natural persons" and not corporations. In the other direction, the number of proposals to ban same-sex marriage declined after marriage equality was upheld by the Supreme Court in 2015 and public opinion had shifted decisively in its favor.

*Table 4.3* Most Popular Constitutional Amendment Proposals (1999–2017)

| Proposal | Number of Amendments Proposed |
| --- | --- |
| Balanced budget | 133 |
| Campaign finance | 71 |
| Term limits | 68 |
| Flag desecration | 28 |
| Direct election of the president | 27 |
| Equal gender rights | 26 |
| School prayer | 24 |
| Prohibiting same-sex marriage | 21 |

Source: Adapted by the author from Pew Research Center, "A look at proposed constitutional amendments and how they seldom go anywhere," September 15, 2017 www.pewresearch.org/fact-tank/2017/09/15/a-look-at-proposed-constitutional-amendments-and-how-seldom-they-go-anywhere/.

The most popular proposal for a balanced budget amendment reflects disquiet over fiscal irresponsibility. From the Founding to the 1960s, deficits were mostly seen as imprudent and unjustified except when borrowing for wars, emergencies, and investments such as territorial expansion and transportation. Incurred debts were paid down diligently. Although the final years of Bill Clinton's administration saw the federal budget in surplus, the deficit returned with a vengeance under the Bush administration and, especially, after the 2008 financial crisis. From 1789 to 2009, successive administrations amassed some $10.6 trillion of national debt (the nation's total accumulated debt). Between 2009 and 2015, in response to the financial crisis, the Federal Government added $7.5 trillion more, and by 2018, the debt exceeded $20 trillion. While the Republican Party won control of the House in 2010, and both the White House and Congress in 2016, fiscal discipline was not restored.

Critics contend that by such profligacy, Congress has acted irresponsibly with American finances: substituting borrowing *for* the future with borrowing *from* the future to finance current consumption of government goods and services and handing immense debt burdens to future generations:

> Since 1961 the United States budget has been in deficit every year except for five. This is not just a string of bad luck; it is the logic of the system. The American Revolution was fought, in part, under the banner "NO TAXATION WITHOUT REPRESENTATION." But who represents future generations who cannot find their way to the ballot box because they have not yet been born? Future generations, whether they like it or not, must rely on patriotism, ethics or, as Tennessee Williams called it, "the kindness of strangers".
>
> (Buchholz 2016: 80)

Using the Constitution to resolve policy problems is not necessarily wise, as Prohibition proved. The United States isn't alone in fiscal irresponsibility, and an amendment requiring balanced budgets would not necessarily resolve the problem. A carefully drafted measure could potentially be beneficial. But without safety valves it could adversely affect the government's ability to manage economic downturns and, especially, economic shocks and financial crises. States that have similar requirements usually have waivers and exceptions and, in recessions, deficit spending is often necessary to stimulate a recovery. Without this, congressional failure could result in the budget being thrown to the courts to resolve, a matter which judges are ill equipped to deal with.

Groups such as the Convention of States and the Balanced Budget Amendment Task Force have campaigned to convince state legislatures to propose holding a constitutional convention to consider such an amendment. But its fate remains unclear. Reducing the budget deficit declined among the public's policy priorities. In 2018, only 48 percent said cutting the deficit should be a top policy priority for the president and Congress, down from 63 percent in 2014 (in 2013, the share citing the deficit as a top priority was 72 percent, the highest point in the 2000s [Pew 2018b]). By that time, the Republicans under Trump had also abandoned fiscal discipline for cutting taxes, boosting spending and going for economic growth.

Passage of a constitutional amendment is rare. Is the process holding up? The evidence is mixed.

First, unanswered questions remain. For example, the time limits by which an amendment can be enacted and whether states can change their minds are unclear. The Eighteenth Amendment – establishing Prohibition, ratified in 1919 – was the first to receive a deadline (of seven years) for ratification from Congress (in 1917). In *Coleman v. Miller* (1939), a case about an amendment over child labor, the Supreme Court ruled that it was up to Congress to decide whether unratified amendments with no deadline were still valid. The Court held that the timeliness of ratification was a "political question" at Congress's discretion. It appears therefore that the length of time elapsing between proposal and ratification is irrelevant to the amendment's continuing validity.

Although that might seem arcane, it remains relevant. For example, the ERA declares that, "Equality of rights under the law shall not be denied or abridged by the United States or any state on account of sex." First introduced in the 1920s, women's advocates were divided over its merits, but support grew over time. By 1972, it passed Congress and thirty of the necessary thirty-eight states ratified it. But by the time the (extended) deadline arrived in 1982, fifteen states had rejected it and five others rescinded ratification. The measure fell short of passage. But efforts to revive it continue.

Second, exactly how – and under what conditions – amendments matter is not always obvious. Strauss (2010: 116–117) makes four arguments about how amendments are secondary to aspects of the "Living Constitution" that more fully drive change:

i   *Extra-textual amendments.* Matters addressed by the Constitution change although the text remains unaltered. Most notably, the scope of federal power has been transformed. Congress regulates matters that 100 years ago were exclusively state preserves, from land use to education, manufacturing, consumer safety and more. The growth of the president's foreign policy power has occurred without textual amendment. Regulatory agencies were not authorized by amendments, but the administrative state is beyond serious constitutional challenge. Article I, Section VIII allows Congress to "raise and support Armies" and "To provide and maintain a Navy" but says nothing about an air force, yet no one objects to the existence of a separate and self-standing US Air Force (as opposed to the aviation wings of the army and navy), despite its not formally being constitutionally authorized.

ii  *Change after rejected amendments.* Some constitutional changes occur even though an amendment that would have established them was rejected. Although the Child Labor Amendment, to restrict children working, was rejected by thirty-eight states and ratified by only six by 1932, Court rulings effectively achieved the same result. Similarly, judicial rejection of sex-based discrimination has meant that "it is difficult today to identify any respect in which the law is different from what it would have been if the ERA had been adopted" (Strauss 126).

iii *Ratification of Change.* Some amendments merely ratify changes that have already taken place. The Seventeenth Amendment requiring direct election of US Senators approved changes that most states had already enacted. Even the Twenty-second Amendment (1951), limiting presidents to two terms, didn't invent a new norm as much as restore a tradition broken by FDR in exceptional circumstances.

iv  *Ineffective amendments.* If amendments are adopted but society has not changed, these can be systematically evaded or make little difference. The Civil War amendments had tragically modest effects. Only when society – institutions, norms and traditions – changed did these truly become operative.

The third issue about the amendment process is that debate continues to surround the desirability of a less rigid requirement.

There is a strong case *against* this. As the supreme law, the Constitution should not be simple to alter. Part of its genius is that, even if Americans do not know the details of case law, they know what the First, Second, or Fifth Amendments stand for. Would a constitution like India's be more desirable ("I plead the 146th Amendment")? A more flexible Constitution would attract even more proposals for change. But the lower the threshold – moving from, say, two-thirds majorities in Congress to three-fifths, or three-quarters of the states to two-thirds – the more amendments become substitutes for legislation.

In addition, the more amendments, the greater the scope for conflict between these, and between amendments and state or local law. No doubt lawyers would applaud the lucrative litigation. But whether most Americans would appreciate even more clashing claims and impediments to clear or lasting resolution of problems is unclear. This explosion of laws and litigation could damage the integrity of the Constitution and its public esteem. A federal constitution with multiple amendments looks less like one deserving Madisonian veneration and more like any other. Finally, courts continually adapt the Constitution through their rulings. If Strauss is right about the relatively limited importance of amendments, why "fix" what isn't broken?

Against this, while constitutions should be conservative forces (with a small "c"), there are good reasons for rejecting overly rigid ones. As with the US Senate, the Framers devised Article V for thirteen states, not fifty. The balanced budget, flag desecration, and ERA examples show that some proposals attract consistent majority support. For these to be frustrated by small minorities compounds the existing anti-majoritarian bias of the constitutional settlement. Even Antonin Scalia, arch conservative defender of a "textual" understanding of constitutional order, was no admirer:

> The one provision that I would amend is the amendment provision. And that was not originally a flaw. But the country has changed so much. With the divergence in size between California and Rhode Island – I figured it out once, I think if you picked the smallest number necessary for a majority in the least populous states, something like less than 2 percent of the population can prevent a constitutional amendment.
>
> (Rayman 2013)

Moving to an Australian or Canadian-style double majority system would make more sense and could provide the requisite mix of democratic input and state safeguards. At present, the core problem is that a small number of states, representing relatively few people, can block any amendment, no matter how popular, either at the proposal stage in Congress – where the Senate gives smaller states enhanced power – or at ratification stage. Shifting to a system where lawmakers, states, and the national population counted would combine high hurdles (supermajorities would still be required) with greater majoritarianism. Such a system could offer a triple lock. Imagine an amendment that required a less demanding set of supermajorities than at present:

i    Three-fifths of the House and Senate
ii   Three-fifths of the states
iii  States representing at least 55 percent of the total population

That trifecta would represent a more formidable hurdle than a bare majority vote. But it would retain the need for federal and state concurrence while lowering the bar for national support. Admittedly, even then, there could conceivably be problems, since a situation could arise in which the larger states, combined with just thirty of the fifty states, passed an amendment. But if that many lawmakers, states, and people were behind it, wouldn't that seem a legitimate change? Moreover, if amending the Constitution gets a little easier, this might take some of the oppressive heat out of ongoing controversies over court rulings. But changing the way that amendments are made would itself require an amendment, to replace Article V.

Enacting an amendment is like pushing a large rock up a steep hill. Failure is more common than success. Partly, that is because many amendments are trivial, symbolic, or position-taking attempts by lawmakers to placate party activists. But, as Sabato (2007: 200–201) notes, Congress is typically too busy, preoccupied, or inert to treat important amendments seriously. There is, nonetheless, a common misunderstanding in the false dichotomy between formally amending the document and informal adaptation. Politicians often assert that the only legitimate route to constitutional change is via the elected branches. If the people wish to overturn a Court ruling, it is said, they can amend the Constitution. But getting an amendment ratified is not the end of the road. For most amendments, their content remains open to interpretation. As with Prohibition, the more specific, the less practicable it often proves. To endure, amendments normally need general and imprecise language, open to competing interpretations.

## Constitutional Interpretation

The high bar for amendments makes courts the key, though not the sole, engine of constitutional change. If America's constitutional journey has resembled a long and winding interstate highway, judicial rulings have provided exit ramps, still linked to the freeway but taking the route in extended directions to new destinations.

As many court decisions as amendments have reshaped America in profound ways. Landmark rulings such as *Brown v. Board of Education* (1954), *Roe v. Wade* (1973), *DC v. Heller* (2008) and *Obergefell v. Hodges* (2015) have left an enduring mark on public life. This practice is so well accepted that it is easy to forget that in most democracies courts play a limited role in constitutional interpretation. Some constitutions, such as the Netherlands, even prohibit courts from declaring acts of parliament unconstitutional. In applying the Constitution to new conflicts, the judiciary has emulated a rolling convention – which has made the role of courts and interpretation subjects of reliably intense controversy.

Part of the reason why the Constitution is venerated is that laws must be tested for their compatibility with the supreme law. Such testing is not straightforward. If it were, decisions could be made by some sophisticated computer algorithm: constitutional law + statute law/executive action/facts of the case = ruling. Matters are rarely so simple. As Bobbitt (1991: xiv) noted, "the interpretation of the Constitution must inevitably be based on principles external to the words of the Constitution itself. Those principles have to be created rather than found: the Constitution does not contain the instructions for its own interpretation." The Court must create doctrine (rules for deciding cases) to give vague textual phrases meaning while uncovering precedents. Carefully reasoned interpretation is necessary to reconciling conflicting claims between the citizen and state, different branches of government, and different tiers of government. The Constitution is the jumping board for these decisions.

Moreover, like any brittle thing, a Constitution that will not bend will break. To endure, every constitution requires "wiggle room." The extent to which any constitution requires interpretation depends heavily on the precision of its provisions. The more detailed and specific, the less discretion and autonomy judges possess. The more general and ambiguous, or "elastic," the constitution, the greater the room for interpretive disagreement. In the latter case, the opportunity for courts to "read into" the Constitution new meanings, pronounce revised understandings, and declare new holdings of what is constitutional are substantial. Although the judicialization of politics has occurred throughout the democratic world, no other courts possess the power and authority of those in the United States.

Courts, though not exclusive arbiters of constitutional meaning, remain the most authoritative. Presidents and lawmakers regularly offer their interpretations of what the Constitution says, and how courts ought to rule. They occasionally seek to constrain judicial actions through tools such as funding, appointments, and jurisdictional and impeachment powers. Moreover, courts lack the executive's coercive arms. Without a police force, army, or bureaucracy to enforce decisions, judicial legitimacy relies on other branches' cooperation and public respect to see court rulings implemented.

But the judicial process, if not necessarily partisan or politicized, is inherently political. As Tocqueville famously observed, "scarcely any political question arises in the United States that is not resolved sooner or later into a judicial question." By the same token, since no rulings are neutral in their effects, scarcely any judicial question is completely put to bed by a decision, and not sooner or later politicized to reemerge. There exists a *Groundhog Day* quality to political issues in the United States. Persistent public divisions and multiple avenues for their redress ensure that issues that elsewhere are "settled" as public policy remain the subjects of ongoing political and judicial conflict and resurface rather than disappear.

The result has produced two constitutional cultures in a judicial polarization over interpretation that reflects and reinforces partisan polarization. Warring philosophies, broadly though not fully corresponding to progressive and conservative readings, employ heavy artillery: "originalists" or "textualists" against "living constitutionalists" or "non-originalists." At its simplest, originalists believe the Constitution should be interpreted as originally written. It is illegitimate to substitute judges' values for those who wrote relevant articles, clauses and what the law plainly says. By contrast, living constitutionalists think courts should interpret the Constitution flexibly, applying what it means to current circumstances.

Although they agree that there exists a constitutional tree and worry that if poorly tended its branches will yield bitter fruit, the choice of approach is less legalistic than political. It is as much about policy and results as a neutral matter of process. This is not merely because it is a search for the meaning of constitutional clauses, but a profound disagreement on how best to go about discovering meaning. It's no accident that the divide here corresponds strongly with the electoral bases of the two parties, structured by opposing coalitions of "transformation" and "restoration" (Brownstein 2016). To the extent there ever was one, there no longer exists a constitutional orthodoxy on interpretation. Originalists and their opponents depict every judicial appointment as the inflection point in constitutional law. And, as Table 4.4 confirms, this is no esoteric disagreement among lawyers. The public is also split.

*Table 4.4* Public Split over Constitutional Interpretation (2014)

|  | What the Constitution Means in Current Times (Percent) | What the Constitution Meant as Originally Written (Percent) |
|---|---|---|
| Total | 49 | 46 |
| Republican | 29 | 69 |
| Democrat | 70 | 26 |
| Independent | 48 | 47 |
| Consistently conservative | 8 | 92 |
| Mostly conservative | 25 | 72 |
| Mixed | 47 | 46 |
| Mostly liberal | 70 | 25 |
| Consistently liberal | 83 | 14 |

Source: Data from Pew Research Center, "Americans divided on how the supreme court should interpret the constitution," July 31, 2014 www.pewresearch.org/fact-tank/2014/07/31/americans-divided-on-how-the-supreme-court-should-interpret-the-constitution/.

Note: Affirmative responses to the statement, "The supreme court should base rulings on what the constitution...".

To conservatives, the "Living Constitution" is an "Etch-a-Sketch" constitution unanchored by enduring principles. A document whose meaning can be creatively re-read according to the whims of the day is alive, but in the sense of an original constitution that has passed away and been reincarnated as something altogether different. The problem is not that this represents bad constitutional law, but that it is not constitutional law. It condemns the actual Constitution into irrelevance and replaces others' values – those who authored the document and the laws or actions held accountable to the higher law – with those of unelected judges making their own interpretations. For those who follow Dahl (2003) in lamenting the Constitution's democratic deficit, it is ironic that they champion an interpretive approach – the paradigmatic case of undemocratic decision-making by a "bevy of Platonic guardians": unelected, unaccountable judges.

On this reading, progressives' "virtual" constitution substitutes for the real one. Abandoning constitutional rigor for empowering courts legitimates the routine exercise of judicial license. It relegates elected parts of government to an afterthought, secondary to a judicial "super-legislature." Instead, living constitutionalists, by expanding the realm of the permissible from the plain language of the text to intentions, inferences, and principles, rob the document of meaning. And in reading provisions according to what most Americans prefer, they turn the Bill of Rights from an instrument *against* majority tyranny into one that expresses majoritarianism.

Take, for example, the Fourth Amendment, which prohibits "unreasonable searches and seizures." Does this mean that the government cannot collect meta-data about phone calls or e-mails to fight terrorism? The measure was never intended to preclude government surveillance but to ensure that government searches and seizures are "reasonable," a term that is deliberately vague. It considers government's need for information to fight crime and provide security as well as the risks of government overreaching. Crudely stated, sometimes government surveillance is reasonable and sometimes not. Drawing the line is the tough part.

To originalists, a "living" approach smacks less of a sophisticated understanding than constitutional philistinism. The only viable constitution is one that is followed; the constitution whose text is ignored is truly deceased. Progressive belief in adaptations is a pretext for judges imposing their values on the people, even when the people reject them. In contrast to breathing new life into a dead document, they desire ending the Living Constitution. As Justice Scalia delighted in noting, "It's not a living document. It's dead, dead, dead" (Tsiaperis 2013).

As a judicial philosophy, originalism offers a clear and elegant counterpoint to the judicial revolution steadily authored during the twentieth century. Politically, it offers a route to conservative policy outcomes. But to progressives, conservatives treat the Constitution as the equivalent of

No Clause Left Behind – every textual provision should be read with the same meaning it was commonly held to have when enacted. It ignores external realities, disregards contemporary social values, and offers a stunted conception of life. It compels an excessively narrow and rigid adherence to electoral means for achieving change that, while superficially attractive in appealing to democratic values and restrictions on judicial license, is effectively an endorsement of pure majoritarianism.

That amounts to originalist homicide of the "Living Constitution." Except where the case before the courts is unequivocally addressed by constitutional clauses as understood when they were adopted, no creative reading of the document is permissible. All modifications to the original document require nothing less than a formal constitutional amendment. Even then, if – say – the Fourteenth Amendment promise of "equality before the law" was not meant *when adopted* to apply to racial segregation in Washington, DC, or to same-sex couples seeking marriage, then it cannot be so interpreted in the twenty-first century.

To progressives, conservatives often speak of interpretive rigor while seeking constitutional rigor mortis. Even pragmatic conservatives reject originalism as too restrictive:

> Eighteenth-century guys, however smart, could not foresee the culture, technology, etc., of the 21$^{st}$ century. Which means that the original Constitution, the Bill of Rights, and the post–Civil War amendments (including the 14$^{th}$), do not speak to today … The Supreme Court treats the Constitution like it is authorizing the court to create a common law of constitutional law, based on current concerns, not what those 18$^{th}$-century guys were worrying about. In short, let's not let the dead bury the living.
>
> (Posner 2016)

Figures such as Justice Stephen Breyer (2005) prefer instead to champion "active liberty." His principles for interpreting what he tellingly termed "our democratic Constitution" include an expansive conception of democratic freedom and political participation. The Framers vested sovereignty with the people, the right to legislate resting with every member of the political community – a clear echo of the Jeffersonian belief in each generation's right and responsibility to revise constitutional order to fit the times. To behave otherwise is not only to freeze public policy but infantilize political life. Instead, as historian Carol Berkin (2003: 8) contended:

> the Constitution invites us to expand its parameters, reinterpret its duties and powers, add to its constituencies, and thus to preserve its fundamental principle of a government of laws rather than men and its fundamental guarantees of rights and liberties to its citizens.

Originalists worship the Constitution with quasi-religious fervor. But endorsing originalism would be to conserve the Constitution in a time-warp, unable to evolve with the society it was intended to order. Like a secular version of the Old Testament or Salafi brands of Islam, originalism offers an austere, hardline, and uncompromising take on the canonical work of American faith. Had it prevailed during earlier decades, the outcome would have been a compassionless constitutionalism that could not survive intact. Advances in civil rights and liberties, and protections for minority groups, that are now taken for granted, could not have occurred – or would have taken even longer than they did. Were courts to embrace originalism now, basic safeguards would be reversed through judicial diktat, since terms such as "privacy" do not appear in the document, much less clearly apply to issues such as contraception, reproductive rights, and sexuality. This is a vulgar constitutionalism that the Framers themselves would surely have rejected as impermissibly restrictive – so rigid as to threaten the survival of the Constitution it purports to preserve.

As judicial philosophies, both approaches have merits and flaws. Living constitutionalism appeals to common sense and rightly highlights how the Constitution protected values as well as rights. In this sense, the approach is validated by the Ninth Amendment, that "The enumeration in the Constitution, of certain rights, shall not be construed to deny or disparage others retained by the people." That certain rights were specified explicitly in 1791 did not mean this was an exhaustive list for all time. Others could be found. But the Ninth Amendment has rarely been used by courts precisely because of its vagueness as to what "undiscovered" rights await revelation.

"Originalism" has appeal. It is not monolithic and admits of important distinctions in how to read the Constitution. Nonetheless, these are heavily weighted toward a parsimonious, narrow reading. The case that there exists a "plain meaning" is seductive in its elegant simplicity. But it is bedeviled by problems. The Framers were not of one accord: many clauses were compromises. The danger also exists than in delegitimizing an evolutionary approach to interpretation, originalism leaves no recourse to discrete minorities that are consistently outvoted by majorities. And as an approach that only gained serious influence from the 1980s, originalism is not ancient but quite original itself. To critics, both sides offer elaborate rationalizations for more elementary political and moral positions (Posner 2008: 324–346).

Regardless of how valid that criticism may be, the debate over interpretation is clearly fused with one over politics. The stakes are such in a polarized and politicized era that progressives and conservatives share a preoccupation with results. In confirmation battles for judicial appointments, they support Justices who will reach the correct results or oppose those who reach the wrong results. Litmus tests are therefore required for nominees. Confirmation hearings become a game of "gotcha," with questioners trying to trip up the other side's nominees and nominees refusing to reveal the only thing their inquisitors truly care about: how they would rule in cases likely to come before the Court. The impression given to the public is that if you can secure enough judges on the right courts, then you have won the argument and effectively changed the law of the land. But if five Supreme Court justices strike down your team's play to establish a fresh interpretation of the Federal Government's powers under the Constitution, you have lost the argument. A corollary is that when decisions disappoint, we chalk it up to the Court's "partisan leanings"; when they please, we praise the majority jurists for their legal wisdom.

Unfortunately for those partisans seeking clarity, both sides are partially right. The fact that Americans are so closely divided makes the task of crafting a consensus to resolve disputes daunting. The problem is that both sides are guilty of selective fidelity to their own approaches: "situational constitutionalism." Although the conservative case can sometimes tilt at imaginary enemies, the critique strikes an undeniable chord. On issues such as capital punishment and abortion, the Court has intervened controversially on matters that are often regarded as matters for the states. On both, the federal judiciary got ahead of public opinion and its interventions politicized and nationalized the issues, sparking a fierce political backlash that lasted for decades.

The contrast with one of the more controversial recent judicial interventions – marriage equality – is striking. In this instance, the Court found itself catching up with, not getting ahead of, public opinion. But the decision spoke directly to the debate over interpretation. Read in values terms, "equal protection" implied that same-sex couples seeking a legal union with the same benefits as a heterosexual couple could not be denied that right, whether by federal or state governments. Read in the plain language of 1868 – as it was understood then – it was never intended and, given the morals of the time, clearly did not, apply to same-sex couples. Somewhere in the 147-year gap between then and the *Obergefell v. Hodges* ruling resided the truth about marriage equality.

As that landmark ruling illustrates, the difficulty in resolving constitutional cases centers on three related concerns.

First, popular discussion of constitutional guarantees often fails to note that no enumerated rights or powers are absolute and unlimited. However broad, protections for freedom of assembly or against unreasonable searches and seizures are relative. They require balancing against competing claims. Civil rights and liberties, though correctly seen as constraints on government, also conflict with each other. For example, even within the terms of a single amendment, such as the First, distinct freedoms – of speech and religion – often collide.

Second, the relative strength of demands for judicial intervention must be weighed against the default assumption of legitimacy accorded action by the elected branches – unless there is a blatantly egregious violation of the Constitution. As a presumptive matter in a representative democracy, it is the judiciary that needs to justify striking down laws, not the Congress and states that need to justify passing them. Striking down federal laws, and establishing new precedents, should be done carefully and sparingly.

Third, constitutional interpretation encompasses different types of issues: those where no constitutional clause exists that expressly addresses the matter in hand (such as on abortion); those where a relevant clause exists but its application is vigorously contested (such as the Second Amendment); and those where different clauses exist in tension (such as the amendments relevant to capital punishment: the 5th, 6th, 8th and 14th). Applying these concerns to matters of literal life and death, the inherent difficulty of interpretation, and its interplay with broader democratic influences, becomes manifest.

## Life and Death as Public Policy: Constitutional Dimensions

Hard cases often make for bad law. But thinking over some controversial issues can illuminate the integral but exceptionally difficult task of constitutional interpretation and its relationship to broader political and social dynamics. As the divides over abortion, firearms, and capital punishment illustrate, the Constitution can address but not fully resolve issues of life and death over which there is no moral consensus.

### Abortion

The United States is comparatively unusual in allowing unelected and unaccountable judges to determine abortion policy. Although every state law is a matter for state legislatures, and many states have held popular referenda on abortion, the key decisions establishing the limits within which states can act are set by the Supreme Court (Perry 2009). *Roe v. Wade* (1973) and its companion case, *Doe v. Bolton* (1973), polarized politics and helped make the issue stubbornly resistant to resolution, for three reasons.

First was the highly emotive and distinctive nature of the issue. Almost all judicial rulings deal either with conflicts between branches and tiers of government or between the individual and the state. But the abortion issue adds a third party. The morality of terminating what some see as unborn life and others as fetal tissue, the autonomy of the woman over her own body, and the relative claims of each against the state vastly complicate and dramatize the issue.

Second, *Roe*'s scope was national rather than narrow, a recipe for resentment and reaction. In 1973, most states had highly restrictive abortion laws that the ruling struck down. To its opponents, judicial fiat replaced deliberation and democratic legitimacy. *Obergefell*, legalizing marriage equality nationwide, was also sweeping, yet it produced almost no political reaction. The contrast could hardly be starker. Public opinion had changed with astonishing speed prior to *Obergefell* (Klarman 2014). The decision seized upon an existing social trend, allowing the Court to ratify rather than challenge public views. But while some states were lifting restrictions before *Roe*, the Justices were well ahead of where the public had reached on reproductive matters.

Third, the substance of the ruling was highly contentious. Justice White, in his dissenting opinion, described *Roe* as "an exercise in raw judicial power." The absence of a compelling constitutional rationale in *Roe* was striking. There was no obvious basis in the Constitution's text, structure, or history – or in embryology – for its trimester policy. The term "right to privacy" or "privacy" did not exist in the Constitution explicitly but was read into this through successive decisions that culminated in *Roe*. Subsequently, the Justices moved the goalposts a little, shifting to whether restrictions placed an "undue burden" on the exercise of the termination right and arguing that *Roe* was established precedent (Devins 2008–2009). Again, by comparison, while some dissenting Justices, including John Roberts, condemned the marriage equality ruling in 2015, there was at least a substantive basis to the majority decision.

Almost five decades after *Roe*, abortion remains controversial. In January 2018, the US Senate failed to pass a twenty-week abortion ban bill. Requiring 60 votes to proceed, the vote failed by 51–46. But Mississippi enacted the nation's toughest state law, with a ban on abortions at fifteen weeks, in March 2018, in the hope that the ensuing legal challenge would encourage federal courts to prohibit abortions before a fetus is viable.

That is unlikely unless and until the composition of the courts change. Reproductive rights are embedded in law and practice. The Supreme Court created a legal regime more liberal than the national consensus in 1973 but that regime has achieved broad support. According to a May 2017 poll, 78 percent of Americans believed abortion should be legal in some or most circumstances (Gallup 2017). Many social conservatives still favor a constitutional amendment against abortion, like the one in Ireland (where the eighth amendment to the Irish constitution, enacted in 1983, gave equal rights to the life of the mother and her unborn child [until a national referendum overwhelmingly approved repeal in May 2018]). Given public preferences, this seems impossible. But the activists who return to Washington each year to protest *Roe* during the March for Life are not alone. In the same 2017 Gallup poll, 49 percent of Americans felt abortion is "morally wrong" (43 percent found it "morally acceptable"). Just 29 percent believed abortion should be legal in all circumstances. As with other activities, from committing adultery to consuming sexually explicit materials, Americans do not wish to criminalize activities of which they morally disapprove: the essence of classical liberalism.

Several states have nonetheless enacted abortion restrictions, such as requiring parental notification or consent for minors, mandating ultrasounds, and directing that providers obtain visiting privileges at local hospitals. Abortion rights groups see such efforts as undermining the legal right to abortion by stealth. By 5–3, the Supreme Court in *Whole Woman's Health v. Hellerstedt* (2016), deemed some of these requirements – such as mandating that abortion clinics meet standards for ambulatory surgical centers – unnecessary, expensive, and an attempt to limit abortion access rather than provide safety to women. But, in the absence of a constitutional amendment, anti-abortion forces still want *Roe* overturned. If it were, the issue would return to the states. The Center for Reproductive Rights estimates that roughly twenty-one states would outlaw abortion while it would remain legal in probably twenty others. Others would reach the sort of compromise adopted by most European nations: legal in the first months, difficult thereafter. Broadly, that is what most Americans – who are not absolutists on either side of the debate – support.

### Guns

Few provisions are more emblematic of the controversies generated by the Constitution than the Second Amendment: "A well-regulated Militia, being necessary to the security of a free State, the right of the people, to keep and bear Arms, shall not be infringed." The twenty-seven words represent the marquee example of a constitutional right that is central to American society but vexatious. For many, the provision expresses American individualism and self-reliance while providing "freedom's insurance policy" to law-abiding citizens: the right to self-defense. For others, it is synonymous with a nation awash in firearms and the associated gun violence that tragically but regularly punctuates American life. Nothing better confirms the Constitution locking America in a deep freeze. Rather than firearms regulation being debated in terms of a rational cost-benefit analysis, it is mired in a short, badly worded, and ambiguous amendment ratified in 1791. Where democracies such as the United Kingdom and Australia responded to public opinion in the aftermath of mass firearms atrocities and tightened their regulatory regimes, the United States remains stubbornly resistant to doing so – even though most Americans have long supported stronger federal gun control (Cook and Goss 2014; Spitzer 2018).

Gun control proponents insist that the first clause links gun rights with the need for a militia. Since no state has the militia that existed in the 1780s (when all able-bodied men were subject to call-up and expected to bring their own weapons), this collective right is redundant and wider curbs on firearms are legal. By contrast, gun rights advocates insist that the second half of the sentence is crystal clear in its application to individual citizens. So, exactly what this provision means is unclear. The first clause implies the right can be regulated, presumably by Congress. But the right cannot itself be infringed. Since, however, no constitutional rights are absolute, what would count as infringement? State firearms laws vary dramatically from the more restrictive in California and New York to the more permissive in Alabama and Arizona.

The stereotype of a static constitution could not be less true. Constitutional law on the Second Amendment's meaning is younger than an iPhone. Ironically, the same charge has been levelled at the Supreme Court over guns as abortion: it created a right not previously recognized: "The Second Amendment, adopted in 1791 with the rest of the Bill of Rights, remained a dead letter as a matter of formal constitutional law until 217 years later, on June 26, 2008" (Cole 2016: 97). Prior to the 5–4 ruling in *District of Columbia v. Heller* (2008), the Court had never invalidated any legislation under the Second Amendment. Nor had the individual right to gun ownership ever been constitutionally recognized. Some laws had been struck down on federalism grounds: *United States* v. *Lopez* (1995), striking down the federal Gun Free School Zones Act (1990); and *Printz v. United States* (1997) on Brady Law background checks. But *Heller* (and *McDonald v. Chicago* [2010], which applied the individual right to the states) upheld an individual right to own and carry guns for hunting, self-defense, or any compelling reason (Tribe and Matz 2014: 154–184). *Heller* allowed prohibition of "dangerous and unusual weapons," those "not typically possessed by law-abiding citizens for lawful purposes." Scalia, who wrote the majority opinion, also held that the militia clause, announcing the law's purpose, could not be used to restrict its scope.

Gun rights have proven less contentious than abortion because the existence of a constitutional provision of relevance was never in popular contention: most Americans – even those who oppose gun ownership – believed it guaranteed an individual right to gun ownership even before *Heller* was decided. But what is striking about the jurisprudence on guns is threefold.

First, as with most controversial Court rulings, the disagreements were intense not only because of their consequences but also as a result of the contested rationale. Although Yale law professor Reva Siegel, referencing the former celebrity National Rifle Association (NRA) president, claimed *Heller* had "more to do with Charlton Heston than with James Madison," (Lepore 2010) both the majority and dissenting opinions adopted an "originalist" search for historical evidence. Moreover, as Scalia's moderate and cautious majority opinion clearly stated:

> Nothing in our opinion should be taken to cast doubt on longstanding prohibitions on the possession of firearms by felons and the

mentally ill, or laws forbidding the carrying of firearms in sensitive places such as schools and government buildings, or laws imposing conditions and qualifications on the commercial sale of arms.

As Cole (2016) notes, the NRA had primed the decision by lobbying shrewdly at state level for decades. *Heller* effectively ratified the extensive existing protections for gun ownership in state constitutions – most of which already recognized an individual right – and highly permissive state laws, such as those allowing concealed or open carry of firearms. But Scalia's opinion made clear that nothing in the Second Amendment precluded "common sense" regulations. Moreover, the Court in *McDonald* treated the Second Amendment as essentially codifying a preexisting "fundamental right of each person to possess the means of self-defense in the home." The court has called this protection a cornerstone of "our system of ordered liberty" – one that preceded the Second Amendment and would remain even without it, embedded explicitly in the Fifth and Fourteenth Amendments' protections of "liberty."

Second, but related, what is instructive is that *Heller* and *McDonald* did not end debate. Subsequently, a raft of litigation arose that required lower courts to offer interpretations on more tailored questions. For example, the Second, Fourth, Seventh, and District of Columbia federal circuit courts upheld the constitutionality of bans on "assault" weapons and large-capacity magazines. Far from striking down laws and regulations or nationalizing them, courts have mostly upheld numerous firearms regulations as not infringing the individual right to bear arms.

Moreover, the Supreme Court has declined to review such lower court rulings. The reluctance reflects the fact that, generally, only blue states enact restrictive laws, and consequently, few conflicts arise among regional circuit courts of appeal for the justices to settle. For example, in 2017, it declined to review a challenge to California's ban on carrying a loaded handgun in public. In 2018, when the Supreme Court by 8–1 declined in *Silvester v. Becerra* to review a challenge to California's ten-day waiting period law, Justice Thomas in dissent described the "right to bear arms" as a "disfavored right" and a "constitutional orphan" due to the Court's "general failure to afford the Second Amendment the respect due an enumerated constitutional right" (Barnes 2018). But even in "red" Texas, the Court in 2014 refused to take a challenge to a state law barring eighteen- to twenty-year-olds from buying guns. Just as *Roe* did not enable every woman who wanted a termination to obtain one, and its reversal would not recriminalize abortion nationwide, so, as Keck (2014: 250) notes, "…gun rights advocates have won a sea change in constitutional doctrine, but the practical policy impact of this doctrinal change has so far been limited."

Third, the United States, with 4.4 percent of the world's population, has approximately 48 percent of the world's civilian-owned guns and the highest homicide-by-firearm rate of developed nations. In comparative terms, what remains striking is not so much how much gun rights and gun control groups differ but how far both are distant to the dominant lens by which firearms regulation is viewed in most nations. While some ban private ownership of handguns (the United Kingdom, Japan) and others (Germany) require psychiatric tests of any-one under twenty-five seeking to purchase a gun, in 2017, Congress revoked an Obama-era regulation that would have made it harder for mentally ill people to buy guns. Toward the end of the year, the House approved reciprocity legislation that would force every state to honor concealed-carry permits, so Louisiana residents could pack heat in Los Angeles or New York City.

Gun control has long been considered the third rail of politics in Washington. The popularity of firearms among a sizeable minority of Americans, their constitutional protection under state and federal laws, the identification of a substantial political sub-constituency as "pro-Second Amendment" (Bishin 2009) and the institutional clout of gun rights groups together pose a formidable quartet of influences sustaining relatively lightly regulated legal access to firearms. But for those urging a second look at the Second Amendment, it is less the constitutional dimension that precludes the stronger federal regulations that most Americans favor than the outsized institutional influence of the NRA (Cook and Goss 2014; Spitzer 2015, 2018). As one Second Amendment "biographer" noted on the relationship between ballots and bullets, Americans can be true to the Amendment and the Constitution's spirit by recognizing that "the ability to make and set gun and other policies through the messy, imperfect democratic process is the ultimate 'right of the people'" (Waldman 2014: 177). The 800-city "March for Our Lives" on March 25, 2018 offered one powerful example of young Americans recognizing the wisdom of electoral routes to regulatory change over repeal of a widely-respected provision in the Bill of Rights.

## Capital Punishment

Capital punishment penalizes those convicted by judges and juries of cer-tain classes of crime by the state killing them. In 2018, the death penalty was legal in thirty-one states (and for the Federal Government and US military) and illegal in nineteen states. According to the Death Penalty Information Center, there were 2,817 prisoners on Death Row in July 2017. Executions had declined from a high of ninety-eight in 1999 to twenty-three in 2017. Since 1977, inmates have been executed by lethal injection, electrocution, the gas chamber, hanging and by firing squad. Between 1973 and 2017, 161 persons were released from Death Row after evidence of their innocence was discovered. While capital punish-ment is illegal in all EU states, "The reason the US is a death-penalty outlier is that it is, in one sense, too democratic ... [and] closer to having government by the people for the people" (Pinker 2018: 210).

The death penalty offers an example where four competing constitutional clauses clash. The Fifth Amendment ("No person shall...be deprived of life, liberty, or property, without due process of law...") and the Fourteenth Amendment ("No State shall...deprive any person of life, liberty, or property without due process of law...") together imply that capital punishment is permissible. Both provide for the taking of life provided due process has been followed. But has due process occurred in every capital case? If the penalty is found to be disproportionately imposed on a particular demographic – such as African Americans – does that indicate that it is discriminatory? Or must discriminatory intent be proven in each individual death row case? The Eighth Amendment states, "Excessive bail shall not be required, nor excessive fines imposed, nor cruel and unusual punishment inflicted." Are certain methods cruel and unusual? Or is the penalty cruel and unusual by definition? The Sixth Amendment requires that the "...accused shall enjoy the right to a speedy and public trial, by an impartial jury...and to have the Assistance of Counsel for his defense." Has an impartial jury of a citizen's peers adjudicated, and has adequate legal advice been provided in every capital trial? All these constitutional factors require weighing against one another before an evaluation of constitutionality can be reached.

In *Trop v. Dulles* (1958), the Court ruled that the Eighth Amendment's "cruel and unusual punishment" clause "must draw its meaning from the evolving standards of decency that mark the progress of a maturing society." That seems sensible. But if the clause is to be read according to what public opinion prefers, it is no safeguard against majoritarianism, but its instrument. (As it happened, the public was for the death penalty back then, so even that proved an illusory hope for abolitionists seeking nationwide prohibition, with the Court concluding that, "the death penalty has been employed throughout our history and, in a day when it is still widely accepted, it cannot be said to violate the constitutional concept of cruelty.") In *Furman v. Georgia* (1972), a divided Court ruled capital punishment unconstitutional by a 5-4 majority: Justices Brennan and Marshall argued it was in principle "cruel and unusual punishment": Douglas highlighted racial and class discrimination; White pointed to its infrequent use; and Stewart focused on its arbitrariness, noting "These death sentences are cruel and unusual in the same way that being struck by lightning is cruel and unusual." But after a public backlash, in *Gregg v. Georgia* (1976), the Court reinstated the death penalty as constitutional providing separate trials for guilt and sentencing existed in state law.

The Court has since chipped away at the death penalty architecture in multiple ways, ruling that states may not execute people with intellectual disabilities (*Atkins v. Virginia* [2002]), juveniles (*Roper v.*

*Simmons* [2005]), or perpetrators of crimes other than murder (*Kennedy v. Louisiana* [2008]). Although it has yet to accept Justice Breyer's invitation to revisit the core issue of capital punishment's constitutionality, many believe it is only a matter of time before the Court does so and strikes the penalty down once and for all.

For traditionalists, the Constitution clearly allows for a death sentence and some heinous crimes exist for which life imprisonment is insufficient punishment. Retribution is sufficient justification and federalism means that states can choose whether to use the penalty. But progressives view "state-sanctioned revenge" as constitutionally impermissible, arguing that the deterrent effect is minimal: States that have the death penalty consistently have *higher* murder rates than non-death-penalty states. Moreover, alternative punishments are available at lesser cost, arbitrary sentencing and enforcement still exists, the measure is racially discriminatory, and wrongful execution cannot be precluded (Perry 2009). From the later 1990s, trends of declining sentences and executions point in an abolitionist direction. Seven states have repealed the penalty over the past decade, sixteen others have moratoria, and thirty have not carried out an execution in five years. Popular support also declined below 50 percent – for the first time in almost half a century – in 2016. As all this illustrates, constitutional protections are inseparable from public practice.

On all three of these emotive issues, the interpretive complexity is self-evident, not least since abstract parchment guarantees must be reconciled with real-world practice. Former Supreme Court Justice John Paul Stevens (2014) proposed concise five word "solutions" to the risk of killing innocents by altering the Eighth Amendment to read, "Excessive bail shall not be required, nor excessive fines imposed, nor cruel and unusual punishments *such as the death penalty* inflicted" (123). He also advised changing the Second Amendment to read, "A well-regulated Militia, being necessary to the security of a free State, the right of the people to keep and bear Arms *when serving in the Militia* shall not be infringed" (132). The former would ban capital punishment nationwide and the latter "return" the Second Amendment to the intent of its authors. (In March 2018, he went on to call for the Second Amendment's repeal.) With no little humility, Stevens proclaimed that the soundness of his proposals would become increasingly evident to his fellow Americans and "ultimately each will be adopted" (13). Yet, bizarrely, he made no mention of how difficult achieving an amendment is, nor of how a nation that remains far from being abolitionist on the death penalty or remotely prohibitionist about firearms is likely to reach the necessary supermajorities.

The most basic choice facing judges is how assertive – or "counter-majoritarian" – they will be against other branches. Will they defer or press their own vision against the president, Congress, or a state? The choice is not between devilish activists and angelic umpires but distinct approaches. Moreover, as the life and death controversies illustrate, the court of public opinion has a major role to play in shaping the differing ways that politics and law interact. Whether a judge aims to apply the law as it was understood at the time it was enacted or by considering the Constitution's underlying moral principles, it is prudent to be careful about claims of judicial supremacy or the Constitution hanging by a thread. Although Posner offered a verdict on the Roberts Court in its infancy, it remains essentially sound:

> ... the Court has been moving rightward from the Warren Court, and, as expected, its decisions have been more conservative than they would have been had all the replacements been as liberal as the average member of the Warren Court ... The expansion of rights brought about by the Warren Court, and to a more limited extent by the Burger Court, has ceased; retrenchment is in the air. But there is no indication of a wholesale rejection of precedents that most of the current Justices may wish had never been created.
>
> (Posner 2008: 55–56)

## Conclusion

Americans look to the Constitution for inspiration but not necessarily instruction. Law-bound societies disagree by reference to the same text. But the inconvenient constitutional truth is that dispute over its meaning is unavoidable, depending on whether "the text," what "the drafters meant" or what "the reader understands" is the chosen standard. Interpretation interweaves history, law, and politics. And while legal formalists proclaim themselves preoccupied with process, not policy, this is disingenuous. Selecting constitutional philosophies is inseparable from the political beliefs animating the choice.

Constitutionalism is not a zero-sum game, but there is some purchase to the argument that what often prevails is "outcome-based constitutionalism": a disintegration of the norms that valued not just *what* happened, but *how* it happened (Weiner 2012), and the use of constitutional provisions as political weapons. Interpreting the Constitution "the way it was meant to be," as President Trump termed it, begs the question. The Constitution often has no plain meaning. Like America's meaning, or what it means to be American, reasonable citizens are divided about how to read the Constitution. Even on issues of whether the Constitution "follows the flag" to apply wherever US officials exercise jurisdiction – such as Guantanamo Bay in Cuba – the notion that constitutional rights confront territorial limits is controversial (Raustiala 2009). It is not, however, the Constitution's fault that disagreement is frequently disagreeable.

As Amar (2012) argues, there exists a complementary relationship between the Constitution's written and unwritten components. Far from endangering constitutional order, the interplay represents an enduring strength. Alongside the elected branches, amendments and interpretation have enabled change in constitutional substance to parallel continuity in structure in a balance that is broadly right between formal revision and interpretation. There is merit in maintaining the appearance of a changeless foundation. In Madisonian terms, it accords the Constitution necessary reverence. But it is perhaps too demanding to obtain the supermajorities needed, and invidious that such a small proportion of Americans can deny change supported by overwhelming majorities. The triple lock suggested here would seem a sensible (but politically unlikely) refinement.

Having such a rigid Constitution makes interpretation inevitable, judicial rulings consequential, and judicial politics controversial. Politicization is unavoidable, even if partisanship is not. That also channels public energies toward unelected officials as agents of change. In a democracy, that is a peculiar, acquired taste. But it is salutary that ordinary Americans can transform laws through advocacy outside as well as within federal courts and pioneer reform from below as much as "heroic" leaders have shaped change from above (Cole 2016).

That said, if the judiciary is not to serve as a constitutional catapult, launching Americans to an unknown destination, the courts should generally defer to elected branches. Most Court decisions are nonetheless "legitimate" less because they are impeccable in interpretation, but because they are "reasonable" and can draw on different rationales: historical lessons; the institutional competence of competing branches; the costs of error; and obvious defects in democracy meriting remedy (Roosevelt 2006).

But we should not deify judges and lawyers. As Vermeule (2016) noted, judges increasingly allow, and show, deference to the administrative agencies of the regulatory state, accepting their greater democratic legitimacy and superior technical expertise on matters from climate change to biotechnology. Judges are also influenced by the discretion they are afforded. If lawmakers articulate clear policy preferences in legislation, judges tend to interpret strictly the plain meaning of the law. But if statutes are imprecise or unclear, legislation allows judges to reach decisions based on their own ideological values and policy preferences (Randazzo and Waterman 2015).

Constitutionalism preserves the founding values while adapting to change. It may not please absolutists and placate purists on either partisan bench, whether proclaiming fidelity to the Founders in perpetuity or redrafting the Constitution to every new majoritarian preference. But it fits a constitutional framework that was animated by an array of intentions and pays due deference to the reality that no constitution is self-executing. To succeed, the Constitution cannot sacrifice popular legitimacy. Logically, if frustratingly, that means that while public opinion is divided, some conflicts can only be managed, not resolved. Yet by allowing for its own revision, the fourth condition of an effective constitution is fully met.

## Summary

- The amendment process and constitutional interpretation are together integral, though distinct, parts of a healthy constitutional ecosystem allowing the means of its own adaptation. Courts are the most authoritative, but not the exclusive, arbiters of constitutional meaning and practice.
- Constitutional amendments are rare, difficult to enact, and the "rigid" requirements would benefit from adopting a more Australian- or Canadian-style "double" or even triple majority system.
- In many respects amendments represent the beginning, not the end, of change as they too are open to interpretation and are sometimes less important to constitutional change than judicial rulings, accumulated precedents, and the actions of governing institutions that set new conventions, norms, and laws.
- Originalists and Living Constitutionalists differ over constitutional interpretation but – as cases such as reproductive rights, gun rights, and capital punishment illustrate – the relationship of interpretation to the other branches of government and public opinion is complex, dynamic, and fluid, not static.

# Conclusion
## Cults, Crises, Conventions, and Crossroads

(W)e must never forget that it is a constitution we are expounding ... a constitution, intended to endure for ages to come, and consequently, to be adapted to the various crises of human affairs.

*McCulloch v. Maryland* (1819)

Liberty lies in the hearts of men and women; when it dies there, no constitution, no law, no court can save it; no constitution, no law, no court can even do much to help it. The spirit of liberty is the spirit which is not too sure that it is right; the spirit of liberty is the spirit which seeks to understand the minds of other men and women; the spirit of liberty is the spirit which weighs their interests alongside its own without bias.

Judge Learned Hand, "The Spirit of Liberty" (1944)

The US Constitution remains America's North Star. Far from being "frozen" or "radically defective," it serves the nation well. Although it has taken an eon to begin achieving its promise, the Constitution meets the four prerequisites for effectiveness: providing a stable framework for government by channeling conflict into everyday politics; allowing the expression of majority preferences while safeguarding individual rights and liberties; ensuring the peaceful transfer of power; and permitting its own revision. That bar for success may seem comparatively low to some. But from the personalized rule of authoritarian regimes to the collapsed central authorities of failed and failing states, it is one that relatively few other constitutions clearly, fully, and consistently meet even now.

Speculating about a better US Constitution is an endlessly fascinating pastime, despite discussion tending to veer unproductively between hopeless idealism and fatalistic cynicism. Reforms that mend, rather than end, problematic features of the existing design are highly desirable, even if such modernization remains politically unlikely: ending equal state representation in the Senate (most importantly), a line-item veto, new presidential eligibility conditions, a proportional state electoral vote, judicial term limits and mandatory retirement, and new amendment requirements. But even without these, far from being terminally ill, the republic is very much alive. This defense therefore concludes its case for enduring soundness on four final themes: the constitution "cult"; constitutional "crisis"; the problems posed by a new convention; and the possibilities of American renewal absent constitutional rewrites.

## Founders Chic: The Founders versus the People?

To some, the tragedy of the US Constitution is all too clear. Americans often seem to exist in an intellectual and political bubble of their own myopic making. Fetishizing the Constitution as a sacred text second to none explains much of what troubles politics. Constitutional blind faith leaves citizens approaching policy dilemmas with eyes wide shut. Founder-worship distorts public life, obscures the depth of contemporary problems, and oversimplifies available alternatives. Unreflective reverence to an outdated text precludes rational evaluation, amounting to a cult of the Constitution.

Cults are always best avoided and unthinking veneration unwise. No doubt, the Constitution is unusual, to the point of being unique, in its iconic status. There is also something distinctive to debates that ostentatiously indulge "Founders chic" and even express this – albeit with unmistakable ambivalence – in bestselling musicals (*Hamilton*). But there is little evidence that such esteem impedes substantive policy discussions. The Constitution is a prism, not a prison. Americans do not think the Founders have all the answers, not least since they were so divided in their own views. Jefferson, Madison *et al.* receive fulsome praise but no legislation triumphs or vetoes fail as a result. On the contrary, whether deploring or "deplorable," pragmatically inclined Americans tend to display an internalized Madisonianism: they expect political leaders to achieve results. Popular frustration occurs when they do not. If anyone believes they have all the answers, it tends to be the politically active, not ordinary folk: activists, donors, "change agents" and organizers. Recent discontents – and their expression in successive election results – arguably reflect not so much failures of the ordinary citizen, but American elites.

That said, and despite the melancholy tone of recent debates about US "decline," twenty-first-century Americans have good reason to be pensive but not pessimistic about their republic. Rather than proclaim its decline and fall, the Constitution remains the nation's past, present, and future. Americans need neither to forget nor forgive their past to secure a compelling future. Intellectual laziness can mythologize, misrepresent, and propagandize the present as much as the past. A wider and wiser perspective suggests that, when many constitutions remain unworthy of the paper on which they are written, there remains good reason to view the United States one with substantial admiration. It has its faults, as does every system that aims to balance principles, values, and interests that exist in intractable tension. But judged either in its own or comparative terms, without militant moralism or ideological hubris, it functions well. The lure of comprehensive change is not seductive. Some reforms look less promising remedies than proponents imagine. Others, offering modest improvements, seem unlikely or impossible to achieve. That somewhat negative mark does not negate a design that still works for a vast, heterogeneous, and fractious society.

That case will displease conservatives standing athwart history, yelling "stop," and resisting the Constitution's steady transformation. Equally, it will frustrate radicals, reactionaries and romantics seeking a fundamental renegotiation of the American social contract, to whom there is an inherent "aside from that Mrs. Lincoln, how did you enjoy the play?" aspect to defending the Constitution while acknowledging its flaws. Such a defense can look anodyne against a design that seems to some increasingly quirky and quaint. But perhaps it is noteworthy that the Constitution has outlived all the authors of its multiple obituaries.

To many, the United States *is* the Constitution; all else is embellishment and detail. America's long trek toward a more perfect union begins and ends at its door. That may be exaggerated, but it captures something enduringly exceptional about the nation. If one isolates a single political value to prioritize, as Dahl (2003) did on its democratic credentials, then the Constitution will inevitably be found wanting. But that sets up a false standard. On the Preamble's more comprehensive goals, the historical record is impressive. On an accounting that marries majoritarianism to minority protections, the Constitution also holds up well over recent decades. But, ultimately, there exists a values dimension to assessing success that precludes a neutral set of metrics. For many, that is about a more equitable distribution of resources. For others, it concerns a more direct democracy. Reasonable people disagree on which values to prize and what outcomes to prefer.

Ultimately, the most powerful expression of the Constitution's continuing relevance is the unerring persistence with which Americans turn to its guarantees at times of political stress. What typically occurs is periodic: less the degeneration than regeneration of constitutionalism. From participation in citizen groups through an adversarial media to renewing the checks and balances of Congress and the courts, challenges within and outside the United States provoke responses that would gladden the Framers' hearts. American politics is deeply uncivil, as it always has been. But government remains limited, liberty vibrant, rights institutionalized, democracy resilient, and America still looks much like America: constantly changing within a framework of basic continuity. Fragmentation of power is the leading feature of the US political system and the Constitution still provides sturdy guardrails that inhibit even reckless drivers careering off the freeway.

Kissinger once said of the Islamic Republic of Iran that it had yet to decide its status as "a nation or a cause." But the same can be said, more positively, of the United States. That America encompasses both explains its episodic "disharmony" (Huntington 1981). Americans tell themselves that, although they are many, they are one. But persistent dis-agreements pervade politics, informed by the Founders' skepticism about human nature and Franklin's wisdom that the Framers had created "a republic, if you can keep it." That "if" has never lost its relevance, nor been more telling. Neither the constitutional design nor the operative or-der is flawless. But blaming the Constitution for what ails politics is like blaming the foundations of a house for its owners' choice of bad interior décor. No constitution, whether new or mature, can assure that political discourse is civil, rights are respected, and institutions operate smoothly. Only politics can. America may not always get the presidents it deserves but, as in all serious democracies, the Constitution and rule of law are only as good as the men and women who uphold them:

> The relative freedom which we enjoy depends on public opinion. The law is no protection. Governments make laws, but whether they are carried out, and how the police behave, depends on the general temper in the country. If large numbers of people are interested in freedom of speech, there will be freedom of speech, even if the law forbids it; if public opinion is sluggish, inconvenient minorities will be persecuted, even if laws exist to protect them.
>
> (Orwell 1945)

Democracies are bound by norms of tolerance and restraint, but these are often informal, unwritten habits. Unless institutions stand up, insurgents can ignore them, and democracies can collapse in a whimper rather than a bang. In the case of several South American states that "cut-and-pasted" the US text, constraints have proven weak (Billias 2009). A constitutional credibility gap is the result: texts that promise but never deliver. In the United States, however, constitutionalism is embedded in the national psyche: "The nation is culturally identified with that document, making it the premier symbol of unity for a diverse and contentious people" (Orren and Skowronek 2017: 8). But when politics frustrates reaching common understandings, and constitutional structures and rights are compro-mised, the Constitution cannot punch above its own weight and the "state finds itself, and the polity it governs, unhinged, unmoored, adrift."

The Constitution continues to set the rules of the American political game but its character, content and outcomes – the "moving pieces" – are another matter. The more we appreciate that, the less likely we are to mistakenly proclaim present discontents as unprecedented or cast the politics of the future as predetermined.

## Constitutional Pathologies: When Is a Constitutional Crisis Not a Constitutional Crisis?

Is American constitutionalism sustainable? On being sworn in as President on August 9, 1974, following Nixon's resignation, Gerald

Ford memorably declared: "Our long national nightmare is over. Our Constitution works; our great Republic is a Government of laws and not men." But that was a little disingenuous. As James Russell Lowell previously warned, the Constitution is not "a machine that would go of itself."

Historical amnesia and political apprehension periodically hamper navigation between the Scylla of constitutional alarmism and the Charybdis of constitutional complacency. More even than Nixon's excesses, whose rhythms it echoed, the Forty-fifth President generated extensive discussion among "Trumpologists" of a clear and present constitutional danger. To some, Trump's "I, the People" presidency posed a hydra-headed threat, from obstructing justice through threatening the Special Counsel, FBI, and Justice Department to blatantly violating the emoluments clause. To others, Trump was less an aberration than logical manifestation of a preexisting decay, one that amply justified the stern warnings of Bruce Ackerman (2013) about a debasement of government decades in the making.

The resiliency of the constitutional system underwent a serious stress test after January 2017. Yet we saw this movie before (mercifully few now recall *The End of America* [Wolf 2008], warning how the George W. Bush presidency paralleled Hitler, Mussolini, and Stalin's earlier paths to dictatorship). Feverish discussion about an America on the brink appeared at once partisan and paradoxical. The former, in that declarations that general faith in democratic principles had declined reflected Democrats' distrust and dislike of Trump as much as disinterested views on public attitudes to the Constitution (Edsall 2018). The latter, in that critics paradoxically regarded the Constitution as worth staunch defense yet so fragile as to be threatened with extinction by a figure they simultaneously ridiculed as a narcissistic know-nothing and national joke. Could the Constitution be so attractive and so weak? Could a monetized "chaos presidency" erode the edifice of constitutional order to create a "constitutional dictatorship"?

Controversy, like conflict, sells. The paths to academic riches or recognition as a "public intellectual" are rarely paved by praising rather than condemning existing arrangements, showing optimism rather than pessimism of the intellect, or emphasizing cock-up over conspiracy. Orwell (1994) perhaps went too far – commenting on British leftists, for whom the presence of US troops in the United Kingdom during the 1940s was not to fight the Nazis but suppress an English revolution – in declaring that "One has to belong to the intelligentsia to believe things like that: no ordinary man could be such a fool." But Eric Hoffer (1971) was surely right that, "The intellectual cannot operate at room temperature." Turning down the heat highlights three problems in the "crisis" prognosis.

The first is to distinguish where politics ends and constitutionalism begins, or what Posner and Vermeule (2008) termed "constitutional showdowns" from crises. The language of crisis is ubiquitous, promiscuously applied to conflicts great and small. But as Levinson and Balkin

(2009: 711) noted, "Conflict in a constitutional system is not a bug – it is a feature ... If a central purpose of constitutions is to make politics possible, constitutional crises mark moments when constitutions threaten to fail at this task" (707). Showdowns are about disagreements between branches over their constitutional powers that end in acquiescence by one branch and set a new constitutional precedent. Crises are about the legitimate uses of power. A genuine constitutional crisis requires a disagreement about constitutional obligations that is impossible to resolve via constitutional means:

> "Constitutional crisis," like "Russian collusion," is not a technical legal term with an agreed meaning. What's clear is that the temptation to define a constitutional crisis as any case in which the meaning of the Constitution is disputed deserves to be avoided. Virtually every clause of the Constitution is disputed, but crises are rare because Americans have shown they accept that ultimately the meaning will be settled by major government institutions.
>
> (Posner 2017)

The Civil War was the one undisputable constitutional crisis in American history: an existential conflict that posed a choice between alternatives allowing for no compromise. Slavery was either wrong and inconsistent with an order founded on the idea that all humans are created equal, or right, and the idea of human equality was not an essential feature of America. When the national government refused to recognize secession, resolution via constitutional means was exhausted. Because the South rejected the national government, neither federal courts nor Congress could resolve the dispute in a constitutional way. War ensued. But even in its midst, rather than postponing the 1864 presidential election, Lincoln submitted to popular accountability. Remarkably, since 1788, national elections have carried on in the United States every two years regardless (unlike, for example, the United Kingdom, which had no wartime general elections between 1911 and 1918 or 1935 and 1945).

This is not to deny that lesser but serious crises had constitutional dimensions. More generally, the Constitution's elaborate checks and balances (and norms giving these effect) could not prevent illiberal outcomes under multiple presidencies. Impropriety is frequently in the eye of the beholder, and partisan lenses have long encouraged equanimity to the erosion of constitutional equipoise. But, as Eric Posner (2017) argues, most conflicts did not rise to the level of crises because they were resolved through constitutional methods. Presidential elections in 1800 (won by Thomas Jefferson), 1824 (by John Quincy Adams), 1876 (by Rutherford B. Hayes), and 2000 (by George W. Bush) resulted in deadlocks due to legal or constitutional ambiguities about voting or voting procedures. But these were resolved by negotiation or (in 2000) the Supreme Court. In other cases – impeachments (Andrew Johnson, Bill Clinton) and near-impeachment (Nixon) – political crises existed. But for all the constitutional hardball, settlement was achieved through constitutional means. Conventional politics stopped while impeachment proceeded but government functioned normally.

That juxtaposition of abnormal politics and constitutionalism-as-usual highlights the second problem with the "crisis" thesis: distinguishing bark from bite. Trump animated "tyrannophobia" on multiple fronts. But the Constitution confronts the three strategies favored by supposed "populists in power" – state colonization, mass clientelism, and systematic repression – with powerful obstacles (Muller 2016; Singh 2017). Frum (2018) claimed the "spirit of thuggery, crookedness and dictatorship" had infiltrated the core of the US state. Levitsky and Ziblatt (2018) also identified four warning signs of an authoritarian leader undermining democratic well-being: a weak commitment to democratic rules; denying the legitimacy of an opponent; the toleration of violence; and a willingness to curb civil liberties. But in focusing on the individual leader they neglected the broader system. In the United States, the latter – an embedded constitutional order to which hundreds of millions subscribe – offers insurmountable barriers to anyone poisoning the constitutional well, creating a "mafia state," buying off clients, or establishing personalized rule.

Moreover, identifying actual violations of the Constitution, rather than rhetorical assaults, was tougher than critics commonly assumed. Trump boasted that "I alone can fix it," disparaged judges, impugned the media as enemies of the people, praised torture, and compared the intelligence community to Nazis. But, without minimizing his affronts and errors, he did not act on those statements:

> Unlike Franklin D. Roosevelt, he hasn't tried to pack the Supreme Court (not that Trump needs to). Unlike Barack Obama, he hasn't (yet) targeted journalists in leak investigations. Unlike George W. Bush, he hasn't actually taken a page from the Nazis by ordering the intelligence community to use coercive interrogation.
>
> (Posner 2018)

And however unwise and counterproductive many presidential actions – on immigration, trade, climate change, and diplomacy – these fell within his appropriate legal authority under the Constitution.

Some urged use of the Twenty-fifth Amendment in response. Eight presidents died in office and, after Eisenhower's heart attacks and JFK's assassination, the provision envisaged a president incapable of carrying on or conceding he was no longer physically or mentally able to govern. Section 4, adopted in 1967, empowers the vice-president and a majority of the cabinet to "declare the president unfit and install the vice-president as acting president." If the president challenges the declaration, Congress must decide the issue within twenty-one days. If both houses vote by a two-thirds majority that the president is "unable to discharge the powers and duties of his office," he is removed. As with "high crimes and misdemeanors," what constitutes sufficient impairment to warrant removal is vague. But to a nation riven by partisan divides, whose citizens view its establishment with disdain, an elite coup offered no more a solution to a wayward Washington than encouraging the "deep state" to revolt. As Glennon (2017) cautioned, "Those who would counter the illiberalism of Trump with the illiberalism of unfettered bureaucrats would do well to contemplate the precedent their victory would set."

This, in turn, raised the third problematic element with "crises." They invariably represent opportunities for constitutional reinvigoration rather than deconsolidation. Institutions push back. After Lincoln used emergency powers in unprecedented ways, Congress reacted against his successor, Johnson, overriding his vetoes fifteen times. FDR's seeking third and fourth terms violated a norm and – two years after his death – Republicans proposed the Twenty-second Amendment. Trump may have tilted the presidency away from *The West Wing* idyll of progressives towards *House of Cards, Veep* and *24* rolled into one. But the Forty-fifth President was less an incipient American dictator that an instigator of political pushback and constitutional reinvigoration.

Ultimately, Trump's encounter with the Constitution was only the most recent, dramatic, and important instance of his proving serially unfaithful after pledging a solemn oath of fidelity. The president's constitutional infidelity destabilized democracy, demoralized institutions, and disrespected the rule of law. Trump championed venality and vulgarity, debased the value of knowledge and expertise, and elevated the dubious overlap of celebrity and politics to a disturbing precedent. But though all this damaged, it did not endanger, the republic. As Michael Nelson (2018: 150) noted, Trump was "taught the hard way what most of the country has rejoiced in for more than two centuries: that the American constitutional system is well designed 'to counteract ambition' when that ambition aspires to roam directionless and unrestrained."

Trump fought the constitutional law, and the constitutional law won. Checks and balances proved resilient enough to roll with the punches. No Caesarism took hold. The American melodrama carried on. Once more, Tom Wolfe (1993: 302–303) was vindicated in identifying one of the unexplained political phenomena of modern astronomy: "the dark night of fascism is always descending in the United States and yet lands only in Europe." There exist unabashed authoritarian rulers in the world, and serious threats to democracy, but they are less in Washington, DC than Beijing and Moscow.

## US Constitution 2.0

The Constitution is much more than the document under glass in the National Archives. Although Leonard Cohen memorably predicted that "Democracy is coming to the USA" (1993: 367), the more scientific Robert Dahl (2003: 154) declared a "measured pessimism" about America's prospects for democratization. But while it has been reshaped by judges and lawmakers, the ultimate arbiters of constitutionalism have been the American people. Millions of citizens have been integral to testing, reframing, and revitalizing constitutionality. Ordinary Americans, as much as lawyers, possess and regularly exercise the means to shape their constitutional futures.

As such, in terms of constitutional kudos, there is ultimately less reason for Jeffersonian angst than Madisonian repose. While the Founders were wary of utopianism, the order they established has become entrenched. But unlike the dreary utopias – "devoid of color, life, art, humanity," as Goethe termed it – of Plato, Thomas More, H. G. Wells, and other dreamers, the Founders had been repeatedly mugged by constitutional realities. They were disabused of the notion that the good society was one where either, at one extreme, there was no need of politics or, at the other, politics was total. The Constitution has consequently proven an example of excellence in design and a "known." It has adapted and escaped any number of potential dead ends and judgment days. The ravages of time and disruption have helped it acquire an "antifragile" quality that few others match: Not only does it resist shock and stay the same, but its tests fortify and improve its character (Taleb 2013).

It is much easier to make a functional constitutional worse than a dysfunctional one better, which is typically a Herculean (or Sisyphean) task. With so many problems at home and challenges abroad, adding a new convention to the mix would potentially resemble the perfect storm. But perhaps overhaul, a "known unknown," represents an offer that can no longer be refused?

## Constitutional Conventions

What would the Founders make of their work today? Would they wish to write something different? After all, in 1787, they initially meant merely to revise the Articles of Confederation, not to create the Constitution as we know it. But they identified a profound disconnect between incremental revision and the more urgent needs of their fledgling nation. Their solution was to start anew. Could history repeat itself over two centuries later or, at least, rhyme?

Constitutional futurology is fraught with problems. But optimism seems unwarranted. A new convention would represent an untested, unlimited mechanism. With immense power to rewrite the existing

Constitution, reformers might well find themselves hoist with their own petard, since it is unlikely to yield anything more than a Pyrrhic victory for those disillusioned with politics. The impracticality of reinventing the entire edifice of government is forbidding and, with no modern precedent – state conventions offer poor comparisons – conducive to much mischief. The probability is less "1787 II: The Sequel" producing a newly bespoke Constitution than a Tower of Babel, not least because of five problems concerning rules, ratification, transparency, duration, and composition.

First, Article V defines no rules for what a convention would need to decide: who attends; whether states that had not called for it would be admitted; what limits to place on delegates; and what majority an amendment would require to be proposed and passed. Even if Congress set rules, the convention could plausibly overturn or disregard these to go its own way. The judiciary would be reluctant to intervene in such an epic political tangle.

Second, once convened, the goalposts could shift dramatically. The subject matter might be initially limited, but this could open a Pandora's Box. While the original convention was a site of constant brokering and paths not taken, it is difficult to imagine how a potentially bewildering range of modern demands could all be accommodated. The Articles, signed in 1777 and ratified by all thirteen states in 1781, required under Article XIII unanimous consent for any changes. But the 1787 convention unceremoniously ignored this, deciding that ratification by nine states would suffice. Imagine the outrage now if a convention decided that only thirty of fifty states were needed to consign the old version to history's ash heap.

Third, a modern convention would not be low-key but, well, unconventional. As Madison declared, "no Constitution would ever have been adopted by the (Constitutional) Convention if the debates had been made public." In 1787, there existed no 24/7 cable news, Twitter, Google, Instagram, or Facebook. The pressures on the new founding parents would be intense and unrelenting. Dispassionate deliberation would be impossible. Behind-the-scenes discussions to facilitate trade-offs would be frowned upon, but public scrutiny would be problematic too: "One trouble with transparency is that people are frequently repelled by what they see" (King 2012: 194). A new convention may avoid being dominated by lawyers, guns, and money, but a thing of beauty it is unlikely to be.

Fourth, given the scale and complexity of the issues, a summer would not suffice to paint a new constitutional masterpiece. Getting the new framework correct would be the overriding task. But would the American people have the patience for a lengthy and labyrinthine convention to thrash out deals about their future from which they were excluded? It seems improbable. Moreover, as a people, Americans remain divided by race, ethnicity, region, religion, language, historical memory, and partisanship. As King (2012: 67) rightly noted:

> The founding fathers found it extraordinarily difficult to devise a constitution for the relatively homogeneous America of the 1780s. Their successors, if they had any, might find it well-nigh impossible to devise an equally acceptable constitution for the far more diverse America of today. That is perhaps why no second constitutional convention has ever been held. The thought of what might happen if such a convention were held is daunting and even appalling. The very pillars of the temple might be brought down.

Fifth, but related, who would attend? The 1787 delegates had flaws aplenty. But even on Washington's K Street, there exists no Rolodex of new James Madisons – disinterested, incorruptible, dedicated public servants, with judicious temperaments and analytical minds, worthy of *Profiles in Courage*. If they exist, these figures have not exactly been hiding in open sight over recent years amid America's increasing political ferment.

Echoing the conservative William Buckley (1963: 134) – "I should sooner live in a society governed by the first two thousand names in the Boston telephone directory than in a society governed by the two thousand faculty members of Harvard University" – Sanford Levinson suggested in 2011 (at Harvard, ironically) that a random lottery select a few hundred Americans to participate:

> If you plucked out the most obscure American and said, "You're going to have a chance to wrestle with the most fundamental issues and to decide how your children and grandchildren would live," they would rise to the occasion ... The fact is, we are not talking about rocket science. We're talking about making fundamental value judgments that require some information, but delegates could get that information during the convention.
>
> (Kreitner 2017)

Perhaps, but on balance that confidence seems misplaced. Entrusting America's future to chance seems a tad imprudent. Indelicate though it is to reiterate, many Americans are indifferent to history and know little about their existing Constitution, much less others'. One need not go as far as Richard Posner (2001: 260) in comparing them to the drugged masses of Aldous Huxley's *Brave New World*: "The society of happy, thoughtless philistines depicted by Huxley seems merely an exaggeration of today's America." Nor need convention delegates be pillars of Socratic wisdom. But expecting a steep upward learning curve and informed judgments over the details of a workable balanced budget amendment in a highly pressured situation is asking quite a lot of a random cohort. Ironically, it also runs against the decidedly un-populist preferences of many younger Americans, 46 percent of whom (ages eighteen to twenty-nine) claim to prefer to be governed by experts (Wike, Simmons, Stokes and Fetterolf 2017).

More important, possessing sufficient information to interrogate proposals closely is no matter for novices. While "the best and the brightest" have sometimes made grievous errors, that is reason to keep them honest, not consigning America's future to (potentially) the worst and the shallowest. As Saunders (2018) noted, "Experienced leaders provide better oversight of foreign policy decision-making because they are more likely to ask hard questions, spot poor planning, or recognize unrealistic proposals." That compelling logic might also plausibly apply to devising a new constitutional settlement.

But suppose the convention did occur, composed of the constitutionally competent rather than the clueless, and armed with more than merely faith-based constitutionalism and a modernizing, future orientation. Would some attractive new governing arrangement emerge?

## What Would Madison Do?

Resort to a convention ultimately represents a candid admission that politics is broken. It might offer unheard of constitutional splendors. But, unless the delegates wished to run roughshod over discrete minorities and impose proposals widely deemed objectionable, the new constitution would have to offer some compromise between deeply discordant preferences. In twenty-first-century America – heterogeneous, cacophonous, individualistic, mindful of rights – the prospect of agreeing to any compact without major compromises would be minimal. Incremental reform, not radical revision, seems more likely. But even a self-consciously modest incrementalism can take America in unintended directions. Central to this assessment are four distinct but overlapping elements.

First, for those who discern substantial flaws in the Constitution, any change would need to be radical. While it is feasible to beg, borrow, or steal any number of selective reforms – revision of an amendment here, abolition of a clause there – the order is too closely integrated for incremental measures to make a huge difference. What some critics have in mind, when all is said and done, is a pure majoritarianism, shorn of the checks and balances that frustrate the popular will in finding its easy expression in federal law. The logical step is a unicameral legislature or parliamentary system.

But would Democrats or Republicans truly want a "Westminster model" for the United States? In a majoritarian democracy, it is conceivable that the Bush administration's response to 9/11 would have been much more aggressive, Obama's increasing of the national debt steeper, and Trump's authoritarian aspirations the unmediated law of the land. For either party, the potential gains of ruling unchecked would be off-set by the costs of being out of power when the other side enjoyed such authority. Even a less brutal change to a unicameral legislature would leave partisans with acute dilemmas: would Republicans have enjoyed Obama and Nancy Pelosi governing in tandem? Would Democrats have rejoiced at a leadership duopoly of Trump and Paul Ryan? As it stands, there is some evidence that Americans dislike "undivided" party control of the White House and Congress. As Mayhew (2017: 107) noted, the alternative to a divided public saying "Don't!" is that, "Every quick, nar-row, temporary majority gets to jam into law whatever its activist base wants. Play that out for a while, especially in a context of ideological polarization, and what level of system legitimacy would result?"

Indeed. Far from a step forward, such a change would represent the antithesis of a legitimate and workable constitutional arrangement for a diverse society, and a disappointment to those dissatisfied with politics. A genuine parliamentary system, with a plurality or, especially, a propor-tional electoral system, would yield small, antagonistic parties with no unifying bond. Whether Americans would relish coalition governments, secretive bargains, and unaccountability that offers no guaranteed cure for policy immobility is doubtful. Already, the days of LBJ giving congressmen "the treatment" to get key bills passed is ancient history. A majoritarian system would make it prehistory.

Second, a less transformative change would be formally to empower the presidency with greater authority. This would reshape the model of separated institutions sharing powers into a more presidential democracy. The purported benefits in theory remedy some of the obvious problems of Congress and offer greater coherence to national policy-making. All this can occur within the existing constitutional framework with limited new amendments.

Despite the logic, however, the move fails to convince. Partly, this reflects the enviable flexibility of the existing design and the undesirability of for-mal change. On matters from war powers to executive orders, the presi-dency has been enabled in ways the Framers could not have envisaged, but mostly with the complicity of Congress and the courts. From Truman to Trump, presidents of both parties have expanded the administrative pres-idency, the reach of executive orders, and presidential unilateralism. In the face of congressional paralysis and indecision, every presidential "decision memo" revs the engine of an otherwise stalled government.

Partisanship invariably conditions responses to presidential power. But a more powerful presidency clearly does not comport with popular wishes. Nor do the costs seem worth the risk. The Framers emphati-cally rejected an American monarch. But the power of the United States and the Federal Government is such that presidents already enjoy more heft than any classical emperor. Beyond institutional checks, and the willingness of those who staff other branches of government, only presidential character tempers its exercise. If the timber of humanity is inherently crooked, as Kant claimed, we have been truly fortunate not to have had more bad luck befall us.

One comparative virtue of the American polity has been the abiding conviction that what government can do *to* you matters as much as what government can do *for* you. Anti-statism has its fringes and violent excesses on the left and right. But it has performed two salutary functions in slowing government's incessant growth and keeping individual liberty alive more fully than elsewhere. The costs of empowering government, and emasculating checks on concentrated power, caution against a more presidential route. For advocates of change, it is telling that there is rarely another constitution from outside the United States that they cite as a petri dish from which Americans can draw for more promising results.

Third, if transformation is undesirable, a more modest reordering might be on the cards. As previously argued, equal state representation in the US Senate, presidential eligibility, judicial term limits and mandatory retirement, and the amendment process represent the most obvious candidates for a modernizing rewrite. But to understate matters, these are all easier said than done. Reform would have costs and not necessarily resolve in full the ills they target. Modest changes would reshape the margins, not the core, of constitutional order. Impolitic though it may be to point it out, the ultimate cause of Americans' unhappiness is, candidly, as much their fellow Americans as "Washington."

Fourth, there exists a danger that changes to the Constitution undermine its standing. Rather than references to "the" Constitution, deepening polarization threatens to yield "their" Constitution. In its infancy, this has already begun. But thus far, despite being episodically weaponized, the Constitution has resisted full entrapment in the partisan battles engulfing American public life. It is therefore ironic that a kind of unholy alliance is developing in which forces both on the left and right perceive the risks of the status quo for their cherished causes as greater than what might emerge from an Article V convention – a macabre alliance of convenience for something less compromised and compromising (Kreitner 2017).

Dahl, Levinson, Sabato, and other eminent American voices notwithstanding, it is worth keeping clear sight of the fact that the aim of constitutionalism remains good government, not people power. Serious constitutionalism – not the faux version that is so widespread – represents a call for restraint. Even for experienced constitutional engineers, dispensing with the existing settlement is a gamble unlikely to pay off. For conservatives, especially, while Thomas Paine's promise to "begin the world over again" once had undeniable power, Edmund Burke's response – that the accumulated wisdom of posterity enshrined in our political institutions deserves respect – remains at least as telling.

## Constitutional Crossroads: Re-Constitutionalizing American Politics

No matter the constitutional design, de-conflicting politics is impossible. Politics is inherently conflictual, and partisanship the natural condition of a self-governing people. Any hope for a functioning democracy relies on healthy party competition (Aldrich and Griffin 2018). Prescriptions for restoring national unity to the United States invariably rely heavily on technocratic solutions, vague pleas for attitudinal change, or fatalistic invocations of shocks (war, financial crisis, recession). But might depolarizing politics, or a "better partisanship," be possible? Might it be possible to lower the fever pitch that sets many Americans against one another with intensity, and a vituperative edge guaranteed to whip up outrage and blind reasonable discussion? In short, might it be possible to deny America's foreign antagonists the kind of domestic discord between the supposedly ethical partisans of my side and evil partisans of yours that they actively seek to spread? After all, Truman and Eisenhower, Vandenberg and Kennedy – not to mention Richard Lugar and Sam Nunn – all knew about strong partisanship but managed, nonetheless, to forge domestic and foreign policies in the national interest.

The key to unpicking gridlock is not about achieving an elusive national unity or shared identity that, historically, only external threats produced. That kind of patriotism is unlikely to displace partisanship. But a sense of national cohesion in which the parties and their electoral coalitions reach a modus vivendi is more modest and feasible. It also has a practical, pragmatic mechanism: more compromise. This entails not a rose-tinted framing of the differences between the two parties and their constituencies but a recognition that those differences may be more reconcilable than the most dedicated partisans claim. This is not wishful thinking or altruism but the most enlightened self-interest, the understanding that dysfunction and stasis ultimately threaten both parties' core values, beliefs, and interests. A willingness to make mutual concessions out of principle has historically underpinned even the most fractious of eras across American history. The Constitution was itself, after all, a set of multiple compromises – the greatest domestic grand bargain and, for all its grievous faults, preferable to all politically feasible alternatives at the time (Robertson 2013).

America is a divided democracy by design and evolution (Singh 2003). But the gains that progressives and conservatives celebrate came through the same constitutional order. US politics remains locked in a struggle between two parties and two visions over what produces the best results. Although this is more complex than a simple battle between collectivism and individualism, the battle lines are clear. Democrats advocate weak social democracy: relatively high taxes (though lower than those of other OECD countries), a relatively strong safety net (though not as strong as others), spending on needs like education and health care, and economic regulation to protect workers, consumers, and the environment. Republicans advocate conservatism: low taxes, less social spending, and less regulation. But such divisions not only impede domestic governance. As Schultz (2018) persuasively argued, partisan polarization also powerfully hinders the US global leadership role by making it more difficult to secure bipartisan support for ambitious or risky undertakings, making it harder to learn the lessons of policy failure, risking dramatic policy swings that undercut US reliability, and increasing vulnerability to foreign intervention in domestic elections and politics. When national polarization incentivizes sub-federal efforts by individual states to craft their own foreign policies, the notion of the United States as a "unitary actor" in international affairs is itself under substantial pressure (Engstrom and Weinstein 2018).

What is especially problematic about the nature of partisan conflict in the present caustic era is fivefold: partisan identity generally precedes position-taking; polarization is so powerful that most voters see the world through thick red and blue lenses, coloring how people experience reality; polarization is in important respects serving as a proxy for more profound battles between illiberal democrats and liberal elitists; geographic polarization advances ideological polarization; and the sides are evenly matched. Absent a change of heart on the part of millions – not least "contested conservatives" who dislike "big government" in the abstract but accept its concrete benefits – partisan tribes will continue to resemble echo chambers in which leaders preach to the converted. As such, the parties increasingly resemble precisely what the Founders feared could render their Constitution inoperable. But they are also reverting to the historical norm. In America's earliest partisan confrontations, John Adams's Federalists and Thomas Jefferson's Republicans saw each other as existential threats to the new republic. And it was the ideologically indistinct, depolarized party system of the middle of the twentieth century – with all its associated problems of a far-from-golden age – that was the unstable anomaly between epochs of intense polarization.

No serious analyst imagines that politics can be transformed. Neither should bipartisanship merit reflexive endorsement. Parties exist for good reason and, at their best, are what make modern democratic politics possible. Under divided government, the combination of polarization and the Constitution's multiple institutional veto points tend to impede functional government. But, as Hopkins (2017: 25) argues, "strengthened bonds of partisanship can foster a productive relationship between the president and Congress during periods of unified party government." Lawrence (2017) also demonstrated that the art of the political deal is still possible. Even in the heat of partisan rivalry, lawmakers can beat the odds to forge serious cross-party agreements. And in their study of prison reform, Dagan and Teles (2016) showed that Americans can shift positions without departing political tribes. Among anti-statist conservatives, the fiscal pressures of recession, the ineffectiveness of "tough" rather than "smart" laws on crime, and increasing engagement by evangelicals allowed a cadre of leaders to reframe criminal justice in terms of rolling back government and redemption. Although the policy results have remained modest, the space was created to reduce mass incarceration. Moreover, federalism continues to allow space for experimentation and difference, a safety valve for the toxicity of Washington.

If, for their own internal reasons, the parties redefine their orthodoxies, some movement on key issues may be possible. But it is easier to reframe issues effectively within a party when internal factions have reasons to concur and the issue is not a core one for the party base; or when the most profound identity crisis prompts change, as may be occurring with the remaking of the Republican Party under President Trump. On many issues – taxes, trade, energy, environment – this is less plausibly accomplished without crises or wrenching battles. As it stands, Republicans and Democrats approach government in fundamentally different ways, reflecting the differences in their partisan cultures and electoral coalitions.

But while the American party system can appear unusually rigid, much is going on beneath the surface that can produce a more fluid politics. If public sentiments change, parties respond. Marriage equality was an eccentric, avant-garde cause in the early 2000s. But a remarkable shift in public opinion resulted in its becoming nationwide law by 2015. The Republicans' transgressive embrace of lax fiscal policy in 2018 was possible because the public no longer saw deficits as a top issue. Such changes inevitably challenge core constituencies and bring about charges of bad faith or hypocrisy. At the same time, the return of bi-partisanship offered no holy grail on tough decisions. The annual gap between spending and revenue in 2019 was projected to eclipse $1.1 trillion, up from $439 billion in 2015 (Paletta and Werner 2018), and to reach $1.7 trillion through the 2020s, almost three times the amount envisioned in 2011. The United States is set to run deficits of 5 percent of GDP for the foreseeable future. Aside from the deep recessions of the early 1980s and 2008–2009, Washington is engaged in greater profligacy than at any time since 1945. Cynics might suggest that if an era of twelve-digit deficits acceptable to both parties is how bi-partisanship works, dysfunction and polarization might be preferable after all.

But that would be to mistake substance for form. Reaching out across cultural divides is a necessary step to resolving political differences. Until cross-cultural understanding is advanced – and that seems some distance away – the existing Constitution is doing a solid job in containing the divisions. Ultimately, constitutional change cannot assuage a continent-sized divide that encompasses values, beliefs, and attitudes on almost every issue. The Constitution offers an elegant and elaborate edifice that structures political actions, law, and political thought. Compared to possible alternatives, it continues to promise Americans the most, and divide them the least. Its institutional system is much less fragile than commonly depicted by commentators who all too often are incentivized and well-rewarded for heated, rather than cool, analysis.

Is the United States facing serious problems? Or is its constitutional order strong? The answer is yes. American politics echoes that famous literary opening in Charles Dickens's *A Tale of Two Cities*: "It was the best of times, it was the worst of times… It was the epoch of belief, it was the epoch of incredulity." But let us keep things in perspective and context: America's problems pale by comparison with much of a world that remains plunged in darkness and despair. Democrats and Republicans are locked into a system they can neither fix nor leave, seemingly intent upon disproving Lincoln by demonstrating that a house divided against itself can nonetheless stand and thrive. Even so, it seems preferable to hunker down where the existing constitutional order has a clear and compelling logic, rather than to hasten to a new dispensation that would guarantee no sure or lasting equilibrium.

Every democracy may be unhappy in its own distinctive way. But comprehensive constitutional change offers no gateway to a new promised land nor the cure for political blues. Although it might seem naïve and Pollyannaish to endorse the sentiment, what Bill Clinton argued more than one-quarter century ago remains true today: there is nothing wrong with America that cannot be fixed by what is right about America. In that regard, the Constitution arguably remains the most important aspect of what remains right. Ironically, a little more constitutional proselytizing might go a long way: more dialogue about the Constitution, its goals, and lessons about imperfect people pursuing enlightened compromise in search of public goods. Mainstreaming constitutional conversation over confrontation would be valuable. The United States remains a rambunctiously free republic, open society, and the world's most stable and powerful democracy. The case for comprehensive change in the American experiment in self-government is "not proven." And there this case for the defense must rest.

# Bibliography

## Books

Abramowitz, Alan I. (2012). *The Polarized Public: Why American Government is So Dysfunctional* (New York: Pearson).

Abramowitz, Alan I. (2018). *The Great Alignment: Race, Party Transformation and the Rise of Donald Trump* (New Haven, CT: Yale University Press).

Ackerman, Bruce (1993). *We the People: Foundations Volume One* (Cambridge, MA: Harvard University Press).

Ackerman, Bruce (2013). *The Decline and Fall of the American Republic* (Cambridge, MA: Harvard University Press).

Aldrich, John H. and John D. Griffin (2018). *Why Parties Matter: Political Competition and Democracy in the American South* (Chicago, IL: University of Chicago Press).

Allison, Graham (2017). *Destined For War: Can America and China Escape Thucydides' Trap?* (Melbourne: Scribe).

Amar, Akhil Reed (2012). *America's Unwritten Constitution: The Precedents and Principles We Live By* (New York: Basic Books).

Baldwin, Peter (2009). *The Narcissism of Minor Differences: How Europe and America Are Alike* (New York: Oxford University Press).

Barnett, Randy E. (2013). *Restoring The Lost Constitution: The Presumption of Liberty* (Princeton, NJ: Princeton University Press).

Barnett, Randy E. (2016). *Our Republican Constitution: Securing the Liberty and Sovereignty of We the People* (New York: Harper Collins).

Beard, Charles A. (2011). *An Economic Interpretation of the Constitution* (Clark, NJ: The Lawbook Exchange).

Berinsky, Adam J. (2009). *In Time of War: Understanding American Public Opinion from World War II to Iraq* (Chicago, IL: University of Chicago Press).

Berkin, Carol (2003). *A Brilliant Solution: Inventing the American Constitution* (New York: Mariner Books).

Berlin, Isaiah (2013). *Against the Current: Essays in the History of Ideas* (Princeton, NJ: Princeton University Press).

Billias, George Athan (2009). *American Constitutionalism Heard Round the World, 1776–1989: A Global Perspective* (New York: New York University Press).

Bishin, Benjamin (2009). *Tyranny of the Minority: The Subconstituency Politics Theory of Representation* (Philadelphia, PA: Temple University Press).

Bobbitt, Philip (1991). *Constitutional Interpretation* (Oxford: Basil Blackwell).

Brady, David A. and Craig Volden (2006). *Revolving Gridlock: Politics and Policy from Jimmy Carter to George W. Bush*, 2nd edition (Boulder, CO: Westview Press).

Breyer, Stephen (2005). *Active Liberty: Interpreting Our Democratic Constitution* (New York: Alfred A. Knopf).

Bruckner, Pascal (2010). *The Tyranny of Guilt: An Essay on Western Masochism* (Princeton, NJ: Princeton University Press).

Buchholz, Todd G. (2016). *The Price of Prosperity: Why Rich Nations Fail and How to Renew Them* (New York: Harper Collins).

Buckley, William F. (1963). *Rumbles Left and Right: A Book about Troublesome People and Ideas* (New York: G.P. Putnam's Sons).

Burns, James M. and L. Marvin Overby (1990). *Cobblestone Leadership: Majority Rule, Minority Power* (Norman, OK: University of Oklahoma Press).

Ceaser, James W., Andrew E. Busch, and John J. Pitney, Jr. (2017). *Defying the Odds: The 2016 Elections and American Politics* (New York: Rowman and Littlefield).

Chafetz, Josh (2017). *Congress's Constitution: Legislative Authority and the Separation of Powers* (New Haven, CT: Yale University Press).

Chemerinsky, Erwin (2014). *The Case Against the Supreme Court* (New York: Penguin Books).

Chua, Amy (2018). *Political Tribes: Group Instinct and the Fate of Nations* (London: Bloomsbury).

Cohen, Leonard (1993). *Stranger Music: Selected Poems and Songs* (London: Jonathan Cape).

Cole, David (2016). *Engines of Liberty: The Power of Citizen Activists to Make Constitutional Law* (New York: Basic Books).

Connelly, Jr., William F., John J. Pitney, and Gary J. Schmitt (eds.) (2017). *Is Congress Broken? The Virtues and Defects of Partisanship and Gridlock* (Washington, DC: The Brookings Institution).

Cook, Philip and Kristin Goss (2014). *The Gun Debate: What Everyone Needs to Know* (New York: Oxford University Press).

Dagan, David and Steven Teles (2016). *Prison Break: Why Conservatives Turned Against Mass Incarceration* (New York: Oxford University Press).

Dahl, Robert A. (2003). *How Democratic is the American Constitution?* (New Haven, CT: Yale University Press).

Dionne, E. J., Norman J. Ornstein, and Thomas E. Mann (2017). *One Nation After Trump: A Guide for the Perplexed, the Disillusioned, the Desperate and the Not-Yet-Deported* (New York: St Martin's Press).

Drutman, Lee (2015). *The Business of America is Lobbying: How Corporations Became Politicized and Politics Became More Corporate* (New York: Oxford University Press).

Easton, David (1965). *A Systems Analysis of Political Life* (New York: Wiley).

Edwards, George C. III (2003). *On Deaf Ears: The Limits of the Bully Pulpit* (New Haven, CT: Yale University Press).

Edwards, George C. III (2009). *The Strategic President: Persuasion and Opportunity in Presidential Leadership* (Princeton, NJ: Princeton University Press).

Edwards, George C. III (2011). *Why the Electoral College is Bad for America*, 2nd edition (New Haven, CT: Yale University Press).

Elkins, Zachary, Tom Ginsburg, and James Melton (2009). *The Endurance of National Constitutions* (New York: Cambridge University Press).

Ellis, Richard J. (1993). *American Political Cultures* (New York: Oxford University Press).

Finer, S. E., Vernon Bogdanor, and Bernard Rudden (1995). *Comparing Constitutions* (Oxford: Oxford University Press).

Fiorina, Morris (2017). *Unstable Majorities: Polarization, Party Sorting, and Political Stalemate* (Stanford, CA: Hoover Institution Press).

Fisher, Louis (2004). *Presidential War Power*, 2nd edition (Lawrence, KS: University Press of Kansas).

Fisher, Louis (2017). *Supreme Court Expansion of Presidential Power: Unconstitutional Leanings* (Lawrence, KS: University Press of Kansas).

Fowler, Linda L. (2015). *Watchdogs On The Hill: The Decline of Congressional Oversight of U.S. Foreign Relations* (Princeton, NJ: Princeton University Press).

Frum, David (2018). *Trumpology: The Corruption of the American Republic* (New York: Harper Collins).

Goidel, Kirby (2015). *America's Failing Experiment: How We the People Became the Problem* (New York: Rowman and Littlefield).

Griffin, Stephen M. (2013). *Long Wars and the Constitution* (Cambridge, MA: Harvard University Press).

Grossman, Matt and David A. Hopkins (2016). *Asymmetrical Politics: Ideological Republicans and Group Interest Democrats* (New York: Oxford University Press).

Hartley, Roger C. (2017). *How Failed Attempts to Amend the Constitution Mobilize Political Change* (Nashville, TN: Vanderbilt University Press).

Hassell, Hans J. G. (2018). *The Party's Primary: Control of Congressional Nominations* (New York: Cambridge University Press).

Henkin, Louis (1996). *Foreign Affairs and the US Constitution*, 2nd edition (New York: Oxford University Press).

Herbert, Ernst Friedrich (Count Munster) (2010). *Political Sketches of the State of Europe, 1814–1867* (Whitefish, MT: Kessinger Publishing).

Hetherington, Marc J. and Thomas J. Rudolph (2015). *Why Washington Won't Work: Polarization, Political Trust and the Governing Crisis* (Chicago, IL: University of Chicago Press).

Hoffer, Eric (1971). *First Things, Last Things* (Titusville, NJ: Hopewell Publications).

Hopkins, David A. (2017). *Red Fighting Blue: How Geography and Electoral Rules Polarize American Politics* (New York: Cambridge University Press).

Howell, William G. (2003). *Power without Persuasion: The Politics of Direct Presidential Action* (Princeton, NJ: Princeton University Press).

Howell, William G. and Jon C. Pevehouse (2007). *While Dangers Gather: Congressional Checks on Presidential War Powers* (Princeton, NJ: Princeton University Press).

Howell, William G. and Terry M. Moe (2016). *Relic: How Our Constitution Undermines Effective Government and Why We Need a More Powerful Presidency* (New York: Basic Books).

Huntington, Samuel P. (1981). *American Politics: The Promise of Disharmony* (Cambridge, MA: Harvard University Press).

Kamarck, Elaine (2016). *Why Presidents Fail and How They Can Succeed Again* (Washington, DC: Brookings Institution).

Keck, Thomas M. (2014). *Judicial Politics in Polarized Times* (Chicago, IL: University of Chicago Press).

Keyssar, Alexander (2018). *Why Do We Still Have The Electoral College?* (Cambridge, MA: Harvard University Press).

King, Anthony (2012). *The Founding Fathers v. The People: Paradoxes of American Democracy* (Cambridge, MA: Harvard University Press).

Klarman, Michael J. (2004). *From Jim Crow to Civil Rights: The Supreme Court and the Struggle for Racial Equality* (New York: Oxford University Press).

Klarman, Michael J. (2014). *From the Closet to the Altar: Courts, Backlash and the Struggle for Same-Sex Marriage* (New York: Oxford University Press).

Klarman, Michael J. (2016). *The Framers' Coup: The Making of the United States Constitution* (New York: Oxford University Press).

Koger, Gregory and Matthew Lebo (2017). *Strategic Party Government: Why Winning Trumps Ideology* (Chicago, IL: University of Chicago Press).

Kriner, Douglas L. and Andrew Reeves (2015). *The Particularistic President: Executive Branch Politics and Political Inequality* (New York: Cambridge University Press).

Kriner, Douglas L. and Eric Schickler (2016). *Investigating The President: Congressional Checks on Presidential Power* (Princeton, NJ: Princeton University Press).

Krutz, Glen S. and Jeffrey S. Peake (2009). *Treaty Politics and the Rise of Executive Agreements: International Commitments in a System of Shared Powers* (Ann Arbor, MI: University of Michigan Press).

Lawrence, Jill (2017). *The Art of the Political Deal: How Congress Beat the Odds and Broke Through Gridlock* (Washington, DC: Independent Publishers).

Lazare, Daniel (1996). *The Frozen Republic: How the Constitution is Paralyzing Democracy* (New York: Harcourt).

Lazare, Daniel (2001). *The Velvet Coup: The Constitution, the Supreme Court, and the Decline of American Democracy* (London: Verso).

Lee, Frances E. and Bruce I. Oppenheimer (1999). *Sizing Up the Senate: The Unequal Consequences of Equal Representation* (Chicago, IL: University of Chicago Press).

Lee, Mike (2016). *Our Lost Constitution: The Willful Subversion of America's Founding Document* (New York: Sentinel).

Leicester, Paul (ed.) (1904). *The Collected Works of Thomas Jefferson* (New York: G.P. Putnam's Sons).

Lepore, Jill (2010). *The Whites of Their Eyes: The Tea Party Revolution and the Battle Over American History* (Princeton, NJ: Princeton University Press).

Levin, Yuval (2016). *The Fractured Republic: Renewing America's Social Contract in the Age of Individualism* (New York: Basic Books).

Levinson, Sanford (2006). *Our Undemocratic Constitution: Where the Constitution Goes Wrong (And How We The People Can Correct It)* (New York: Oxford University Press).

Levinson, Sanford (2012). *Framed: America's Fifty-One Constitutions and the Crisis of Governance* (New York: Oxford University Press).

Levinson, Sanford and Cynthia Levinson (2017). *Fault Lines in the Constitution: The Framers, Their Fights, and the Flaws that Affect Us Today* (Atlanta, GA: Peachtree Publishers).

Levitsky, Steven and Daniel Ziblatt (2018). *How Democracies Die: What History Tells Us About Our Future* (New York: Viking Press).

Levy, Bernard-Henri (2006). *American Vertigo: On the Road from Newport to Guantanamo* (London: Gibson Square).

Lichtman, Allan J. (2017). *The Case for Impeachment* (London: William Collins).

Magliocca, Gerard (2018). *The Heart of the Constitution: How the Bill of Rights Became the Bill of Rights* (New York: Oxford University Press).

Mann, Thomas E. and Norman J. Ornstein (2008). *The Broken Branch: How Congress Is Failing America and How to Get It Back On Track* (New York: Oxford University Press).

Mann, Thomas E. and Norman J. Ornstein (2012). *It's Even Worse Than It Looks: How The American Constitutional System Collided with the New Politics of Extremism* (New York: Basic Books).

Manuel, Paul C. and Anne Marie Cammisa (1999). *Checks and Balances? How a Parliamentary System Could Change American Politics* (Oxford: Westview Press).

Mayhew, David R. (2017). *The Imprint of Congress* (New Haven, CT: Yale University Press).

Mezey, Michael L. (2017). *(S)electing the President: The Perils of Democracy* (New York: Routledge).

Miller, Aaron David (2014). *The End of Greatness: Why America Can't Have (and Doesn't Want) Another Great President* (New York: Palgrave Macmillan).

Milner, Helen V. and Dustin Tingley (2015). *Sailing The Water's Edge: The Domestic Politics of American Foreign Policy* (Princeton, NJ: Princeton University Press).

Morgan, Edmund S. (2013). *American Slavery, American Freedom* (New York: W. W. Norton).

Muller, Jan-Werner (2016). *What Is Populism?* (Philadelphia, PA: University of Pennsylvania Press).

Murray, Charles (2013). *Coming Apart: The State of White America, 1960–2010* (New York: Crown Publishing).

Nelson, Michael (2018). *Trump's First Year* (Charlottesville, VA: University of Virginia Press).

Neustadt, Richard (1991). *Presidential Power and the Modern Presidents: The Politics of Leadership from Roosevelt to Reagan* (New York: The Free Press).

Nichols, Tom (2017). *The Death of Expertise: The Campaign against Established Knowledge and Why it Matters* (New York: Oxford University Press).

O'Sullivan, Meghan L. (2017). *Windfall: How the New Energy Abundance Upends Global Politics and Strengthens America's Power* (New York: Simon and Schuster).

Orren, Karen and Stephen Skowronek (2017). *The Policy State: An American Predicament* (Cambridge, MA: Harvard University Press).

Pacelle, Jr., Richard L., Brett W. Curry, and Bryan W. Marshall (2011). *Decision Making by The Modern Supreme Court* (New York: Cambridge University Press).

Penguin Classics (2017). *The Constitution of the United States* (London: Random House).

Perry, Michael J. (2009). *Constitutional Rights, Moral Controversy, and the Supreme Court* (New York: Cambridge University Press).

Piereson, James (2015). *Shattered Consensus: The Rise and Decline of America's Postwar Political Order* (New York: Encounter Books).

Pinker, Steven (2018). *Enlightenment Now: The Case for Reason, Science, Humanism and Progress* (London: Allen Lane).

Posner, Eric A. and Adrian Vermeule (2013). *The Executive Unbound: After the Madisonian Republic* (New York: Oxford University Press).

Posner, Eric A. and E. Glen Weyl (2018). *Radical Markets: Uprooting Capitalism and Democracy for a Just Society* (Princeton, NJ: Princeton University Press).

Posner, Richard A. (2001). *Public Intellectuals* (Cambridge, MA: Harvard University Press).

Posner, Richard A. (2003). *Law, Pragmatism, and Democracy* (Cambridge, MA: Harvard University Press).

Posner, Richard A. (2006). *Not a Suicide Pact: The Constitution in a Time of National Emergency* (New York: Oxford University Press).

Posner, Richard A. (2008). *How Judges Think* (Cambridge, MA: Harvard University Press).

Prakash, Saikrishna B. (2015). *Imperial from the Beginning: The Constitution of the Original Executive* (New Haven, CT: Yale University Press).

Putnam, Robert D. (2015). *Our Kids: The American Dream in Crisis* (New York: Simon and Schuster, 2015).

Randazzo, Kirk A. and Richard W. Waterman (2015). *Checking the Courts: Law, Ideology and Contingent Discretion* (New York: State University of New York Press).

Raustiala, Kal (2009). *Does The Constitution Follow The Flag? The Evolution of Territoriality in American Law* (New York: Oxford University Press).

Reynolds, Molly E. (2017). *Exceptions to the Rule: The Politics of Filibuster Limitations in the U.S. Senate* (Washington, DC: Brookings Institution Press).

Robertson, David Brian (2013). *The Original Compromise: What the Constitution's Framers Were Really Thinking* (New York: Oxford University Press).

Roosevelt, Kermit (2006). *The Myth of Judicial Activism: Making Sense of Supreme Court Decisions* (New Haven, CT: Yale University Press).

Rosenberg, Gerald N. (1991). *The Hollow Hope: Can Courts Bring About Social Change?* (Chicago, IL: University of Chicago Press).

Sabato, Larry J. (2007). *A More Perfect Constitution: 23 Proposals to Revitalize Our Constitution and Make America a Fairer Country* (New York: Walker and Company).

Sartori, Giovanni (1994). *Comparative Constitutional Engineering: An Inquiry into Structures, Incentives and Outcomes* (London: Macmillan Press).

Schake, Kori N. and Jim Mattis (eds.) (2016). *Warriors and Citizens: American Views of Our Military* (Stanford, CA: Hoover Institution Press).

Schmitt, Gary J., Joseph M. Bessette, and Andrew E. Busch (eds.) (2017). *The Imperial Presidency and the Constitution* (Lanham, MD: Rowman and Littlefield).

Sehat, David (2015). *The Jefferson Rule: How the Founding Fathers Became Infallible and Our Politics Inflexible* (New York: Simon and Schuster).

Shafer, Byron E. (2016). *The American Political Pattern: Stability and Change, 1932–2016* (Lawrence, KS: University Press of Kansas).

Shapiro, Ira (2018). *Restoring the U.S. Senate: Looking for the Nation's Mediator* (New York: Rowman and Littlefield).

Singh, Robert (ed.) (2003). *Governing America: The Politics of a Divided Democracy* (Oxford: Oxford University Press).

Sitaraman, Ganesh (2017). *The Crisis of the Middle-Class Constitution: Why Economic Inequality Threatens Our Republic* (New York: Alfred A. Knopf).

Smith, Keri E. Iyall, Louis Edgar Sparza, and Judith R. Blau (eds.) (2017). *Human Rights Of, By, and For the People* (New York: Routledge).

Spitzer, Robert J. (2015). *Guns Across America: Reconciling Gun Rules and Rights* (New York: Oxford University Press).

Spitzer, Robert J. (2018). *The Politics of Gun Control*, 7th edition (New York: Routledge).

Stevens, John Paul (2014). *Six Amendments: How and Why We Should Change the Constitution* (New York: Little, Brown and Company).

Strauss, David A. (2010). *The Living Constitution* (New York: Oxford University Press).

Sundquist, James L. (1992). *Constitutional Reform and Effective Government* (Washington, DC: Brookings Institution Press).

Suri, Jeremi (2017). *The Impossible Presidency: The Rise and Fall of America's Highest Office* (New York: Basic Civitas Books).

Taleb, Nassim Nicholas (2013). *Antifragile: Things that Gain from Disorder* (New York: Penguin).

Thurber, James A. and Antoine Yoshinaka (eds.) (2016). *American Gridlock: The Sources, Character and Impact of Political Polarization* (New York: Cambridge University Press).

Tocqueville, Alexis de (1966). *Democracy in America*, eds. J.P. Mayer and Max Lerner, trans. George Lawrence (New York: Harper and Row).

Tribe, Laurence H. and Joshua Matz (2014). *Uncertain Justice: The Roberts Court and the Constitution* (New York: Henry Holt and Co.).

Vermeule, Adrian (2012). *Law and the Limits of Reason* (New York: Oxford University Press).

Vermeule, Adrian (2013). *The Constitution of Risk* (New York: Cambridge University Press).

Vermeule, Adrian (2016). *Law's Abnegation: From Law's Empire to the Administrative State* (Cambridge, MA: Harvard University Press).

Vile, John R. (1991). *Rewriting the United States Constitution: An Examination of Proposals from Reconstruction to the Present* (New York: Praeger).

Waldman, Michael (2014). *The Second Amendment: A Biography* (New York: Simon and Schuster).

Ware, Alan (2011). *Political Conflict in America* (New York: Palgrave Macmillan).

Weiner, Greg (2012). *Madison's Metronome: The Constitution, Majority Rule, and the Tempo of American Politics* (Lawrence, KS: University Press of Kansas).

Whittington, Keith E. (1999). *Constitutional Construction: Divided Powers and Constitutional Meaning* (Cambridge, MA: Harvard University Press).

Whittington, Keith E. (2007). *Political Foundations of Judicial Supremacy: The Presidency, the Supreme Court, and Constitutional Leadership in U.S. History* (Princeton, NJ: Princeton University Press).

Williams, Joan C. (2017). *White Working Class: Overcoming Class Cluelessness in America* (Cambridge, MA: Harvard Business Review Press).

Wills, Garry (2010). *Bomb Power: The Modern Presidency and the National Security State* (New York: Penguin Books).

Wilson, Graham (1998). *Only in America? The United States in Comparative Perspective* (Chatham, NJ: Chatham House Publishers).

Wittes, Benjamin and Pietro Nivola (eds.) (2015). *What Would Madison Do? The Father of the Constitution Meets Modern American Politics* (Washington, DC: Brookings Institution Press).

Wolf, Naomi (2008). *The End of America: Letters of Warning to a Young Patriot* (Hartford, VT: Chelsea Green Publishing).

Wolfe, Tom (1993). *The Purple Decades* (London: Picador).

Zeisberg, Mariah (2013). *War Powers: The Politics of Constitutional Authority* (Princeton, NJ: Princeton University Press).

Zirin, James D. (2016). *Supremely Partisan: How Raw Politics Tips the Scales in the Supreme Court of the United States* (New York: Rowman and Littlefield).

## Articles and Reports

Aaronovitch, David (2017). "Trump Knows There Aren't Really Any Rules," *The Times* May 11, p. 29.

Abbott, Greg (2016). "Governor Abbott Unveils Texas Plan, Offers Constitutional Amendments to Restore the Rule of Law," *Office of the Texas Governor* January 8.

Abramowitz, Alan and Steven Webster (2016). "The Rise of Negative Partisanship and the Nationalization of U.S. Elections in the 21st Century," *Electoral Studies* 41 March, pp. 12–22.

Acemoglu, Daron and Simon Johnson (2017). "It's Time to Found a New Republic," *Foreign Policy* August 15.

American Council of Trustees and Alumni (2016). *A Crisis in Civic Education.*

Annenberg Public Policy Center (2014). "Americans Know Surprisingly Little about Their Government, Survey Finds," September 17.

Annenberg Public Policy Center (2015). "Is There a Constitutional Right to Own a Home or Pet? Many Americans Don't Know," September 16.

Associated Press/GfK Roper Public Affairs and Corporate Communications poll (2011). "The AP-National Constitution Center Poll," August.

Bacevich, Andrew J. (2017). "Saving 'America First': What Responsible Nationalism Looks Like," *Foreign Affairs* 96 (5), pp. 57–67.

Barnes, Robert (2018). "Thomas Dissents from Supreme Court Decision Not to Review California Gun Law," *The Washington Post* February 20.

Barone, Michael (2016). "The End of History Not Turning Out as Hoped," *Washington Examiner* August 9.

Bennetts, Marc (2016). "Russia Runs Out of Money After Oil Crash and Sanctions," *The Times* September 8, p. 32.

Berenson, Tessa (2018). "Inside Trump's Plan to Dramatically Reshape U.S. Courts," *Time* February 8.

Blau, Judith R. (2017). "Why Revise?", chapter two in Keri I. Eyall Smith, Louis Edgar Esparza, and Judith R. Blau (eds.), *Human Rights Of, By, and For the People* (New York: Routledge), pp. 9–29.

Bolton, John R. (2016). "What Trump's Foreign Policy Gets Right," *The Wall Street Journal* August 21.

Borger, Julian (2017). "Trump Blames Constitution for the Chaos of His First 100 days," *The Observer* April 30, 2017, p. 28.

Brands, Riley (2017). "Congress' Job Approval 19% at Start of New Session," *Gallup* January 13.

Brownstein, Ronald (2016). "Why the Democrats Keep Winning Presidential Elections," *The Atlantic* August 25.

Burgat, Casey (2018). "Five Reasons to Oppose Congressional Term Limits," *Brookings Blog* January 18.

Burns, Sarah (2017). "Debating War Powers: Battles in the Clinton and Obama Administrations," *Political Science Quarterly* 132 (2), pp. 203–223.

Bush, Jeb (2016). "Where Republicans Go From Here," *Wall Street Journal* November 24.

Calandra, Lion (2010). "Why Do Americans Get the Constitution So Wrong?" *The Christian Science Monitor* September 17.

Campbell, Kurt M. and Ely Ratner (2018). "The China Reckoning: How Beijing Defied American Expectations," *Foreign Affairs*, 97 (2), pp. 60–70.

Carney, Jordain (2017). "Senate Votes Down Paul's Bid to Sunset War Bills," *The Hill* September 13.

Carter, Ralph and James Scott (2012). "Striking a Balance: Congress and U.S. Foreign Policy," in Steven Hook and James Scott (eds.), *US Foreign Policy Today: American Renewal?* (Washington, DC: CQ Press), pp. 36–53.

Caryl, Christian (2016). "Let's Face It: The U.S. Constitution Needs a Makeover," *Foreign Policy* November 11.

Chicago Council on Global Affairs (2016). *America in the Age of Uncertainty* October 6.

Chokshi, Niraj (2015). "The Astonishing State-By-State Rise in Food Stamp Reliance," *The Washington Post* March 3.

Clement, Scott and Jim Tankersley (2016). "Is America Still Great? Clinton and Trump Voters Have Starkly Different Views," *The Washington Post* September 15.

CNN (2016). "Khzir Khan's Powerful DNC Speech."

Cohen, Eliot A. (2017). "Rex Tillerson Doesn't Understand America," *The Atlantic* May 5.

Congressional Management Foundation (2017). *State of the Congress: Staff Perspectives on Institutional Capacity in the House and Senate* (Washington, DC: Congressional Management Foundation).

Cook Jr., Charles E. (2016). "Doubting a Down Ballot Wave," *National Journal* August 8.

Cook Jr., Charles E. (2018). "The Demographic Trends That Should Worry Republicans," *The Cook Political Report* March 30.

Cutler, Lloyd (1980). "To Form a Government," *Foreign Affairs* 59 (1), pp. 126–143.

Daley, William M. (2016). "Dump the Electoral College? Bad Idea, Says Al Gore's Former Campaign Chairman," *The Washington Post* December 4.

Davidson, Paul (2017). "Median Household Income Hits $59,039 Rising for 2nd Straight Year," *USA Today* September 12.

Deudney, Daniel (1995). "The Philadelphia System: Sovereignty, Arms Control, and Balance of Power in the American-States Union, Circa 1787–1861," *International Organization* 49 (2), pp. 191–228.

Devins, Neal (2008–2009). "How Planned Parenthood v Casey (Pretty Much) Settled the Abortion Wars," *Yale Law Journal* 118, pp. 1318–1354.

DeYoung, Karen (2016). "Trump Proposes Ideological Test for Muslim Immigrants and Visitors to the US," *Washington Post* August 15.

Dionne, E. J. (2016). "Elitism Won't Defeat Trumpism," *Real Clear Politics* August 8.

Dionne, E. J. (2017). "The Norms of Government are Collapsing Before Our Eyes," *The Washington Post* July 26.

Dionne, E. J., Thomas Mann, and Norman Ornstein (2017). "Why the Majority Keeps Losing on Guns," *The Washington Post* April 10.

Dropp, Kyle, Joshua D. Kertzer, and Thomas Zeitzoff (2014). "The Less Americans Know about Ukraine's Location, the More They Want US to Intervene," *Monkey Cage* blog, *Washington Post* online, April 7.

Dubner, Stephen J. (2016). "Ten Ideas to Make Politics Less Rotten," http://freakonomics.com/ July 27.

Dueck, Colin (2016). "If Asked, National Security Conservatives Should Serve the New Administration," *National Review* November 18.

Edsall, Thomas B. (2018). "Trump's Tool Kit Does Not Include the Constitution," *The New York Times* February 8.

Engstrom, David Freeman and Jeremy M. Weinstein (2018). "What If California Had a Foreign Policy? The New Frontier of States Rights," *The Washington Quarterly* 41 (1), pp. 27–43.

Epps, Garrett (2016). "Trumpism Is the Symptom of a Gravely Ill Constitution," *The Atlantic* September 20.

Federal Reserve Board (2016). *Report on the Economic Well-Being of U.S. Households in 2015.*

Fingerhut, Hannah (2018). "Why Do People Belong A Party? Negative Views of the Opposing Party are a Major Factor," *Pew Research Center* March 29.

Fiorina, Morris (2018). "The Meaning of Trump's Election Has Been Exaggerated," *Real Clear Politics* January 10.

Foa, Roberto Stefan and Yashca Mounk (2016). "The Democratic Disconnect," *Journal of Democracy* 27 (3), pp. 5–17.

Freedom House (2018). *Freedom in the World 2018.*

Fukuyama, Francis (2014). "America in Decay: The Sources of Political Dysfunction," *Foreign Affairs* 93 (5), pp. 5–26.

Gallup (2017). "In Depth Topics A-Z: Abortion."

Glennon, Michael J. (2017). "Security Breach: Trump's Tussle with the Bureaucratic State," *Harper's* June.

Gourevitch, Peter (2002). "Reinventing the American State: Political Dynamics in the Post-Cold War Era," in Ira Katznelson and Martin Shefter (eds.), *Shaped by War and Trade: International Influences on American Political Development* (Princeton, NJ: Princeton University Press), pp. 301–330.

Gramlich, John (2017). "How Countries Around the World View Democracy, Military Rule And Other Political Systems," *Pew Research Center* October 30.

Greenberg, Scott (2017). "Summary of the Latest Federal Income Tax Data, 2016 Update," *Tax Foundation* February 1.

Gross, Samantha (2018). "Is the United States the New Saudi Arabia?" *Brookings blog* January 26.

Haas, Peter (2017). "Does It Even Work? A Theoretical and Practical Evaluation of the War Powers Resolution," *Congress and the Presidency* 44 (2) May–August, pp. 235–258.

Hains, Tim (2016). "Kissinger: Give Trump International Order a Chance," Real Clear Politics December 11.

Hallard, Vic (1996). "In Defense of Legislatures," *The Council of State Governments* February 1996, p. 9.

Hamel, Liz, Bryan Wu, and Mollyann Brodie (2017). "Data Note: Modestly Strong but Malleable Support for Single-Payer Health Care," *The Henry J. Kaiser Family Foundation* July 5.

Hewitt, Hugh (2017). "Why Ryan and McConnell Should Go for a Big Deal with Democrats," *The Washington Post* July 18.

Hill, Catey (2016). "45 Percent of Americans Pay No Federal Income Tax," *Marketwatch* April 18.

Hitchens, Christopher (1993). "Away with Them and Their Overweening Power," *Independent* February 6.

Hitchens, Christopher (1998). "Ireland," *Critical Quarterly* Spring.

House of Representatives Armed Services Committee (2018). "Testimony of Secretary of Defense James Mattis," February 6.

Jacobson, Gary C. (2016). "The Triumph of Polarized Partisanship in 2016: Donald Trump's Improbable Victory," *Political Science Quarterly* 132 (1), pp. 9–41.

Jacoby, Susan (2008). "The Dumbing of America," *Washington Post* online, February 17.

Jaffe, Sarah (2016). "The Sanders Campaign is Over. The Political Revolution is Not," *Washington Post* August 22.

Johnson, Gary (2016). "Gary Johnson: Our Two-Party System Has Failed Us, Just Like Our Founders Said It Would," *The Washington Post* September 7.

Jones, Charles O. (1990). "The Separated Presidency," chapter 1 in Anthony King (ed.) *The New American Political System*, 2nd edition (Washington, DC: American Enterprise Institute), pp. 1–28.

Jones, Jeffrey M. (2017). "Trust in Judicial Branch Up, Executive Branch Down," *Gallup* September 20.

Kady II, Martin (2009). "Boehner Mixes Up Constitution and Declaration," *Politico* May 11.

Keillor, Garrison (2016). "Make the Most of Your Brief Time on Earth," *Washington Post* August 17.

Kennedy, John F. (1962). "Remarks at a Dinner Honoring Nobel Prize Winners of the Western Hemisphere," April 29.

Kiley, Jocelyn (2017). "Public Support for 'single-payer' Health Coverage Grows, Driven By Democrats," *Pew Research Center* June 23.

Klarman, Michael (2010). "A Skeptical View of Constitution Worship," *Balkinization blog* September 27.

Kreitner, Richard (2017). "The US Constitution Is Over 2 Centuries Old and Showing Its Age," *The Nation* November 2.

Lempert, Richard (2016). "Two Cheers for the Electoral College: Reasons Not to Abolish It," *Brookings blog* November 29.

Lepore, Jill (2011). "The Commandments: The Constitution and Its Worshippers," *The New Yorker* January 17.

Lerner, Max (1937). "Constitution and Court as Symbols," *Yale Law Journal* 46 (8), pp. 1290–1319.

Lessig, Lawrence (2016). "The Constitution Lets the Electoral College Choose the Winner. They Should Choose Clinton," *Washington Post* November 24.

Levinson, Sanford (2012). "Our Imbecilic Constitution," *The New York Times* May 25.

Levinson, Sanford and Jack Balkin (2009). "Constitutional Crises," *University of Pennsylvania Law Review* 157 (3), pp. 707–753.

Loschky, Jay (2018). "Countries Disapproving of U.S. Leadership Triples in 2017," *Gallup* January 19.

Main, Thomas (2011). "The Constitution and Its Critics: Taking Another Look at America's Fundamental Document," *Policy Review* no. 167.

Mann, Thomas E. (2016). "Trump, No Ordinary President, Requires an Extraordinary Response," *Brookings blog* December 20.

Marshall, Thurgood (1987). "Remarks of Thurgood Marshall at the Annual Seminar of the San Francisco Patent and Trademark Law Association," May 6.

McCarthy, Justin (2015). "Confidence in U.S. Branches of Government Remains Low," *Gallup* June 15.

Miller Center of Public Affairs (2008). *National War Powers Commission Report* (University of Virginia).

Monmouth University (2018). "Low Public Confidence in American System," January 4.

Movement for Black Lives (2016). *A Vision for Black Lives.*

Muirhead, Russell and Nancy L. Rosenblum (2015). "The Uneasy Place of Parties in the Constitutional Order," chapter 11 in Mark Tushnet, Mark A. Graber and Sanford Levinson (eds.), *The Oxford Handbook of the U.S. Constitution* (New York: Oxford University Press), pp. 217–239.

Muller, Jerry (2008). "Us and Them: The Enduring Power of Ethnic Nationalism," *Foreign Affairs* 87 (March/April), pp. 18–35.

Newport, Frank (2013a). "Most in U.S. Say Politics in Washington Cause Serious Harm," *Gallup* January 7.

Newport, Frank (2013b). "Most in U.S. Still Proud to be an American," *Gallup* July 4.

Newport, Frank (2016). "The American Public and Extreme Policy Positions," *Gallup* April 25.

Newport, Frank and Andrew Dugan (2017). "Five Ways America Changed During the Obama Years," *Gallup* January 27.

Norman, Jim (2016). "Americans' Confidence in Institutions Stays Low," *Gallup* June 13.

Norman, Jim (2018). "Political Splits Widen on Satisfaction with Life in U.S.," *Gallup* January 25.

Orgad, Liav (2010). "The Preamble in Constitutional Interpretation," *International Journal of Constitutional Law* 8 (4), pp. 710–738.

Orwell, George (1945). "Freedom of the Park," *Tribune* December.

Orwell, George (1946). "In Front of Your Nose," *Tribune* March 22.

Orwell, George (1994). "Notes on Nationalism," in George Orwell, *Essays* (London: Penguin Books).

Osnos, Evan (2017). "Endgames: What Would It Take to Cut Short Trump's Presidency?' *The New Yorker* May 8, pp. 34–45.

Paletta, Damian and Erica Werner (2018). "Republicans are Completely Reversing Themselves on the Deficit," *The Washington Post* February 7.

Patten, David A. (2008). "Obama: Constitution is 'Deeply Flawed'," *Newsmax* October 27.

Peele, Gillian (2014). "An Emerging Constitutional Debate," chapter one in Gillian Peele, Christopher J. Bailey, Bruce E. Cain and B. Guy Peters (eds.), *Developments in American Politics Seven* (New York: Palgrave Macmillan), pp. 14–31.

Pew Research Center (2016). "Few Clinton or Trump Supporters Have Close Friends in the Other Camp," August 3.

Pew Research Center (2017a). "The Partisan Divide on Political Values Grows Even Wider," October 5.

Pew Research Center (2017b). "Large Majorities See Checks and Balances, Right to Protest as Essential for Democracy," March 2.

Pew Research Center (2018a). "Majorities Say Government Does Too Little for Older People, the Poor and the Middle Class," January 30.

Pew Research Center (2018b). "Economic Issues Decline Among Public's Policy Priorities," January 25.

Pillar, Paul R. (2016–2017). "American Good Fortune and Misperception about the Outside World," *Political Science Quarterly* 131 (4), pp. 685–715.

Polling Report (various years). "Direction of the Country."

Posner, Eric A. (2017). "America Is Nowhere Near a Constitutional Crisis," *Foreign Policy* December 26.

Posner, Eric A. (2018). "Trump Has Plenty of Bark. His Predecessors Had More Bite," *The Washington Post* February 2.

Posner, Eric A. and Adrian Vermeule (2008). "Constitutional Showdowns," *University of Pennsylvania Law Review* 156, pp. 991–1048.

Posner, Richard A. (2016). "The Academy is Out of Its Depth," *Slate* June 24.

Public Policy Polling (2013). "Congress Less Popular Than Cockroaches, Traffic Jams," January.

Publius Decius Mus (2016). "The Flight 93 Election," *Claremont Review of Books* September 5.

Putley, Jeremy (1997). "The Moral Vacuum and the American Constitution," *Political Quarterly* January, pp. 68–76.

Putnam, Robert D. (1988). "Diplomacy and Domestic Politics: The Logic of Two-Level Games," *International Organization* 42 (3), pp. 427–460.

Rauch, Jonathan (2016). "How American Politics Went Insane," *The Atlantic* July/August.

Rauhala, Emily (2018). "China Approves Plan to Abolish Presidential Term Limits, Clearing Way for Xi to Stay on," *The Washington Post* March 11.

Rayman, Noah (2013). "Justice Antonin Scalia Thinks He Has Gay Friends," *Time* October 7.

Rochelle, Shawnette and Jay Loschky (2014). "Confidence in Judicial Systems Varies Worldwide," *Gallup* October 22.

Romano, Andrew (2011). "How Ignorant Are Americans?" *Newsweek* March 20.

Ross, Kenneth (2017). "We Are on the Verge of Darkness," *Foreign Policy* January 12, 2017.

Saad, Lydia (2016). "Gallup Vault: A Supreme Court Power Play," *Gallup* February 26.

Saad, Lydia (2017). "Gallup Vault: Praise for U.S. Constitution at 200 Years," *Gallup* September 21.

Samuels, Gabriel (2016). "Michelle Obama's 2016 DNC Speech: Read the Transcript in Full," *The Independent* July 26.

Samuelson, Robert J. (2017). "Are We on the Road To Impeachment?" *The Washington Post* May 28.

Sandbrook, Dominic (2016). "Court Politics," *The Sunday Times, Culture*, November 13, pp. 32–33.

Sandstrom, Aleksandra (2017). "God or the Divine is Referenced in Every State Constitution," *Pew Research Center* August 17.

Saunders, Elizabeth (2018). "Is Trump a Normal Foreign-Policy President? What We Know After One Year," *Foreign Affairs* January 18.

Schake, Kori (2016). "The Disconnect Beneath the Praise for U.S. Military," *The Wall Street Journal* August 24.

Schuetz, Jenny (2018). "Does TV Bear Some Responsibility for Hard Feelings Between Urban America and Small-Town America?" *The Avenue, Brookings* February 12.

Schultz, Kenneth A. (2018). "Perils of Polarization for U.S. Foreign Policy," *The Washington Quarterly* 40 (4), pp. 7–28.

Schwartz, Ian (2017). "Trump Weekly Address: The 230th Anniversary of the Signing of the Constitution," *Real Clear Politics* September 16.

Shaban, Hamza (2018). "Google for the First Time Outspent Every Other Company to Influence Washington in 2017," *The Washington Post* January 23.

Shambaugh, Jay, Ryan Nunn, Patrick Liu, and Greg Nantz (2017). "Thirteen Facts About Wage Growth," *The Hamilton Project* September 24.

Sheppard, Noel (2009). "Maddow Apologizes for Constitution Gaffe with Schoolhouse Rock," *MRC Newsbusters* November 7.

Siegel, Benjamin (2016). "Donald Trump Says He'll Protect Constitution's 'Article XII'," *ABC News* July 8.

Singh, Robert (2005). "Are We All Americans Now? Explaining Anti-Americanisms," chapter 2 in Brendon O'Connor and Martin Griffiths (eds.), *The Rise of Anti-Americanism* (London: Routledge), pp. 25–47.

Singh, Robert (2017). "'I, The People': A Deflationary Interpretation of Populism, Trump and the United States Constitution," *Economy and Society*, 46 (1), pp. 20–42.

Singh, Robert (2018). "The United States Congress and Nuclear War Powers: Explaining Legislative Nonfeasance," *The Journal of Legislative Studies* 24 (3).

Sollenberger, Mitchel A. (2004). "The Presidential Veto and Congressional Procedure," *Congressional Research Service report for Congress* February 27.

Stokes, Bruce (2018). "Europeans want Direct Democracy," *Real Clear World* January 31.

Steuerle, C. Eugene (2012). "The Government We Deserve" *blog*, May 4.

Sullivan, Andrew (2016). "The Republic Repeals Itself," *New York* magazine.

Sustainable Development Solutions Network (2017). *World Happiness Report 2017*.

Tarrance, V. Lance (2018). "The Peril of Midterms: Can Trump Defy the Odds Once Again?" *Gallup* January 5.

Tribe, Laurence H. (2017). "Trump Must Be Impeached. Here's Why," *The Washington Post* May 13.

Tribe, Laurence H., Richard Painter, and Norman Eisen (2017). "No, Trump Can't Pardon Himself. The Constitution Tells Us So," *Washington Post* July 21.

Tsiaperis, Tasha (2013). "Constitution a 'dead, dead, dead' document, Scalia Tells SMU Audience," *Dallas News* January 28.

Turley, Jonathan (2017). "Yes, Trump Can Legally Pardon Himself or His Family. No, He Shouldn't," *Washington Post* July 21 2017.

Tushnet, Mark, Mark A. Graber and Sanford Levinson (eds.) (2015). *The Oxford Handbook of the U.S. Constitution* (New York: Oxford University Press).

United Nations (2016). *Human Development Report 2016: Human Development for Everyone* (New York: UN Development Program).

Vance, J. D. (2016). "Why Race Relations Got Worse," *National Review* August 29.

Wheeler, Russell (2018). "Trump's 1st State of the Union: Is He Really Reshaping the Judiciary?" *Brookings* January 25.

White House (2016). "Remarks of President Barack Obama—State of the Union Address as Delivered," January 13.

White House (2017). "Statement by President Donald J. Trump on signing the 'Countering America's Adversaries through Sanctions Act'," August 2.

Wike, Richard, Katie Simmons, Bruce Stokes, and Janell Fetterolf (2017). "Globally, Broad Support for Representative and Direct Democracy," *Pew Research Center* October 16.

Will, George F. (2016). "The Sinking Fantasy that Trump Would Defend the Constitution," *Washington Post* April 7.

World Economic Forum (2017). *The Global Human Capital Report 2017*.

Wright, Thomas (2016). "Trump's Team of Rivals, Riven by Distrust," *Foreign Policy* December 14.

Zakaria, Fareed (2011). "Are America's Best Days Behind Us?" *Fareed Zakaria blog* March 3.

Zelizer, Julian E. (2018). "Out of Control," *The Atlantic* January 25.

# Index

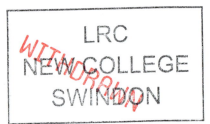